REMAKING THE UNION
Devolution and British Politics in the 1990s

THE CASS SERIES IN REGIONAL AND FEDERAL STUDIES
ISSN 1363-5670
General Editor: John Loughlin

This series brings together some of the foremost academics and theorists to examine the timely subject of regional and federal issues, which since the mid-1980s have become key questions in political analysis and practice all over the world.

The Political Economy of Regionalism
edited by Michael Keating and John Loughlin

The Regional Dimension of the European Union: Towards a Third Level in Europe? *edited by Charlie Jeffery*

Remaking the Union: Devolution and British Politics in the 1990s
edited by Howard Elcock and Michael Keating

REMAKING THE UNION
Devolution and British Politics
in the 1990s

Edited by

HOWARD ELCOCK and
MICHAEL KEATING

FRANK CASS
LONDON • PORTLAND, OR.

First published in 1998 in Great Britain by
FRANK CASS PUBLISHERS
Newbury House, 900 Eastern Avenue, London IG2 7HH

and in the United States of America by
FRANK CASS PUBLISHERS
c/o ISBS, 5804 N.E. Hassalo Street
Portland, Oregon 97213-3644

Website http://www.frankcass.com

British Library Cataloguing in Publication Data

Remaking the union : devolution and British politics in the
1990s. – (Cass series in regional and federal studies; 3)
1. Decentralization in government – Great Britain. 2. Great
Britain – Politics and government – 1979–
I. Elcock, Howard, 1942–   II. Keating, Michael, 1950–
941'.0859

ISBN 0 7146 4876 0 (cloth)
ISBN 0 7146 4430 7 (paper)
ISSN 1363-5670

Library of Congress Cataloging-in-Publication Data:

Remaking the union : devolution and British politics in the 1990s /
edited by Howard Elcock and Michael Keating.
        p.   cm. – (The Cass series in regional and federal studies,
ISSN 1363-5670)
    Includes bibliographical references and index.
    ISBN 0-7146-4876-0 (hbk). – ISBN 0-7146-4430-7 (pbk.)
    1. Regionalism – Great Britain. 2. Decentralization in government –
Great Britain. I. Elcock, H. J. (Howard James). II. Keating,
Michael, 1950–   . III. Series.
JN297.R44R46   1998
320.941'09'049 – dc21   98-10066
                                                                  CIP

This group of studies first appeared in a Special Issue of *Regional & Federal Studies*
(ISSN 1359-7566), Vol.8, No.1 (Spring 1998), published by Frank Cass and Co. Ltd.

Printed in Great Britain by
Antony Rowe Ltd, Chippenham, Wiltshire

Contents

Introduction: Devolution and the UK State   *Michael Keating and Howard Elcock*   1

Devolution and Europe: Britain's Double Constitutional Problem   *Graham Leicester*   10

Financial Arrangements for UK Devolution   *David Heald, Neal Geaughan and Colin Robb*   23

Scottish Home Rule: Radical Break or Pragmatic Adjustment?   *Lindsay Paterson*   53

What Could a Scottish Parliament Do?   *James Mitchell*   68

Reactive Capital: The Scottish Business Community and Devolution   *Peter Lynch*   86

Deepening Democracy: Women and the Scottish Parliament   *Alice Brown*   103

The Devolution Debate in Wales: The Politics of a Developing Union State?   *Jonathan Bradbury*   120

Strategies of Autonomist Agencies in Wales   *Jonathan Snicker*   140

English Regionalism and New Labour   *John Mawson*   158

Territorial Debates about Local Government: Or Don't Reorganize! Don't! Don't! Don't!   *Howard Elcock*   176

What's Wrong with Asymmetrical Government?   *Michael Keating*   195

Index   227

Introduction:
Devolution and the UK State

MICHAEL KEATING and HOWARD ELCOCK

The United Kingdom, having given constitutions to so many countries of
the world, has proved extremely conservative in its own constitutional
practice, evolving gradually largely on the basis of unwritten convention
and practice, and only occasionally having to confront large issues of
principle. At the end of the twentieth century, however, it appears to be on
the brink of large-scale changes in the way it is governed, in the
relationships of its constituent parts, and in the bonds between citizens and
governors. As usual, this is being done piecemeal, with little regard to an
overall plan or even consistency, but a process is being set in train which
could have radical implications. The constitutional agenda is large, covering
the UK's position in Europe, citizen rights, the House of Lords and the
electoral system, but the issue with the most urgency and perhaps the most
far-reaching consequences is the reform of territorial government. This
includes a legislative parliament for Scotland, an executive assembly for
Wales, the possibility of regional governments in England, and the search
for a solution to the problem of Northern Ireland. This collection of essays
looks at the reform of territorial government in Britain – that is, in Scotland,
Wales and the regions of England, assesses proposals on offer and addresses
the principal challenges of the future.

There are two interpretations of the territorial constitution of the UK
state. The first sees it as a unitary state, based on the sovereignty of
Parliament and the absolute concentration of power there. In practice, as
Bagehot observed in the last century, given party discipline and an electoral
system which normally produces government majorities with a mere
plurality of the vote, parliamentary sovereignty translates into the power of
the Cabinet. This unitary interpretation of the constitution is espoused by
radicals on both right and left. For many in the Labour Party, the
concentration of authority at the centre provides a reservoir of power to be
used for their schemes of social transformation. For right-wing radicals in
the mould of Margaret Thatcher, parliamentary sovereignty was also seen as
a form of absolute power, enabling a very different political programme to
be pushed through regardless of societal opposition. There was always a
degree of inconsistency in all this. Labour radicals proposed to use the state
to achieve socialism, while at the same time arguing that it was controlled

either by the civil service elite or, for the most Marxist-influenced, by the bourgeoisie. The inconsistency in the Thatcherite vision was the use of the state and a single-minded concentration of power in its hands, in the interests of a programme whose ostensible aim was the liberation of citizens from the oppressive and intrusive presence of the state.

The second interpretation of the British state is as a balanced constitution. Parliamentary sovereignty certainly is there, but it is tolerable and tolerated only because governments exercise a certain self-restraint, respecting the independence of civil society and of local communities. So while the UK has an apparently untrammelled central authority, it did not establish the centralized bureaucracies found in Napoleonic states, and left important matters, including the regulation of the professions, private-interest associations, trade unions, universities, the financial system and ecclesiastical affairs, to self-governing bodies in civil society. One element in this is the tradition of local self-government, which was achieved quite early in England because of the lack of a gulf between the state and local political elites, since it is the latter who were represented in Parliament where they negotiated with royal power and later assumed the right to make and break governments. Under the 'dual polity' (Bulpitt, 1983), the centre could entrust the management of local affairs to the localities themselves, secure that the right people were in charge. In the twentieth century, party politics provided a link and a common identity for centre and locality. There were occasional confrontations, for example Poplarism in the 1920s, when socialist councils sought to defy central financial restraints, or the fights over housing finance under the Heath government in the 1970s. Generally, however, the Labour Party accepted the terms of central–local relations, in government and in opposition, adapting it to the needs of the welfare state and modern planning.

A second element in this interpretation of the constitution is the idea of the union state (Rokkan and Urwin, 1982; Mitchell, 1996), best exemplified by the Anglo-Scottish union of 1707. This was a bargain by which Scots elites surrendered their Parliament but retained key elements of their distinct civil society, including the Church of Scotland, the law, the education system and the burghs. There were certainly many breaches of the Union, starting with the restoration of lay patronage in 1712, and the assumption by the new British Parliament that it was the continuation of the old English Parliament, when in fact both parliaments had been suppressed to create the new one. Yet the idea of the union has persisted and the distinct elements of Scots civil society and government have been preserved and considerably extended, notably in the form of the Scottish Office and its associated agencies. Scots have carved out their own niche in UK institutions, and conventions have remained to the effect that Scots actors should have a certain degree of autonomy and self-regulation (Paterson,

1994). None of this was entrenched constitutionally, but relied on a self-restraint and mutual understanding which has been more in evidence at some periods than at others. It was also underpinned by an implicit exchange, in which Scots elites traded off autonomy for access to the British market and to central decision-making in Westminster and Whitehall, and for resources (Keating, 1975).

The Union has undergone periodic crises, calling for adjustment or renegotiation of its terms but, given the doctrine of parliamentary supremacy, it has proved very difficult for British governments to negotiate or to undertake radical constitutional reform. Instead, adjustments are made to administrative arrangements, local government is reformed, or policy concessions are granted. The late nineteenth century saw the rise of nationalism across Europe, challenging multinational states and empires. Expansion of the interventionist state brought government, central bureaucracy and educators into peripheries with their own culture and traditions. Agrarian and industrial class conflicts broke out as a new division of labour was imposed. Many of these conflicts assumed a territorial dimension, challenging central state management or the chosen model of development and this was certainly true of the United Kingdom. In the late nineteenth century, Irish home rule crises broke the British party system, consigning the Liberals to long periods of opposition and bringing the country to the edge of civil war by 1914. It was resolved only with the concession of what became full independence to the southern part of the country and the establishment of the UK's only example of devolved government in the north. Scotland proved more tractable, and rises in home rule and nationalist sentiment in the late nineteenth century and after the two world wars were contained by administrative devolution and economic concessions. Wales was less of problem for the state. Non-conformism led to pressure for the disestablishment of the Church of England there, finally successful after the First World War. Later, language demands were met through policy concessions.

The union-state reading of the constitution, familiar up to the late nineteenth century, was so some extent lost in the twentieth century, as the national party system and the construction of the interventionist welfare state imposed a uniformity in policy and practice, while citizen demands centred on equity rather than the recognition of diversity. After the Second World War, politicians continued to pay lip service to local self-government but few made it a priority and, far from coinciding with other concerns or being seen as a means to attain substantive goals, it often seemed to conflict with them. By the 1990s, however, this had changed. Self-government for the nations and regions of the United Kingdom is seen not as a nostalgic remnant of the past but as a central element in political, social and economic modernization. This owes something to particularly British factors, but also forms part of a broader European trend.

One general factor is the crisis of the nation-state. The rise of multinational corporations, mobility of capital and the imperative of competition, together with the rise of market and neo-liberal ideology, have deprived the nation-state of many of the instruments of territorial economic management which underpinned broader territorial management strategies in the post-war era. In those states with existing territorial fractures, the crisis of the state has deepened these and politicized them, as territorial minorities seek to preserve and develop a public space which the nation-state seems unable any longer to sustain. Minority nationalism was often dismissed in the past as atavistic and tribal, since it did not fit the dominant modernization paradigm or the world view of metropolitan intellectuals. This attitude still persists (see Hobsbawm, 1992; Dahrendorf, 1995) but there is a broader recognition that in places like Scotland and Wales it represents a search for civic community, for new principles of solidarity, and a mechanism for retaining social cohesion in the face of the disintegrative effects of the global market.

European integration has also weakened states' capacities for territorial management, while the single market tends to increase territorial disparities. Regions have reacted in a variety of ways. At one time, peripheral and poorer regions tended to take a hostile stance to Europe, seeing it as more remote and threatening than the national government, while self-governing regions, like the German Länder, saw that Europe tended to concentrate power in the hands of national governments, at their expense. From the 1980s, with the further development of a European political space, and the establishment of more active European policies, notably in regional development, but also in research, environment, agriculture and industry, regions turned to a more positive engagement with Europe. Those with their own historic, cultural or national identities even began to see it as an opportunity to increase their own autonomy, to pursue their own distinct interest, and to project themselves as more than mere dependencies of the state. For some, like the Scottish National Party, the aim is independence in Europe, as a full member state of the European Union, while for others, like Catalonia's Convergència i Unió, Europe is evoked more vaguely as a framework for nation-building and is used pragmatically as a complex series of opportunities.

Another factor which has brought territorial government back on the political agenda is the shifting relationship between function and territory, which has seen the emergence of the intermediate or regional level as a key area for the management of change (Keating, 1998). This is especially true in relation to the needs of economic development in a globalizing economy and the single European market. The old paradigm of regional economic development, based on diversionary policies managed by nation-states, on infrastructure and inward investment, has given way to a new paradigm based on the qualities of regions themselves. Emphasis is now placed on human capital, education and training, entrepreneurship and the construction of territorial networks which can diffuse innovations, encourage the production of public goods and balance market competition with social co-operation. So globalization, which in one sense erodes territorial distinctiveness, in other ways enhances the importance of territory and gives impetus to the construction of territorial societies. Regional planning, dismissed by neo-liberals of the 1980s as ineffective interventionism, has also come back into fashion, as fiascos such as the Channel Tunnel, the third London airport, or the Docklands project have shown up the limitations of non-planning.

Also widely found across Europe is a democratic impulse, to confront the technical bureaucracy of the modern state with more effective mechanisms for citizen input and control, and to match functional systems of policy making with democratic forums. Successive British governments have expanded the role and responsibilities of the Scottish and Welsh Offices, partly in response to nationalist pressures, but also in the interests of effective and integrated administration. Regional administration in England has had a more chequered history. The emerging institutions of regional planning and intervention of the 1960s failed to evolve into a regional level of government, and were run down by the Thatcher administration after 1979. Yet in the 1990s there has been a return to regional administration, with the Integrated Regional Offices and Labour's proposed regional development agencies. These institutional changes have both responded to, and in turn encouraged, a sense of territorial identity and focused political debate on the Scottish, Welsh and English regional levels. They have also highlighted a democratic deficit, as they are not responsible to the populations they administer. The proliferation of quangos, used to bypass elected local government especially in areas of weak Conservative support, was another concern under the late government, notably in Wales.

A peculiarly British factor is the territorialization of the party system in the 1980s, as the Conservatives fell back in Scotland, Wales and the north of England, while maintaining their strength in the south. By 1997, they had lost all their parliamentary seats in Scotland and Wales, and were eliminated from the cities of northern England and from Cornwall. Scottish and Welsh nationalists held four and six seats respectively and the Liberal Democrats were strongly present in the Celtic Fringe of Highland Scotland and the English south-west. There is no doubt that being forced back to the periphery caused the Labour Party to strengthen its decentralist credentials, renewing its commitment to Scottish devolution, while new local government leaders in the cities of England were at the forefront of innovation in the 1980s. The centralizing impetus of the Thatcher government was a reinforcing factor in this, forcing Labour on the defensive. Thatcher, as we have noted, subscribed to a centralist vision of the constitution, and paid scant respect to the conventional restraint which underpins the union formula. This led many on the left who had previously regarded written constitutions with suspicion to change their minds and think about ways in which rights and some sort of balance of power could be entrenched. In so far as demands for constitutional change were a reaction to a centralizing, right-wing government with little support in the periphery, we might expect them to fade with the advent of a new Labour government. Yet there are good reasons to expect the issue to remain alive. The party programme contains proposals for radical constitutional change and limitations on the power of government, but the leadership seems set on maintaining an iron grip on the party itself and on ensuring uniformity in policy, even for devolved governments. On the other hand, home-rule movements in Scotland, Wales and even the English regions are reflections of social demands which will not go away and which in many cases conflict with New Labour priorities.

The response to these factors has been a considerable movement for constitutional reform. Civic movements like Charter 88 and the Campaign for a Scottish Parliament have pressed for change and, along with think tanks, have produced proposals. Labour has been converted from its centralist vision, picking up the less statist and pluralist elements of its early history, although the process has been halting and uncertain. Forced in the 1970s to adopt Scottish and Welsh devolution, it was defeated by dissent within its own ranks, and made little progress on proposals for English regions. In the 1980s, it began to take the issue more seriously, and the party in Scotland largely united around the cause of home rule, but there is less enthusiasm elsewhere, and some members of the new Labour Cabinet of 1997, notably Home Secretary Jack Straw, were open in their hostility to the whole project. The Conservative Party has once again opted for resistance to any change. Combined with the challenge of Europe, constitutional reform has produced something of an identity crisis for British Conservatism. The party has long prided itself on its pragmatism and its ability to change with the times and tailor its ideology accordingly. It accepted the welfare state and Keynesianism in the post-war years, played with monetarism in the 1980s, and discovered privatization. Important though these issues are, they do not touch on questions of identity and sovereignty. Europe and devolution, however, challenge a fundamental tenet of British Conservatism, the Union and its basis in parliamentary sovereignty. It is for this understanding of the constitution that an earlier generation of Conservatives in 1912–14 was prepared to defy the law and countenance military rebellion. In 1992 and again in 1997, John Major sought to make the defence of the Union a centrepiece of his campaign. Yet in the 1990s, the Conservative Party, forced back into England, is defending a Union of which they hardly form a participating element, and is defying Europe in the name of a British nationalism which looks ever more like mere Little Englander sentiment. So neither party has a clear vision of the union state or a doctrine to underpin it. A series of issues is unresolved as the country embarks on its constitutional voyage.

The election of a Labour government in May 1997 put the issue of devolution at the centre of political debate. A White Paper on Scotland surprised some by the strength of the proposals, notably the decision to specify powers reserved to Westminster, leaving Edinburgh with a general competence over all other matters. The proposals for Wales were, in line with Labour policy, less generous, offering an executive assembly with tightly defined competences and no legislative powers. Referendums were set in Scotland and Wales for September 1997, taking advantage of the government's honeymoon and the disarray of the opposition. On 11 September, Scots voted by 75 per cent to support the principle of a Scottish Parliament and by 65 per cent for the power to vary taxes, on a turnout of 60 per cent. This was generally considered decisive, and it is expected that, after 300 years, a Scottish Parliament will be restored. The Welsh vote a week later was much less conclusive. On a turnout of barely 50 per cent, Welsh voters supported the assembly proposals by a margin of 50.3 per cent to 49.7, showing a country still divided geographically and culturally. The government pledged to plough on with its plans, but the bill seemed much more vulnerable to guerrilla opposition than its Scottish counterpart. The government also proposes a referendum in London for the restoration of a strategic authority and mayor, but proposals for extending devolution to the English regions were set back by the tepid support in Wales. At the time of writing, then, the territorial constitution of Great Britain is still a matter of uncertainty and speculation. The chapters in this collection look at the implications.

The first chapters are overviews. Graham Leicester explores the issues that devolution raises for the constitution, especially in the light of the growing impact of European law and practices on the British constitution. David Heald and his colleagues look at the vexed question of finance, including the matter of taxation powers for the Scottish Parliament, an issue decided in principle in the referendum but whose implications have yet to be spelled out fully.

The next four papers discuss Scotland. Here it is reasonable to say that, after September 1997, the principle of devolution has been secured, but the details and implications are still to be explored. Lindsay Paterson puts the issue in historical perspective, arguing that what is involved is an adjustment of the union, and asking whether the establishment of the parliament will be just one more incremental change, or whether it may lead to ultimate statehood. James Mitchell also assesses the significance of the parliament, looking not, as is conventionally done, at formal powers and responsibilities, but at policy capacity and control of governing instruments. Scottish devolution has, with some exceptions, been associated with the left-of-centre part of the political spectrum and business has tended to stand aloof, where not taking an openly hostile stance. Yet the future of Scottish government will depend in no small measure on the relationships between devolved political institutions and the business sector. Peter Lynch explores business attitudes and concludes that, while business has taken a generally negative view of the process, it will in the end accept reality and live with a Scottish Parliament. Devolution is about the territorial decentralization of power, but it is also tied into a broader agenda of democratization and making government more representative. Alice Brown addresses this question in the context of the Scottish Parliament, exploring the efforts to secure greater representation for women than is the case in Westminster or local government.

Two papers on Wales present different perspectives on the issue of devolution there. Jonathan Bradbury recounts how devolution became re-established as an issue, particularly in the Labour Party but also notes the weaknesses on the pro-devolution side, weaknesses that were apparent in the referendum campaign and result. Both he and Jonathan Snicker trace the growing Welsh consciousness under the Major government which, unwittingly, helped national, if not always nationalist, sentiment by its concessions on administrative structures, language and culture.

The future of English devolution is in great doubt as we write. John Mawson follows Labour's long journey towards English regionalism and assesses the prospects for change under the new government. As in Scotland and Wales, the ground has been prepared by the Conservatives who, for functional reasons, felt obliged to institutionalize a regional level of sorts in the 1990s. Labour has already promised regional development agencies to answer one of the most serious complaints of English regionalists, but the political way forward remains uncertain. Howard Elcock discusses the adverse impact of repeated reorganizations of English local government and proposes that the issue of further such reorganization should be uncoupled from the devolution debate, as well as arguing that rational reorganization is unlikely to be accepted if it violates established community identities.

There is no tidy formula for reorganizing territorial government in the union state, and the events since the election of 1997, with strong support for devolution in Scotland, lukewarm support in Wales, and confusion in the English regions, suggests that uniformity is less likely than ever. In the final chapter, Michael Keating explores the issue of asymmetrical government, arguing that the problems in practice are a great deal less acute than in theory, that the British constitution is already asymmetrical in important respects and that we need to rethink our model of the state to take account of the complex and changing reality of modern government.

REFERENCES

Bulpitt, J. (1983), *Territory and Power in the United Kingdom* (Manchester: Manchester University Press).

Dahrendorf, R. (1995), 'Preserving Prosperity', *New Statesmen and Society*, Vol.13, No.29 December.

Hobsbawm, E. (1992), 'Nationalism: Whose Fault-line Is It Anyway?', *Anthropology Today*, February 1992.

Keating, M. (1975), The Role of the Scottish MP, PhD thesis, Glasgow College of Technology and CNAA.

Keating, M. (1998), 'The New Regionalism in Western Europe. Territorial Restructuring and Political Change (Aldershot: Edward Elgar).

Mitchell, J. (1996), *Strategies for Self-Government. The Campaigns for a Scottish Parliament* (Edinburgh: Polygon).

Paterson, L. (1994), *The Autonomy of Modern Scotland* (Edinburgh: Edinburgh University Press).

Rokkan, S. and D. Urwin (1983), *Economy, Territory, Identity: Politics of West European Peripheries* (London: Sage).

Devolution and Europe:
Britain's Double Constitutional Problem

GRAHAM LEICESTER

Under the new Labour government, the United Kingdom is set for a period of far-reaching constitutional change. The programme promises devolution to Scotland, Wales and the English regions, reform of the House of Lords, incorporation of the European Convention on Human Rights, freedom of information legislation and a referendum on moving to a proportional voting system for general elections.

These proposed changes in the UK political system will in turn take their place in a framework set by membership of the European Union (EU). That framework too will change in the years ahead. The Amsterdam Treaty did little more than tidy up the loose ends from Maastricht, but more fundamental institutional reforms will be needed before enlargement. The introduction of the single currency planned for 1999 will also have repercussions for the system as a whole, perhaps presaging the development of a more flexible structure for all.

That these two reform processes, at the UK and at the European level, are linked cannot be in doubt. A recent study of Britain in the EU drawn from an Irish perspective eloquently made the case for seeing Britain's difficult relationship with Brussels and with its own constitutional arrangements as two sides of the same coin:

> The common point at issue is sovereignty. At European level it centres on the extent to which sovereignty is to be shared externally with other nation states. At national level it revolves around the question as to how it is to be shared internally within the nation state. Looked at from the vantage of the British state as currently constituted, there is a dual concern. Sovereignty could be simultaneously drained from the centre in two opposite directions: outwards towards Europe and inwards towards the regions. Britain has a double constitutional problem. The key ... lies in the debate about Britain, rather than the debate about Europe. The solution to the first is the precondition for the solution to the second. (Institute for European Affairs, 1996)

Britain's 'double constitutional problem', on this analysis, is at root a consequence of uncertainty about British identity. When Britain lost an Empire it not only lost a role in the world, it lost an identity based on the projection of 'Britishness' overseas. Britain's sense of itself is now challenged by changing transatlantic relations – the waning of the special relationship, by the challenge to unionism represented by the Irish peace process, by changing relations between Britain and Europe – in particular the threat that the other member states will abandon 'the slowest ship in the convoy' and by proposals for constitutional and institutional change at home which, among other things, assert national identities other than the British one. Hence the conclusion that Britain must first come to terms with a new sense of itself before it is able fully and confidently to engage with the external world again.

This article will return to the fundamental theme of identity. First it considers devolution. That is the issue in the domestic programme which raises the double constitutional question most sharply. To be effective devolution will have to take account of the evolving European framework. Indeed, developments in Europe can be seen to have acted as a spur to devolution and to wider constitutional change in the UK. The EU has entrenched the concept of subsidiarity and encouraged regional mobilization to compete for Community funds. More generally, EU membership has encouraged a closer examination of domestic constitutional arrangements and stimulated new thinking by challenging traditional concepts of Westminster's absolute sovereignty.

At the same time, the need to design reforms at the national level within the framework provided by the EU treaties can constrain the options available. Part of the challenge of constitutional reform in the UK in the late 1990s is the need to adapt the resulting system to mesh with a pervasive set of larger cogs at the EU level. The twin solutions to Britain's double constitutional question must connect and cohere; and devolution will be the first testing ground.

ALLOCATION OF POWERS: SOVEREIGNTY AND SUBSIDIARITY

Perhaps the most important connection between EU and UK reform is the principle of subsidiarity. Most of the complexities that arise from attempting to devolve power locally while at the same time pooling it supranationally arise from the failure to make subsidiarity work as an effective organizing principle for the allocation of powers in a coherent system of multi-tiered government.

Since its inclusion in the Maastricht Treaty, subsidiarity has become an established principle governing the structure of the European Union. It is a principle with a long history in the European debate, but the full practical and legal effects of its application within the EU are still contested and developing (see Duff, 1993; Toth, 1994). What is clear is that the principle as now enunciated as part of the Community's legal order is intended to apply only to the relationship between the Community (or the Union) and its member states. Although the regional tier of government in some member states is tempted to pray the Treaty in aid, the subsidiarity principle does not apply within the EU member states simply by virtue of its inclusion in the Maastricht Treaty.

Nevertheless, inevitably subsidiarity has gained a new resonance in discussions about the internal allocation of powers, responsibilities and competences within a number of member states. The point is an especially pertinent one in the United Kingdom where subsidiarity was hailed by the Major government as a significant force for decentralization within the EU, promising the return – or 'repatriation' – of powers which fall within the competence of the Community back to the competence of the UK government.

The Labour Party and the Liberal Democrats have also championed the principle of subsidiarity, but as one that ought to apply within the UK too. The Liberals have always supported subsidiarity as underpinning a federal UK. The principle is now enshrined in Clause IV of the Labour Party's constitution as adopted in 1995. That looks forward to 'a community in which power, wealth and opportunity are in the hands of the many not the few … an open democracy in which government is held to account by the people [and] decisions are taken as far as practicable by the people they affect'. In short, both parties agree that subsidiarity is as good a principle in Britain as it is in Europe.

APPLYING SUBSIDIARITY IN BRITAIN AND IN EUROPE

The practical difficulty in implementing this ideal is the perception in some quarters that there may be a tension between the application of subsidiarity in the EU to enhance the position of the state, and its application in the state to enhance the position of the region. Resolving that tension requires a sophisticated view of the role of the central state.

Such sophistication was clearly absent from the debate about UK constitutional reform in the early 1970s. At that time, for example, two members of the Royal Commission on the Constitution which reported in 1973, Lord Crowther-Hunt and Professor Alan Peacock, published a Memorandum of Dissent from the Commission's conclusions. They did so partly because they saw a tension between simultaneously devolving and pooling sovereignty and they thought the problems insurmountable: 'We believe it makes no sense today to seek to move 'sovereignty' downwards when in more and more subjects it is actually moving upwards – to Brussels' (Royal Commission on the Constitution, 1969–73).

In theory the consistent application of the principle of subsidiarity should solve this apparent problem at a stroke. If decisions are taken 'as closely as possible to the citizen' (Maastricht Treaty, Article A), then autonomy in decision-making should logically occur at the appropriate level in the system. There should be no overlap, no draining of the same sovereignties upwards and downwards simultaneously.

The application of subsidiarity in this way would lead to a clearer division of competences between vertical levels of government, from the European to the local. Its implicit strength as an organizing principle in a federal system would be made explicit. There would still be grey areas – all boundaries are contestable – but the consistent application of the principle throughout the EU and within the member states at least holds out the promise of greater certainty about where competence lies. The analogy might be with the German federal constitution in which the principle, although not mentioned by name, lies behind the distribution of competences between the Federal and the Land governments.

'SUBSTANTIVE SUBSIDIARITY'

Using subsidiarity to allocate decision-making powers to the appropriate level of government has been termed 'substantive subsidiarity' (Scott *et al.* 1994). But there are clearly limits to how it can be applied in that way within the EU. First, as noted above, responsibility for implementing the principle within each member state falls to national governments rather than the EU itself. A thorough-going application of the principle down to local level needs matching action from the member states. Second, the question of which is the appropriate level for a given function is intensely political, and one which can receive a different answer in different member states.

Third, the debate since Maastricht has moved away from discussion of competence generally: the Amsterdam Treaty concentrates on how the Union should discharge its responsibilities rather than on what those responsibilities should be. Hence early ideas that the Treaty might provide lists of competences – of the Community and the member states – came to nothing. The limits of the Community's legislative competence have been established over time by the action of legislating. Those limits evolve. The Community's area of competence expands through its exercise and is bounded only by the will of the member states and the objectives written into the Treaty.[1]

For these reasons the principle of subsidiarity has been interpreted within the Union in a less demanding, more mechanical fashion – as 'procedural subsidiarity'. That places the emphasis on the three tests in Article 3b of the Maastricht Treaty, elaborated at the Edinburgh summit of

1992 and written into a protocol at Amsterdam: whether the Community has the power to act under the treaties, whether it can achieve an objective better than the member states acting alone and whether the action is proportionate with the desired objective. This interpretation of the principle includes no criterion of democracy or accountability or closeness to the citizen and so offers no prospect of a clear allocation of responsibilities between the Community and the member states.

It is no easier to apply the principle in the UK to provide a comprehensive allocation of powers. The doctrine of Westminster's parliamentary sovereignty militates against any neat division. The Scottish Constitutional Convention's scheme for devolution contemplates three lists of powers on the German federal model: reserved (to the centre), devolved and shared. Technically however two of those lists – of devolved and shared powers – are redundant (Scottish Constitutional Convection, 1995). So long as the Westminster Parliament is sovereign then devolution can only be seen as a temporary sharing of competence, which can be reversed at any time by the simple act of legislating. All powers are 'shared': power devolved is power retained.

There are constraints, therefore, in realizing the principle of subsidiarity at either the EU or the UK level. But they are compounded by the fact that the application of the principle at national level tends towards a mirror image of the EU level application, rather than a linear continuum. This is the source of the Peacock/Crowther-Hunt critique. The overlap between the powers likely to be transferred to a lower tier within the UK under devolution and the legislative competences now exercised by the European Community is striking – environment, training, public health, transport etc. Powers and competences will not trickle smoothly down from the federal centre through national, regional and local tiers of government under the consistent application of subsidiarity.

What is actually happening in both debates is a growing focus on core activities. In an EU driven by the threat of growing diversity, there is pressure to define a common core of policies which must be accepted by all members of the Union. Likewise at home many experts have argued that any devolution bill for Scotland should follow the model of the Government of Ireland Act of 1920 in listing powers reserved to Westminster rather than those devolved to Edinburgh (Scotland's Parliament, 1996). The domestic debate too is therefore likely to focus on the core policies which cement the union that is the United Kingdom. Both debates pose sharp questions about what the machinery of the British state is for.

UK EUROPEAN POLICY AND THE 'NATIONAL INTEREST'

In practical terms the answer may turn out to be a procedural one: the state acting to balance the demands of supranational and subnational political systems which are largely responsible for the same policy areas. That role will be most evident in the changes which will have to occur after devolution in the official machinery for co-ordinating the 'UK position' in EU negotiations. Defining the 'national interest' that is to be defended in Brussels is already a complex task of balancing interests and departments. After devolution there will also be strong national and regional interests to be taken into account. That will mean that the system of co-ordination will move from an internal machinery within government to an intergovernmental machinery between governments.

This is not a problem unique to the UK. Other member states have also had to cope with pressure from their regions for a greater say in EU policy. The experience of other member states with regional governments is instructive.

OTHER MEMBER STATES: GERMANY, BELGIUM, SPAIN

The best developed system is in Germany, where arrangements for the incorporation of Länder interests in federal government policy date back to the 1950s. Those arrangements were steadily eroded over the years in the Bund's favour. More recently the Länder have used the leverage they possess by virtue of the Bundesrat's role in the ratification of European treaties to restore and formalize their position. The Länder made Bundesrat approval for the ratification of the Maastricht Treaty conditional on a number of demands which were met by the inclusion of a new Article 23 in the federal constitution. Among other things, Article 23 stipulates a qualified majority in both the Bundestag and the Bundesrat for the transfer of any sovereign powers into Community competence, it makes the position of the Bundesrat decisive in those areas which affect the exclusive legislative competences of the Länder and it provides that the Federal Republic may be represented by a Länder delegate in the Council where those legislative competences are being discussed.

Belgium is another example in which formalized arrangements have had to be concluded to recognize the fact that Belgium is a 'decomposed state' in which the regions have substantial powers. There the federal government, the three regional and three community governments concluded a co-operation agreement in 1993 laying down the composition of the Council delegation for EU meetings and decision rules concerning negotiating strategy and voting when there is no agreement. The co-operation agreement was finalized in an Inter-Ministerial Conference for External Affairs, which is now the main forum for joint EU policy-making. The directorate for EU affairs within the Foreign Ministry and the Belgian Representation to the EU in Brussels act as the 'two diplomatic gatekeepers' of Belgian policy, ensuring that the policy presented in the Community institutions is coherent and has been arrived at in the right way.

Since the constitutional changes of May 1993, the Belgian regions and communities are fully competent to enter into international agreements themselves within the scope of their competences. Treaties which affect shared competences require the assent of all assemblies involved. This means that the Amsterdam Treaty is likely to require ratification in the Federal Parliament and in all Belgian regional and community assemblies. That has made co-operation in European policy a necessity for the central government.

Belgium and Germany have federal systems, in which the states' positions in insisting on adequate involvement in EU policy-making derives from their exclusive domestic competences. In Spain the position is different, in that asymmetric devolution has given some states greater competence than others. That position is matched in relation to the EU where no very clear formal arrangements have proved possible. The government proposed in 1986 an 'Agreement for Co-operation in Community Matters' based on early German practice. But the negotiations stalled in 1988 because Catalonia and Euskadi in particular wanted too much autonomy in the Council delegation. There is for the moment formal co-operation only in access to information and in specifically regional policy, although Catalonia enjoys considerable influence on central government and for a long time Andalucia benefited from the fact that Prime Minister Gonzalez was a native of that region.

UK EUROPEAN POLICY CO-ORDINATION

In the UK elaborate arrangements already exist for co-ordinating a national position in EU negotiations. These will have to be adapted to incorporate national and regional interests presently covered largely by the territorial departments in Whitehall. Given the overlap in the areas of competence of the EU and the devolved legislatures proposed in the UK, it is simply unsustainable to suggest that regional influence on the UK position in these areas can be allowed to wither away.[2] That goes against the whole spirit of devolution and would make any devolved system unworkable.

The overall effect of refashioning the system for devolution will be to open it up far more than at present. The same faces might appear at the same tables, but some subtle changes in the chemistry will have been performed by the mechanism of devolution. The Scottish officials involved, for example, will speak with a stronger voice than some of their former counterparts from small-spending departments. They will be backed by an autonomous political system with elected legitimacy. They may well have greater sources of independent information, gathered both by an office in Brussels and from independent contacts and attendance at meetings. They will have their own Scottish overview of negotiations as a whole and their own strategic objectives. They might be in a better position to promote cross-Council trade-offs than allowed by the present issue-by-issue bargaining co-ordinated by the Cabinet Office. They will have different political motives for what they reveal in public about discussions in progress in Brussels and in London.

The net effect must be to promote more open, less centralized policy-making machinery in which the public is likely to see very much more of the process of formulating the 'national interest' in EU negotiations than it does now. It is possible, then, that the impact of devolution might add to the already existing case for stronger authority at the centre of the process: forging the national interest will no longer be something that simply requires a lowest common denominator inter-departmental consensus. It will involve a far more politically active and positive approach from the top.

In other words, the process of negotiating and agreeing domestic EU policy will come to resemble far more closely the actual processes followed by other member states in agreeing policy within the EU. There sophisticated bargaining operates across Councils and within shifting coalitions of interest, but guided in most cases by a common strategic view of the Union's overall sense of purpose. Similarly, the looser, more flexible co-ordination process described above can only really work, as it does in Germany, if there is a clear strategic view from central government. That strategy sets out the government's overall national objectives in the EU, including how it wishes its relationship with the Union to develop over time. Within such a clear framework regional and other interests can be more readily accommodated.

The UK machinery has never operated in this way largely because of confusion and division within governments of both parties. That may be about to change. The new government has pledged a 'fresh start' in relations with the EU and wishes to make Britain a leading protagonist in the European debate. The opening up of the European policy-making process after devolution may well provide the necessary catalyst to force the government to follow through on this promise. Devolution should encourage central government to think strategically about where the true 'national interest' lies in our relations with the EU. If that happens it could bring benefits all round, but there will be a painful transition from the comfort of absolute national sovereignty.

THE EU AND DEMOCRACY

Another issue which will come into sharper focus following devolution is democracy. The addition of a new tier of elected institutions in the UK will highlight structural issues within the EU as a whole, in particular the overlap between the multitude of democratic bodies with a legitimate interest in EU affairs. The democratic operators in the EU legislative process already include the European Parliament (EP), national parliaments, regional parliaments (acting through influence on their national government's position), the indirectly elected Council of Ministers and the EP-approved Commission.

The relationship between the Commission and the EP may well become closer in the years ahead. There is a commitment to enhancing the Commission's accountability to European citizens by making its composition more dependent on the EP than on the member states. The effect could well be to transform it from a collegiate administration into an indirectly elected representative institution. The function of the Committee of the Regions does not look set to develop markedly beyond its present consultative role, but it too is likely to become more democratic in the sense that all members will be elected representatives.

The irony is that while democratic bodies are proliferating in the EU and the democratic credentials of existing EU institutions are being enhanced, participation in EP elections is falling. The simple theory that people would take the EP elections seriously only once the EP was given substantial power and influence in the Community was proved false when the turnout in the 1994 elections, post-Maastricht, fell compared with 1989. In fact the average turnout has fallen in every election since the first in 1979.[3]

One reason might be that the Community's legislative process has now become so complex that it is less easy than ever to determine where responsibility for European legislation lies. This undermines confidence and interest in the system at both the European and the national level. Yet while the Union expresses good intentions about simplifying procedures, in practice each fresh development introduces further complexities – the proliferation of special majorities in the Amsterdam Treaty, for example, with the prospect of 'double majorities' (of votes and of population) to come following enlargement. Flexibility and enlargement could also lead to complexity rather than simplicity.

The periodic calls for a constitution for the European Union are borne out of the increasing complexity of the Union's decision-making processes.

A constitution, it is argued, would clarify the present untidiness. Such a constitution would be likely to bring out the elements of a federal structure already present in the Union: it would be a federal constitution.

While a European constitution is an unlikely, but not impossible, development in the foreseeable future, there will certainly be more consideration of how to consolidate and simplify the Union's structures around a set of constitutional principles. That discussion might begin to unbundle the concept of democracy as it applies in the EU, perhaps distinguishing between critical democracy – that is, policing the rules and scrutinizing their application, and affirmative democracy – making the rules and setting the objectives of the project as a whole.[4] The EP might gravitate towards the first role, with national parliaments remaining crucial to the second.

At the same time there will be greater efforts to isolate certain parts of the system from popular and political pressures altogether. The European Central Bank is a prime example, although France is still pressing for greater political oversight of the Union's monetary policy. Suggestions to split the Commission into agencies, including an agency dealing with competition policy, also aim at the same result: to isolate certain types of decisions from popular and political pressures.

Such a debate at the European level would stimulate a similar debate within the United Kingdom itself. The introduction of an additional elected tier in the UK will lead to a debate about the proper roles of each level of government, and the purpose of a multi-faceted democratic input that is ultimately based on different groups and sub-groups of the same electorate. Difficult questions arise about the possibility of voter fatigue and the inter-relation between elections for different levels of government. There must also be changes in Westminster's role following a measure of constitutional reform and in response to devolution in particular.

It is difficult to predict the overall outcome. Much depends on the calibre of the regional political élites which emerge to govern in the devolved order. But it is Westminster that would have to change the most to adapt to the process, just as it has had to adapt to the process of European integration. A new activism on the part of MPs in policing the devolution settlement, coupled with a fresh emphasis on better European scrutiny, might be one response to a perceived decline in Westminster's importance. On that analysis, Westminster itself – rather than the UK government – could become a central actor in balancing competing and overlapping spheres of interest at the supranational and subnational levels.

IDENTITY

It is possible that the only practical answer to the problem of untangling the mixed roles of the many democratic institutions now involved in European policy will be to root democratic structures in secure identities. The processes of democracy may be exercised at any level, but the results command legitimacy and respect only when the *demos* they operate in has some substance. This is, fundamentally, the weakness of the European Union at present. In spite of attempts to foster the idea of European citizenship, European political parties and uniform European elections on or around the same day throughout the EU, European politics remains stubbornly national (Weiler, 1996).

The process of 'unbundling democracy' described above might well come to recognize that, building the processes of the Union on the solid foundation of national electorates, while working in the meantime to consolidate a transnational electorate which feels a common sense of European identity. That electorate is already a formal reality which largely supports the critical democracy function within the Union. National electorates are still crucial to more fundamental questions such as Treaty revision. It should be possible to build a political process like this on the basis of multiple but not competing identities.

Britain faces the same challenge. The pressure for democratic reform – both for PR and for devolution – stems from a sense that the present political system is insufficiently responsive to regional concerns and to the concerns of political parties where they are in the minority. This flaw in the democratic process has become increasingly obvious in Scotland since the Conservative vote went into decline:

> If the different political rhetoric deployed in Scotland inspires voters to vote for one political party, that party gains no prizes unless it has secured victory elsewhere in the UK. That matters not at all if the party system is able to transcend the border, and by and large since 1707 the party system has done so.... Two conditions have produced constitutional stability: first that the party winning power has always enjoyed support throughout the UK, and secondly that both parties have had broadly equal chances of gaining power (Jones, 1992).

Since the late 1950s the first condition has not held; and throughout the 1980s the second failed too.

Correcting these defects through the mechanism of devolution is a way of recognizing a distinct political identity in Scotland. But its success in addressing a sense of injustice in the present system rests on the Scottish people recognizing themselves as a legitimate *demos* for the purposes of a discrete democratic process. Devolution will work in Scotland precisely because that sense of community and identity is present already. Whether the same can be said of Wales will be an important and perhaps the determining factor in their referendum, as it will in winning regional referendums in England.

Devolution to Scotland, to Wales and to any of the English regions which share a similar sense of identity and are prepared to demonstrate that in a referendum is therefore the easy course. It is analogous to the suggestion that the EU consolidate its democratic credentials by rooting them in existing structures which command loyalty and respect rather than relying on an EP which does not yet spring from a truly transnational electorate. But it raises the same challenge – to build and consolidate a sense of the wider community while simultaneously recognizing the smaller.

The Irish study quoted at the beginning of this article concludes that through the process of devolution and the reform of other central institutions Britain will be forced to recognize the shallow foundations of British identity, the weakness of cohesive forces holding the union together. An active process of reforming British identity around new co-ordinates will be necessary, the study argues, and preoccupation with this task will make Britain less able to play a central part in the analogous process at the European level.

Conversely, the fact that the United Kingdom will be addressing these issues within its own system at the same time as similar questions arise at the European level might thrust the UK into a pivotal position in the debate. Its role might be to gain insights from the reform process at home and reflect them in the EU debate. Principal among such insights might be the recognition that it is possible to develop a model of integration which is not federalism, which builds on existing identities and which provides a coherent framework in which practitioners and electors know who is responsible for what, and how and why the democratic elements in the system apply.

Experience of a rolling programme of asymmetric devolution at home might convince us that such a model exists. We might in turn then be able to convince others to accept that model as constructive of European Union rather than destructive – as our partners on the basis of past experience might be inclined to suspect.

That will be a good thing. At present there is a false debate in the UK about Europe, dominated by twin images of irresistible integration in a central 'super state' and renegotiating the *acquis communautaire* to 'repatriate' national powers and competences: federalism or nationalism. Neither bears any relation to what is actually happening in Europe: the gradual development over a number of years of a complex political system, full of checks, balances and intricacies, which exercises an increasingly dominant pull on our own constitutional arrangements. More coherent constitutional thinking at home might allow us both to understand the EU system better (and therefore make us better partners) and to make a more considered and credible contribution to the debate about its future development.

NOTES

1. For a discussion of the extent of the Community's exclusive competence see Nicholas Emiliou, 'Subsidiarity: Panacea or Fig Leaf?' In D. O'Keefe and P. Twomey (eds) *Legal Issues of the Maastricht Treaty* (Chancery Lane Publishing), 1994.
2. Then Foreign Secretary Malcolm Rifkind suggested as much in the Scottish Grand Committee debate on 'Scotland in the World', Edinburgh, 13 January 1997.
3. Average turnout was 61.4% in 1979, 59.0% in 1984, 57.2% in 1989 and 56.5% in 1994.
4. For a discussion of the distinction see Ian Harden, 'Democracy and the European Union', in *Political Quarterly*, 1996.

REFERENCES

Duff, Andrew. (1993), *Subsidiarity within the European Community,* Federal Trust, 1993.

Institute for European Affairs. (1996), 'Britain: A Crisis of Identity' in Paul Gillespie (ed.) *Britain's European Question – the Issues for Ireland.*

Jones, Peter (1992), 'Politics' in Magnus Linklater and Robin Denniston (eds) *Chambers Anatomy of Scotland.*

Royal Commission on the Constitution 1969–1973, Cmnd.5460. *Report*, HMSO.

Scotland's Parliament (1996), *Fundamentals for a New Scotland Act*, The Constitution Unit, June.

Scott, A., J. Peterson and D. Millar (1994), 'Subsidiarity: A Europe of the Regions vs the British Constitution?' *Journal of Common Market Studies*, March.

Scottish Constitutional Convention (1995), *Scotland's Parliament. Scotland's Right*, Novermber.

Toth, A. (1994), 'A Legal Analysis of Subsidiarity', in D. O'Keefe and P. Twomey (eds), *Legal Issues of the Maastricht Treaty* (Chancery Lane Publishing)

Weiler, J.H.H. (1996), 'European Neo-Constitutionalism: In Search of Foundations for the European Constitutional Order' *Political Studies*, Vol.44.

Financial Arrangements for UK Devolution

DAVID HEALD, NEAL GEAUGHAN and COLIN ROBB

Referendums in Scotland and Wales, conducted on the basis of sharply differentiated proposals for devolution (Scottish Office, 1997c; Welsh Office, 1997), have provided the necessary indications of public support sought by the Labour government before embarking upon constitutional legislation. Devolution in Northern Ireland – and there alone – was the policy of the Conservative government defeated in May 1997. The 1982 scheme (Northern Ireland Office, 1982) remains on the table, though the obvious caveat relates to the security situation. Much further down the track, if at all, would be some form of devolution to England or to regions within England.

Although this article concentrates upon financial arrangements, this introductory section will briefly address broader constitutional and political issues so that the reader will be able to locate the technical issues within their proper context. Accordingly, the following issues are discussed: the question of asymmetry; the need to address matters of institutional design and political culture; and the need to establish financial arrangements for Scottish devolution generalizable to other parts of the United Kingdom and consistent with European Union (EU) obligations. Inevitably, the case of Scotland receives the most attention, because debates there will be crucial to outcomes across the United Kingdom.

First, a degree of asymmetry in constitutional arrangements is inevitable whenever there are differentiated circumstances (Keating, 1997). If fully symmetrical 'solutions' to the governance problems of the United Kingdom were regarded as essential, only three options would be available:

- *Full integration* would involve abolishing the three territorial departments (Scottish Office, Welsh Office and Northern Ireland Office/Departments);
- *Federalism* would involve having four separate parliaments for England, Scotland, Wales and Northern Ireland, and also a Federal Parliament; and
- *Independence* for one or all of Scotland, Wales and Northern Ireland would either abolish the United Kingdom or narrow its geographical coverage, in which latter case either full integration or federalism could be implemented in the remaining United Kingdom.

Wales, which was annexed to England by the unilateral *Act of Union 1535*, was in most respects fully integrated.[1] This was not the case for Scotland (whose parliament voted by the *Act of Union 1707* for its own abolition) nor for Ireland (which, following the abolition of its parliament by the *Act of Union 1800* passed by the Westminster Parliament, was annexed to Great Britain). The resulting political entity was the United Kingdom of Great Britain and Ireland. There are many ways in which Scotland has been differentially governed since 1707 (Kellas, 1989),[2] a pattern reinforced by the creation in 1885 of the Scottish Office and the post of Secretary for Scotland (Gibson, 1985). In our view, majority opinion in Scotland and Wales would strongly oppose full integration, and no UK government would be likely to adopt the policy of the UK Unionist Party for full integration of Northern Ireland, not least because of how that would be interpreted by world opinion.

The key obstacle to federalism is the lack of interest in England. Our own position is that, *if* the circumstances were conducive to federalism, that would produce the best possible resolution of the United Kingdom's governance problems. As these circumstances seem unlikely to arise, asymmetrical devolution is both desirable and workable. The independence option is outside the scope of this article.

All schemes of asymmetrical devolution raise issues about parliamentary representation. The 'West Lothian Question' (so named in the 1970s after the then constituency of the Labour MP Tam Dalyell) draws attention to Scottish MPs at Westminster voting on the English counterparts of devolved services whereas they cannot vote on such matters affecting Scotland. However, this same question existed as the West Belfast Question from the date of the establishment in 1921, under the *Government of Ireland Act 1920,* of the Northern Ireland Parliament, until its prorogation in 1972. The abolition of the Northern Ireland Parliament eventually led to the convening of a Speaker's Conference on Northern Ireland parliamentary representation. After this had reported in 1978, processes were set in motion which led to an increase in the number of Northern Ireland MPs from 12 to 17 in the 1983 election. This increase was interpreted as the removal of the 1920 Act's 'devolution discount' (that is, one-third less Westminster representation than population would then have indicated) (McLean, 1995). Nevertheless, the Conservative government's Northern Ireland devolution plans (Northern Ireland Office, 1982, 1995) did not propose the reintroduction of any such discount.

Although there is a good case for avoiding unnecessary asymmetry, certain asymmetries are inevitable in the United Kingdom. What ultimately matters is whether particular asymmetries (of governmental structure or of parliamentary representation) are regarded as acceptable or unacceptable.[3]

Intriguingly, it has recently been those who claim to be defenders of the Union who have been attempting to convince public opinion in England that *proposed* asymmetries would be unacceptable, without regard to the *existing* asymmetries which have been endemic and often unremarked (Crick, 1995).

The second general point is that devolution, as now proposed, will be a considerable shock to the highly centralized political and governmental institutions of the United Kingdom, even though – when viewed in international terms – these same proposals look rather cautious. For example, both Australia and Canada adopted federal rather than unitary forms of government, and the United Kingdom played a significant role in the post-1945 establishment of a federal basis for Germany. There is one practical consequence of this history of centralism. Elsewhere in the world there is a vast amount of experience of the technical aspects of handling the vertical relationships between tiers of government and of ensuring that such systems work, albeit with (varying) degrees of fractiousness. Professor Russell Mathews, a distinguished Australian academic who served on the Commonwealth Grants Commission, expressed amazement in the 1970s at the apparent determination in the United Kingdom to re-invent the wheel.[4] The difficulties confronting successful devolution will not be technical, rather they will be political. Potential for centralism existed in the United Kingdom long before the 1979–97 Conservative government, but during this period it was unleashed, seriously undermining the role of local government (Select Committee on Relations between Central and Local Government, 1996). Increased centralization affects devolution as well as the future role of local authorities. With great prescience, Farquharson (1995) warned of the tension between the centralist party management characteristic of New Labour and devolution proposals which claimed to return certain areas of Scottish life back to Scotland for decision.

It is therefore necessary to ensure that this legacy of centralism does not generate a situation in which relationships and systems which work in countries with different political cultures fail to work in the United Kingdom. For that reason, institutional design requires a great deal of thought and care. During the 1990s, the period during which the activities of the Scottish Constitutional Convention (SCC) raised the UK political profile of Scottish devolution, there were a number of statements from those hostile to constitutional reform which might brutally, but accurately, be summarized as warnings that 'London will take revenge'. This theme had two variants: unilateral abolition by Westminster of a Scottish Parliament; and the threat of financial penalties. Stephen Dorrell, then Secretary of State for Health, said in February 1997 that a future Conservative government would abolish a Scottish Parliament if such had been established by Labour

(Parker, 1997). The flavour of the threats about money will later be illustrated by quotations from Cabinet ministers in the Major government, including those made by Jonathan Aitken (Chief Secretary to the Treasury, 1994–95) and Lord Mackay of Clashfern (Lord Chancellor, 1987–97). Limiting needs-based equalization to a situation in which decentralization remains administrative (Aitken) or linking block grant reductions to the exercise of tax-varying powers in either direction (Mackay) are simply wrecking propositions. Such threats corrode the threads which bind the United Kingdom together; their implementation would be a conclusive demonstration that the Union – ostensibly being supported by such actions – had ceased to be worth defending.

The third general point relates to the need to keep in mind when designing institutions and technical systems that there may in future arise the possibility of generalizing the model of Scottish devolution to other parts of the United Kingdom. The only valid reason for treating Wales differently from Scotland would be that the constitutional debate was held to be at a different stage of development and that proposals for a non-legislative, non tax-raising Assembly better conformed to majority opinion. Developments in Northern Ireland are contingent upon a lasting peace settlement. Devolution to Scotland cannot wait until changes in Wales, Northern Ireland and perhaps England make a parallel form of governance preferred in these countries and acceptable to the UK Parliament. Nevertheless, wherever possible, the arrangements made for Scotland should be sufficiently robust to accommodate later extensions. As will be shown below, these debates have to be conducted within the framework of the obligations which flow from membership of the European Union.

FISCAL RESPONSIBILIZATION AS THE CENTRAL ISSUE

Making devolved government fiscally responsible is the central issue which has to be addressed. It will be argued in this article that there was substantive logic for voting in the pre-legislative referendum[5] for:

- *Yes, Yes* (those who supported legislative devolution and tax-varying powers) or
- *No, Yes* (those who opposed legislative devolution but, in the event of a Scottish Parliament being established, wanted it to be fiscally responsible).

However, there was no substantive logic, though there was undoubted tactical appeal,[6] in voting:

- *Yes, No*
- *No, No*

The basis for these categorizations is developed below.

As a preliminary, a clear distinction should be drawn between post-legislative referendums on completed schemes (such as the 1979 referendums in both Scotland and Wales) and pre-legislative referendums on draft schemes (such as the September 1997 referendums). If there had been a post-legislative referendum on a completed scheme adapted from the SCC proposals, the question would have simply asked for approval or rejection of a Scottish Parliament with legislative and tax-varying powers. In practice, while the SCC scheme was largely reproduced in the Scotland White Paper the Scottish referendum unbundled one particular issue (tax-varying powers), though not others (such as the Additional Member form of proportional representation). Asking stupid questions for reasons primarily of electoral tactics runs the risk of receiving a stupid answer.[7] Alexander (1996) warned against the trap:

> When the [Scottish] Parliament is created Britain will have established a quasi-federal system. In any federal system there are three principal levels of government – national, state and local. If Scotland chose a Parliament with no taxation powers it would create the unstable nonsense in which the 'top' and 'bottom' levels of government had fiscal powers and the middle one ... had not. That is the real danger of a two-question referendum and I hope that the Scottish people will not fall into the trap (p.7).

Indeed, scaremongering on the second question[8] did reveal vulnerability on the Yes side, which appeared to grow as both sides to the debate came to expect a convincing Yes majority on the first question.[9] Alexander (1997) considered that a Yes:No outcome would resolve nothing, leaving a scheme which satisfied few:

> ... a Parliament without a power of taxation will produce a feeling of still unfinished business and the question of Scotland's constitutional arrangements will remain open for the foreseeable future (p.2).

A Yes:No vote would have involved legislating for a Scottish Parliament which commanded support in Scotland only on the basis that it was the only Parliament on offer. The arguments used by the Yes side for tax-varying powers would then have been recycled by those opposed to devolution as a means of keeping the issue alive. Simultaneously, there would have been bitter recriminations on the Yes side, concerning, *inter alia*, the behaviour of Labour's UK leadership in imposing the double-question referendum and the damaging sleaze allegations affecting Labour MPs and councillors in the West of Scotland.

Returning to the substantive issue of tax-varying powers, it is useful to separate this into two parts:

- whether a Parliament with legislative powers should have tax-varying powers; and
- whether fiscal responsibilization requires that such a Parliament raise *all the money it spends* or that its electors face the *full cost of marginal expenditure*.

The Imperative of Tax-Varying Powers

The kernel of the argument for tax-varying powers is that – *when differentials in needs and resources have been addressed* – the marginal expenditure decided upon by sub-national governments should be *self-financed* from an *economically appropriate* and *politically acceptable* tax base. This argument is carefully worded, and the wording receives detailed attention below.

The link between elected office and responsibility for revenue-raising is deliberate. All those who spend public money by virtue of elected office should have responsibility for raising some of that money through taxation and/or user charges. Just as 'no taxation without representation' was the battle cry of those who fought for American independence, so 'no representation without taxation' is a maxim which deserves equal priority. Tony Blair, then Leader of the Opposition, was heavily criticized in Scotland during the 1997 general election campaign for seeming to compare a Scottish Parliament with an English parish council.[10] The fact that his eloquence seems to have failed him on that occasion should not obscure the serious point he was attempting to make, namely that the link between election and tax-raising is an accepted feature of democratic societies. Indeed, election to office confers a legitimacy and (time-limited) permanence which does not attach to those who are appointed – and can summarily be dismissed – by ministers. Taxation powers are not conferred upon those public bodies loosely described as 'quangos', the appointees to which must either manage within the budgets allocated by ministers or resign their posts if budgets are thought so inadequate that satisfactory performance is impossible.

Moreover, these arguments about the link between election and tax-raising apply even more forcefully to an elected body which possesses extensive legislative powers, ranging over a substantial part of public expenditure:

No meaningful Parliament anywhere in the world is without revenue-raising powers (Canavan, 1997).

... Labour is proposing both an Edinburgh Parliament and an option for the Scots to deny it any tax powers. A Parliament with no powers over taxation is not worth the name (Adonis, 1997).

A study undertaken by the Institute for Fiscal Studies (IFS) strongly emphasized the importance of tax-varying powers, before extending the argument to note that, without them, the decisions of sub-national governments would be dominated by the centre:

> If regional governments are to function as genuine democratic units, with the power to make decisions concerning the level and pattern of public services, they will need to have access to some form of tax revenues under their own control. Reliance on fiscal transfers from central government will undermine the ability of regional government to make their decisions free from central influence (Blow, Hall and Smith, 1996: 62).

Full Self-financing versus Self-financing at the Margin

A number of commentators have begun to argue that fiscal accountability can only be achieved if a devolved Scottish Parliament were to be responsible for raising all the money it spends. Even though this argument is often used as a spoiler – knowing that this condition is incapable of being fulfilled – the argument requires a proper answer.

The most eloquent advocates of 'full self-financing' are those opposed in principle to devolution but willing to engage in serious debate, notably the journalists Andrew Neil and Michael Fry:

> Any Scottish parliament which is not responsible itself for raising from the Scottish people *all the money* it intends to spend on our behalf will only perpetuate the unhealthy myth which has dominated Scottish political culture for too long, that big government is a free ride. Worse, when the overwhelming source of that parliament's funds (even if the tartan tax were to be levied at full whack) is a grant from Westminster, then you have a system tailor-made for exploitation to Nationalist advantage. An Edinburgh parliament will be run by the outdated collectivist consensus that still dominates Scottish politics. It will want to spend, spend, spend. But instead of having to go to the Scottish people to raise the money, it will rattle the begging bowl in London; and when Westminster refuses to stump up more cash, the Nationalists will have a field day ... The only way to avoid a bust-up would be to make the Edinburgh parliament responsible for raising

every penny it plans to spend (Neil, 1997a, italics added).

Instead of [a Scottish Parliament] being funded by a block grant from London (which the Nationalists will always insist is never enough) there ought to be a far closer correlation between what a Scottish Parliament spends and the taxes it levies on the Scottish people. That is the only way to undermine the collectivist consensus which dominates Scottish politics; it is also a pre-condition for any Scottish Tory revival (Neil, 1997b).

Others [Scottish Tories] might split their votes, Yes-No or No-Yes, the latter being my own preference … The [outcome] which appears most promising to me is *full fiscal responsibility* for a Scottish Parliament (Fry, 1997, italics added).

Our view is that fiscal accountability at the margin of decision is what can practically be achieved in contemporary economic and political circumstances. The same conclusion was drawn by the IFS study team which investigated the financing of regional government:

… explicit equalising grants from central to regional government could be used – regional accountability is satisfied even where, on average, most spending is grant financed, as long as *extra* spending is financed by extra taxes. However, grant finance also makes regional government less autonomous (Institute for Fiscal Studies, 1996).

The sting in the tail of the IFS quotation – too much grant dependence curtails freedom of action – indicates that it would be preferable to secure independent sources of revenue to the maximum extent possible under the specific circumstances of the case.[11]

However, an insistence upon a strict interpretation of full self-financing (one which saw control over tax rates as an integral part of the concept) would:

• breach EU law;
• involve serious economic inefficiencies and weaken safeguards against tax avoidance and evasion; and
• preclude needs and resources equalization.

Indeed, in the context of EU developments, even national governments will find it more difficult to vary tax rates.

There are four factors shaping these conclusions. First, on a general level, economic globalization and deregulation, and, on a specific level, European economic integration and possible monetary union, have all combined to limit fiscal discretion. Capital and labour have become much more mobile. With regard to corporate taxes, the fact that jurisdictions find it more difficult to protect their own tax bases strengthens long-standing arguments against the use of such taxes by sub-national governments (King, 1984). Moreover, certain categories of labour are now internationally mobile to an unprecedented extent: good examples are managerial labour (such as those who work in financial sectors) and professional sportspersons (for example, footballers such as Paul Gascoigne and Paolo di Canio). In such circumstances, mobile labour may be able to shift personal taxation back to the employer, through the ability to bargain about net wages. More generally, this is a signal that progressive taxation, which is coming under strain even at a national level, cannot be sustained at a sub-national level. This reinforces a standard conclusion of the public finance literature, emphasizing that, in the context of greater income inequality, even a proportional sub-national income tax may have to have a cap on total individual liability.

Second, membership of the European Union involves acceptance of extremely strict limits on the extent of variation in consumption taxes, which the European Commission has been attempting to standardize across member states. When the November 1975 White Paper on devolution (Lord President of the Council *et al.*, 1975) was being prepared, European constraints on territorial variations in VAT and on the introduction of a retail sales tax were not recognized for some time. The use of such taxes as one of the revenue sources of the German Länder is covered by derogations in regard of pre-existing taxes which, even before the big push for tax harmonization, would not have been extended to the United Kingdom (Heald, 1980).

Third, there have been remarkable changes over the last 20 years in the technology of consumption and in the organization of retailing. Even without the presence of EU constraints, there would be powerful revenue protection arguments for keeping VAT as simple as possible and for not complicating matters by introducing regionally variable rates and/or supplementary retail taxes. It should also be noted that reductions in real transport costs have lowered the costs of shopping in other jurisdictions, as indicated by the controversies about the extent of cross-Channel shopping. In any case, effective distances in the United Kingdom are small in international terms, thereby ruling out many of the revenue sources from consumption taxes which are used by states in Australia[12] and provinces in Canada.

Fourth, proper attention has to be paid to the macroeconomic context. Just because the power of central government over local authorities was seriously abused during the 1980s and 1990s does not imply that there is no legitimate central government interest in the expenditure and financing of sub-national governments. Central governments have the responsibility for securing macroeconomic balance, an undertaking which must affect sub-national governments when they account for a significant proportion of General Government Expenditure (GGE) and of GDP. This issue most obviously arises when sub-national governments overwhelmingly depend upon central grants. More subtly, the issue reappears when local authorities have access to buoyant tax bases, as in Sweden, which would elsewhere be the preserve of central government. Nevertheless, the most pressing concern for the finance ministries of EU member countries relates to the obligations under the Maastricht Treaty's Excessive Deficits Protocol: member states have pledged themselves to 'avoid excessive government deficits', interpreted as ceilings of 3 per cent for the ratio of the government deficit to GDP at market prices and of 60 per cent for the ratio of government debt to GDP at market prices. In consequence, the main concerns will relate not to expenditure financed by sub-national taxes[13] but rather to central grants and sub-national borrowing.[14]

The culmination of these developments has clearly been to favour tax-raising being effected at higher levels of government. Moreover, strong arguments can be mobilized that the best taxes for variation at sub-national levels are highly visible ones such as personal income taxes (though the variation band has to be kept modest) and property taxes, supplemented by user charges. There is no reason to be too depressed by these conclusions about limitations on which taxes can be devolved: these are fiscal dilemmas that confront other states. Musgrave (1997), who firmly rejects the Leviathan view of the state advanced by public choice theorists, cautioned that arguments for pushing tax-raising down to lower tiers of government are, in part, designed to reduce tax progressivity and to increase the economic costs[15] and political obstacles associated with generating the revenues required for (what he would regard as) an efficient and equitable level of public expenditure.

THE SCOTTISH CONSTITUTIONAL CONVENTION'S FINANCING FRAMEWORK

The purpose of this section is to consider the overall design of the SCC's financing framework, set out in proposals published in 1990 and revised in 1995 (Scottish Constitutional Convention, 1990, 1995). Accordingly, the following structure is adopted: the main features of the SCC proposals are summarized; recent threats that devolution means the end of needs-based equalization are exposed as spoiling tactics; the suggestion that the exercise of tax-varying powers in either direction would lead to block-grant reductions is shown to be either misinformed or malicious; and, finally, there is further discussion of the proposition that the financial framework will generate unmanageable conflict.

Financing Proposals of the Scottish Constitutional Convention

The final scheme published by the Scottish Constitutional Convention (1995) based the financing package upon a block grant (described as an 'assigned budget' for presentational reasons), supported by the 3p each-way income tax-varying power. Mitchell (1995, p.20) made the reasonable complaint that there was considerable vagueness, noting that 'The Convention scheme has less detail than the 1978 [Scotland] Act.' In defence of the SCC, the increasingly difficult political environment needs to be recognized. Between 1990 and 1995, Labour had lost the 1992 general election for reasons widely believed to be connected with tax, and there was obvious nervousness in its UK leadership about the repercussions in 'middle England' of a Scottish debate increasingly dominated by Michael Forsyth (Secretary of State for Scotland from July 1995) who had dubbed the SCC's tax-varying powers the 'tartan tax'. In the event, the UK leadership bounced its SCC partners into abandoning assigned revenues, which had formed part of the 1990 financing scheme (Scottish Constitutional Convention, 1990):

> The shift from assigned revenues to assigned budget was foreshadowed in *A Parliament for Scotland: Labour's Plan* which proposed the system subsequently adopted by the Convention. There was some concern within the Convention that the change was adopted to suit the electoral fortunes of the Labour Party. Labour has noted that the assignment of taxes to Scotland would have left a shortfall on current Scottish Office expenditure requiring a top-up grant from the Treasury, and considers that a well-established formula-driven public grant would be more stable. However, the change raised fears that the tax-raising powers of the Parliament might be under attack (Gay *et al.,* 1995: 13).

Heald (1990) advocated some tax assignment, though differently structured from the SCC's 1990 scheme, for exactly the same reasons of fiscal pyschology as motivated the SCC: namely, to emphasize that such revenues were not subsidy from central government.[16] If Gay *et al.* were correct in their attribution of Labour's motives, this hope of diverting attention was misplaced: an inevitable consequence of devolution, especially asymmetrical devolution, will be to bring far greater transparency to territorial public finances (Heald, 1992, 1994).

Although not specified in the SCC's 1995 scheme, the block grant system should operate in the following way. The first step is to make arrangements for a systematic needs assessment, covering each of the four constituent parts of the United Kingdom; how this should be done is discussed below. The second step is to determine a formula which automatically controls changes in each territorial block relative to changes in comparable English expenditure. This would be the third such formula, following in the tradition of the Goschen formula (established in 1888) and the Barnett formula (established in 1978) (Heald, 1994). In the unlikely event that each constituent part's expenditure relative exactly matched its assessed needs relative, the new formula would allocate expenditure changes on the basis of weighted population. The formula, once determined, would be set to run for a period of, say, ten years, thereby establishing a degree of certainty about future shares. If, as is more likely, there were divergences between the expenditure and assessed needs relatives, the new formula would be set to lead to convergence over a manageable period, say, ten or 20 years.[17] There is substantial experience in the National Health Service of convergence mechanisms, though these have operated for the health authorities of each territory, rather than across the United Kingdom as a whole.

A key task of the devolution legislation will be to establish the framework both for the needs assessment exercise and for the determination of the formula: the first task should be exclusively allocated to a Territorial Exchequer Board (Heald and Geaughan, 1996), to which any governmental or private body would be able to make representations; proposals for the content of the formula would also be made by this Board, though the final decision would be the subject of negotiation between the UK government and devolved governments. It would be helpful to establish arbitration procedures for use in cases of failure to agree on formula revisions consistent with the terms of the devolution legislation.

Threatened Withdrawal of Equalization

Lurking behind threats about the financial consequences of devolution for Scotland can be found certain issues of principle; these have to be recognized now and acted upon. The following quotations are some of the best examples, both in content and tone:

> As the Cabinet minister concerned with the level of overall public expenditure I am very conscious of the benefits Scotland enjoys under the UK's system of public expenditure. Identifiable government expenditure per head in Scotland in 1992–93 is estimated to have been 16 per cent higher than the equivalent UK figure. The conclusion must be that under the present constitutional arrangements Scotland derives substantial financial benefit from the Union. There is nothing wrong in that, but it should not be lost sight of either in the current debate …

A devolved or independent Scotland no longer underpinned by the present UK public expenditure formula would have to raise extra taxation on a scale which could seriously damage Scotland's competitive position (Aitken, 1995).

...higher income tax would inevitably follow if devolution became a reality. That is because higher spending in the end has to be paid for by higher taxation. Already, identifiable government expenditure in Scotland in 1993–94 was 21 per cent higher than in England. That is over £600 more per person a year and over 16 per cent more than the United Kingdom average. If a devolved Assembly were set up in Edinburgh many English taxpayers would undoubtedly expect more of this higher public spending in Scotland to be raised in Scotland (Clarke, 1995).

'So just to maintain spending ... a Scottish Parliament would have to levy additional taxes.' Labour has said that the maximum figure by which a Scottish Parliament could vary income tax would be 3p in the pound, but Mr Lang said this would raise only £450 million. 'If a British Chancellor decided to reduce the funding transferred to a Scottish Parliament to the same level as the rest of the UK, funding would be cut by almost £2,845 million. To replace that would need additional taxation in Scotland, on top of UK taxation, of 19p on Scottish income tax.' (Ian Lang's Dimbleby interview on London Weekend Television, as reported by MacAskill in the *Scotsman*, 13 February 1995).

The common thread in these quotations is that needs equalization, in recognition of Scotland's higher per capita expenditure needs, is explicitly linked to the status quo of administrative decentralization; this would be withdrawn if there were to be devolution within the United Kingdom. The Aitken (1995) quotation failed to distinguish between a devolved Scotland (which would contribute to, and draw from, the common pool of UK resources) and an independent Scotland (which would depend upon its own resources). In 1995, the year of all these quotations, the irony was not lost in Scotland that the Major government had been promoting schemes of devolution for Northern Ireland which did not involve the termination of needs equalization.

Two principles need to be clearly enunciated. The first is that the entitlement to needs equalization of any component part of the United Kingdom is not affected by the form of devolved government chosen by its citizens. The second is that successful devolution requires much greater transparency about territorial public finances than has been the case when territorial allocation was a process internal to a single government (Treasury, 1997). This transparency will be required to sustain public confidence throughout the United Kingdom that expenditure relatives properly reflect need relatives, and that corrective action is being taken when divergences emerge. This point remains valid despite the IFS caution that:

> In the longer run, if the current interregional transfers become more explicit, this may reduce public willingness to maintain these transfers at current levels (Institute for Fiscal Studies, 1996: 1).

Without proper transparency, a commitment to matching expenditure with needs will undoubtedly be transformed into a reluctance to sustain needs equalization.

Financial Penalties for Using Tax-varying Powers

The Revenue Support Grant system for local authorities is structured in such a way that, if all local authorities were to spend at their centrally assessed expenditure need, they would all declare the same Band D council tax. The corollary is that divergences of actual expenditure above assessed expenditure lead to a higher-than-norm council tax, just as cases of actual expenditure below assessed expenditure lead to a lower-than-norm council tax. Grant penalties have never been exacted for 'underspending' whereas 'overspenders' have faced grant penalties and tax capping.

With regard to the exercise of tax-varying powers conferred upon devolved government by the UK Parliament, Lord Mackay of Clashfern, then Lord Chancellor and a member of the Major Cabinet, speculated that there might be penalties:

> And on the vexed tax question, Lord Mackay believes that it would be 'meaningless' to ask the Scottish people to approve of a tax-raising parliament, without knowing the consequences of their actions. 'What will be the consequences of the financial arrangements between Scotland and the rest of the United Kingdom if Scots decide to raise income tax by 3p in the pound? Will the government of the United Kingdom be expected to put the same amount into Scotland than if the income tax was the same in England and Wales?' Similarly, he said that if the Scots decided to cut their tax rates, would the English taxpayer be expected to make up the difference? (Cochrane, 1997).

The answers to Lord Mackay's questions are straightforward. Upwards use of the tax-varying power would allow the Scottish Executive to incur higher expenditure on, for example, education, the block grant being increased by an amount equivalent to the positive yield net of administrative costs.

Similarly, downwards use would require the Scottish Executive to reduce its expenditure on, say, education, the block grant being reduced by the negative yield plus administrative costs. It would be remarkably futile to confer delimited tax-varying powers upon a devolved parliament, and then penalize their use. The Scottish Council Foundation (1997) urged that the size of the block grant should be formally insulated from the exercise of the tax-varying power. This might most effectively be done by making such insulation explicit in the devolution legislation and by requiring the separate identification of both the (positive, zero or negative) proceeds of the tax-varying power, and the administrative costs reimbursed to the Inland Revenue.

The Prospect of Perpetual Crisis and Instability

There have been several variants of this line of criticism of the SCC scheme; the one considered here is associated with Midwinter and McVicar (1996a, b). Their argument might be summarized as involving three linked propositions:

- the SCC's financing package would provide inadequate fiscal autonomy, leading to a 'fiscal relationship ... with Westminster of dependency' (1996a: 51), resulting in both
- political conflict, and
- challenges to 'Scotland's preferential funding' (1996a: 50).

Together these lead to the implied conclusion that such a devolved parliament is not worth having.[18]

There is not the space here to work through all the stages of this argument. Comment will therefore be restricted to three points. First, Midwinter and McVicar developed their case in such a forceful way that they unwittingly invite the conclusion that no form of political decentralization is viable. Given Midwinter's long-standing commitment to local authority autonomy, this is highly paradoxical as this argument can be readily extended to local authorities. The reasons why full self-financing is infeasible for either devolved governments or local authorities have been explored earlier in this article. Midwinter and McVicar attach too much importance to the proportion of expenditure which is self-financed and too little importance to self-financing at the margin. Whatever the position on the proportion of self-financing, central government has possessed administrative instruments, such as capping and targets, which have allowed ministers to override local decisions. What has to be sought for both devolved governments and local authorities are financing frameworks in which the scope for choice at the margin is transparent, and which regulate intergovernmental relationships.

Second, considerably more fiscal discretion can be exercised within Scotland than is usually portrayed. The estimated yield of the maximum upwards use of the tartan tax is about three per cent of the Scottish Parliament's likely total budget. Some commentators argued that, even if the tax-varying power was fully used upwards, the additional £450 million would be a trivial amount, leading to a grant dependency of 97 per cent. Given that the Labour Party had pledged itself not to use this power during the period 1997–2002, the grant dependency was likely to be 100 per cent. These figures of 97 per cent and 100 per cent are seriously misleading, because they fail to probe beneath the financing of the Scotland Programme, which is effectively what a devolved Scottish Executive would take over from the Scottish Office.[19] Although satisfactory data are not in the public domain, certain observations can be made. In terms of 1996–97 estimated outturn, central government support to local authorities represented 41 per cent of the Scotland Programme outturn (excluding the Forestry Commission) (Scottish Office, 1997b). For technical reasons, it is not possible to match up this data source with figures published in the local government financial statistics. However, in respect of local authority general fund services,[20] council tax accounted in 1994–95 for 14.4 per cent[21] of total revenue income, while income from sales, fees and charges accounted for 5.5 per cent (Scottish Office, 1997a, Table 1). These figures, excluding non-domestic rates which accounted for 15.6 per cent of total revenue income for general fund services, indicate that there is a considerable amount of revenue generation, and hence discretion, within this part of the Scotland Programme. There is an urgent need for better data in the public domain about the extent of such revenue generation (both the difference between gross and net expenditure, and the yield of other taxes controllable within Scotland).[22]

Third, as stressed by Mair and McAteer (1997), devolved parliaments will be able to draw on considerable political resources, including those that can be derived from the devolution legislation and those from the recognition that Scotland is a nation within the United Kingdom. With reference to the 1970s' devolution debates, MacKay concluded that:

> ... the efficient operation of the devolution settlement requires the development of a workable and reasonably harmonious relationship between the Assembly and Westminster (MacKay: 16).

The decisive 1997 election result will be important in this regard, as the prospect of a five-year parliament provides an opportunity to establish sound working relationships in an environment where there are no incentives for deliberate destabilization. Moreover, the fact that the Scottish

Parliament is to be elected by proportional representation will not only add to its legitimacy, but will also provide strong incentives for devolutionists to support proportional representation for elections to the UK Parliament, as the best guarantee of the long-term survival of devolved parliaments in the absence of any mechanism for entrenchment.

DEFENDING THE TARTAN TAX

Two mutually exclusive criticisms have often been made of the tartan tax: that it would cripple the Scottish economy, and that it would raise so little money that it is an irrelevance.[23] Amusingly, these criticisms are made by the same people, with it being a matter of judgement whether they are dissembling or unaware of the contradiction. Simultaneous use is open to ridicule, as when Michael Forsyth, then Secretary of State for Scotland, contended that '… devolution would bring a parish council which would impoverish the country' (Stewart, 1997). In the case of the first criticism, a constrained power to vary personal income taxes is implausibly forecast to cause momentous damage to the Scottish economy:

> Any form of additional regional tax can only handicap Scottish business and commerce and discourage vital investment by UK and overseas companies – and thus the all important creation of wealth and jobs (Sir Bruce Pattullo, Governor of the Bank of Scotland, quoted in Ballantyne and MacMahon, 1997).

In contrast, economists at the Fraser of Allander Institute at Strathclyde University concluded that the macroeconomic effects would be modest, either way:

> If the Scottish people genuinely wish increased government expenditure in Scotland and, importantly, if they are prepared to pay for this in the form of higher income taxes without seeking compensating changes in their gross wage, then the fiscal innovation of the 'tartan tax' may have significant beneficial effects on employment, output and migration. However, even in the worst likely scenario [full compensating changes in gross wages] the adverse macroeconomic impact is relatively small and spread over a considerable time period (McGregor *et al.,* 1997: 82).

A key factor in determining the impact would be the extent of tax shifting by employees back to their employers. The available evidence suggests that there would be some shifting and that the valuation placed by employers and employees upon the outputs produced with that incremental expenditure would be important (Helms, 1985; Day, 1992; Wallace, 1993).[24]

The SCC's scheme specifically avoided taxes directly levied on business, with corporation tax ruled out and the business property tax (known as 'non-domestic rates' or 'business rates') judged unsuitable (McCormick, 1996). Earlier controversies about Scotland–England differences in non-domestic rates led to the policy of having a Unified Business Rate (a common poundage in Scotland and England), with the staged implementation being completed as from 1995–96. There are few advocates in Scotland of a return of the power to set business rate poundages to local authority control.[25]

On the issue of 'irrelevance', the following views have been attributed to Jim Stevens, an economist with the Fraser of Allander Institute and a member of the Labour Party's Scottish Executive:

> Economically, the tax-levying powers contained in the proposals are insignificant. A 3p increase in basic income tax would raise £400 million or so and once that money is spread across the entire Scottish Office budget its macro-economic impact will be very slight. It is enough money to build a few miles of motorway or keep the Forth Bridge in paint for a few years (Donegan, 1997).

Leaving aside the point that the Scottish Executive will not be responsible for painting the Forth Rail Bridge (which is the metallic structure), such a view misses the point that the fiscal discretion of sub-national governments – increasingly of all governments – is exercisable at the margin.

It is necessary to make three further points about the tax-varying power. First, it was always a matter of political judgement on how to define its extent, and in that sense the band of variation was arbitrary:

> ... there is no particular reason why the 3p maximum should have been chosen. However, politically it would probably be difficult now to propose a higher ceiling. It would have been possible to plan for a much higher proportion of funding to be tax-based, in order to increase accountability (Bell et al., 1996: 67–8).

On the contrary, both the imposition of the referendum and the eventual 10.8 percentage points (14.5 per cent) differential Yes vote in Scotland between the two questions provides support for the soundness of the SCC's political judgement. Second, there is a fundamental distinction between the definition of the powers to be conferred upon a Scottish Parliament by the devolution legislation and the intended use of those powers by the Labour Party in the event that it controlled the Scottish Parliament.[26] At the due date, it will be for the Scottish electorate to decide whether to vote for this policy or to support other parties which might propose to use these powers upwards or downwards. Third, one factor which should be borne in mind during the early years of the Scottish Parliament is that the political obstacles to the use of tax-varying powers, in either direction, would be likely to grow during an extended period of non-use, and the administrative and compliance arrangements originally put in place would atrophy.

Needs Assessment and Equalization

From the earlier discussion, the pivotal role of needs equalization within the devolved financing system is self-evident. Throughout the period of Conservative government, there was no repetition of the Treasury's (1979) needs assessment study. Instead, the only significant change to the mechanism for determining changes in the Scottish Block was the recalibration of the Barnett formula in 1992.[27] The Scottish Office did not consider that it was in Scotland's interests to propose such a review. During the 1980s, the Scottish Office and its ministers favoured 'talking down' issues of territorial allocation, so as not to provoke developments which might imperil the Scottish expenditure relative. During the 1990s, the position has been remarkably different, with ministers queuing up to proclaim the fact of higher Scottish expenditure and publicize 'threats' to the formula – a tactic which Mitchell (1992) uncharitably suggested was intended to portray the then Secretary of State, Ian Lang, as the defender of Scottish interests. During the Secretaryship of Michael Forsyth, all caution was abandoned; the recklessness of some later statements, which suggested that higher levels of expenditure were unjustifiable, became a scorched-earth policy (Dinwoodie, 1997; Scott and MacMahon, 1997). Regrettably, one consequence was to prejudice the reception given to important new work on government revenues and expenditure in Scotland (Scottish Office, 1992, 1995, 1996); data which ought to have provoked a serious debate were glibly dismissed as politically motivated.

There are two urgent tasks. The first is to incorporate the principle of needs equalization in the forthcoming legislation, together with adjustment mechanisms of the kinds discussed above. The second is to set in motion the steps for conducting a UK-wide needs assessment. Conduct of the needs assessment will have to await the establishment of the Territorial Exchequer Board after the passage of the legislation (Constitution Unit, 1996). However, much can now be done in preparation, particularly with regard to the design of data collection systems. There are several areas in which action is urgently required: two ready examples relate to the territorial analysis of public expenditure and to the sample size of the Survey of Personal Incomes. Those who have complained in recent years about insufficient resources devoted to these tasks have been firmly told that the allocation of resources to statistical activities had to meet the policy and operational needs of current ministers, not the hypothetical ones of hypothetical ministers. These issues now have high policy and operational salience.

Our best guess is that, on devolved services, such a needs assessment exercise might show that Scotland's expenditure relative is higher than its needs relative, necessitating a downwards adjustment through time. There is a powerful case for accepting that such an exercise should be undertaken as soon as the institutional framework is in place, rather than postponing it to a later date, when tension or hostility between the UK and devolved governments may have arisen. There can be no doubt that differences in per capita expenditure need new legitimization, which can only be provided through the processes discussed above. Moreover, the purpose of a territorial formula, namely that these issues are not re-opened every year, needs to be re-asserted after a period in which the mechanics but not the spirit of the formula have been observed.

OTHER ASPECTS OF THE FINANCING SCHEME

There are several important issues which have not been addressed in this article, but which are worth listing as topics for debate:

- the treatment of EU funds, about which there would be concern to ensure that the Scottish and Welsh Executives are properly incentivized to secure such funds without there being unintentional 'double compensation' for additional needs (for example, through both the block grant and EU funds); this is yet another manifestation of the issue of additionality.
- the implications of the introduction of Resource Accounting and Budgeting (accruals accounting, in which capital assets are valued and depreciated) for the measured size of the block grant and the operation of the formula which controls changes in its size.
- the treatment of National Lottery funds.
- the treatment of assets financed through the Private Finance Initiative.
- the monitoring of tax expenditures granted by the UK government which touch upon devolved programme areas.
- the structuring of relationships between the devolved parliament and local authorities.

CONCLUSION

As a prelude to drawing the argument together, it is instructive to juxtapose the observations of two professors of political science, both of whom have explicitly identified themselves as Scots resident in other parts of the United Kingdom:

I am an expatriate Scot who has until now always been an ardent unionist ... The current plan for Scottish devolution is so unworkable that, if implemented, it must either lead back to unionism, or on to federalism or independence. The state of Scottish opinion makes a return to unionism impossible. Federalism would mean designing institutions for England that nobody wants. So I have taken a deep breath and decided to support independence ... England should offer a fair devolution scheme which would end Scotland's favourable treatment. The Scots could take it or leave it ... [The offer would be] on terms that are fair to all parts of the country – say, a Scottish parliament with no secretary of state, with 45 Scottish MPs at Westminster (currently 72), and with a block grant to the Scottish parliament comprising the UK mean expenditure per head on the services that the Scottish parliament will run ... (McLean, 1997a: 80; the last two parts of the quotation above have been resequenced).

There were two main reasons for the failure of the last referendum. One, for non-Labour voters, was that the assembly would be dominated by the Strathclyde majority. The second was not only that a parliament without economic powers would be a 'talking shop', but also that their absence would reduce political debate to an unseemly competition over who could 'screw the most money out of Westminster' ... If people in Scotland fail now to endorse proposals which go to the heart of what they regarded as wrong last time, they will not deserve to be heard again and the world at large will be entitled to think of them as whingers (Meehan, 1997).

Undoubtedly, the greatest threat to the future of the Union lies in the deliberate closing of constitutional options, in the attempt to polarize opinion between the status quo and independence. Recourse to this device was widely believed to have contributed to the Conservative Party's better-than-expected 1992 general election result in Scotland, though its use in 1997 did not prevent the loss of all its Scottish seats. The devolution scheme offered by McLean (1997a) would involve: a devolution discount on Westminster representation;[28] a block grant set at UK mean expenditure per head on devolved services, thus ending UK-wide needs equalization; and (presumably) no tax-varying powers. His wording would suggest that his stated conversion to independence is mocking, and that his objective is to devise a scheme which Scotland would reject. Article titles such as 'Yes, yes! Begone with Scotland!' (McLean, 1997b) and use of the 'velvet divorce' analogy[29] (McLean, 1997c) do not resonate with constructive motivation, but rather with a threat to throw Scotland out of the Union.

The context of UK devolution is that the government of a hitherto highly centralized unitary state is being fragmented. It is often the context that federations are created by hitherto independent states unifying their governmental structures. Decisions with long-term consequences are then made about the extent to which needs and resources will be equalized across the federation; marked differences in outcome can be detected among Australia (where the tradition of needs and resources equalization is strong), Canada (where the emphasis is on partial resources equalization), and the United States (which has little systematic equalization). Devolution within the United Kingdom will not work unless there is an explicit recognition that the forms of government chosen by a country or region do not affect its claims upon the pool of UK resources on the basis of differential need.

McLean drew comfort from the deliberate impression created in the 1990s by Ian Lang and Michael Forsyth that Scotland's present expenditure relative is unfair to England, in that the present level of spending is far too high in relation to needs (expenditure relative greatly exceeds the needs relative). Forsyth's scorched-earth tactics to resist devolution are bizarrely portrayed as evidence of the 'success' of his incumbency. McLean's conviction that Scotland's expenditure is too high relative to needs leads on to his proposal to abolish Scotland's access to UK-wide needs equalization as the 'price' of legislative devolution. Logically, however, it should lead to a proposal for a new needs assessment.

Moreover, the UK pool of resources embraces oil revenues from the UK Continental Shelf, defined for UK statistical purposes as a separate region. These revenues would come back into the political reckoning were Scotland either to be independent or, post-devolution, implausibly denied access to UK-wide needs equalization. In the run-up to the 1997 general election there was extensive controversy about the Scottish National Party's (SNP) proposed budget, the news appeal of which was greatly enhanced by the Treasury unexpectedly providing a written parliamentary answer, on the basis of the SNP's hypotheticals (Waldegrave, 1997a, b). The resulting calculation represented Scotland's General Government Borrowing Requirement (GGBR), expressed at 1996–97 prices, as a surplus of £26.7 billion over the years 1978–79 to 1994–95.[30] Though a good propaganda number, these figures – even if accepted – refer to byegones and not to Scotland's present budgetary position, stated by the same written answer as a GGBR in 1994–95 of £6.5 billion (at 1996–97 prices) on the same assumptions (Waldegrave, 1997a). The benefits to England projected by McLean (1997b: 21) from Scottish independence ('the English will gain from the ending of its £6 billion transfer payment') constitute a misinterpretation of Scotland's share of the UK GGBR as 'a structural deficit between Scotland and the rest of the UK of £6 billion a year' (p.19).[31]

Four concluding points are appropriate. First, the SCC fulfilled an invaluable function by keeping devolution on the political agenda during a period in which the UK government was hostile to the idea, except for Northern Ireland. Following the 1997 election, the Scotland White Paper published by the incoming Labour government was well received by its SCC partners; they largely held their silence on the issues of a pre-legislative referendum and the separating out of the taxation issue. In the longer-term, however, the work of the SCC may have created the basis for new alliances in Scotland, which will be resistant to unilateral impositions of policy by the UK Labour leadership. There was a questionable assumption during the referendum campaign that Labour would overcome the hurdles of the Additional Member system and be able to impose its will, notably on the exercise of tax-varying powers.

Second, the United Kingdom, which has exported its system of government across the world, must now be willing to learn from elsewhere. Obvious examples relate to how the Commonwealth Grants Commission in Australia organizes the data collection systems which underpin its judgements on relative needs,[32] and how the Loans Council co-ordinates borrowing activities. Closer to home, there is a much to be learned from the experiences of the devolved Northern Ireland Parliament, about which there are several authoritative accounts (for example, Lawrence, 1965; Birrell and Murie, 1980; Bloomfield, 1996). The reaction in Great Britain to most things to do with Northern Ireland – communitarian strife discouraging interest and understanding – should no longer inhibit learning from the United Kingdom's only experience of legislative devolution, notably about how *not* to undermine financial autonomy.

Third, to repeat what has already been stressed, devolution makes elected bodies responsible for territorial management, rather than this being internal to one government. Many relationships, especially financial ones, must become more explicit and hence more transparent. Where this is not arranged through formal machinery, the information will be leaked out or forced out later, with damaging repercussions.

Fourth, there should be no illusions about how tough the public expenditure climate will be, both because of UK-level pressures (Heald, 1997) and because the Scotland (and Northern Ireland) expenditure relatives have received a dramatically higher public profile as result of their flaunting by those opposed to Scottish devolution:[33]

> Everyone knows that sooner or later Westminster will refuse to continue funding the much higher health, education and housing expenditure in Scotland than is spent in England and Wales. Devolution will bring that moment of truth far closer and will result in either heavier taxation in Scotland or massive cuts to deal with the deficit (Rifkind, 1997).

The moment of truth, in the different sense that expenditure relatives will now have to be publicly justified, was dawning well before the referendum verdict. The crucial task of relegitimating the territorial allocation system can now be joined by a Scotland with renewed self-confidence, having stepped over Alexander's (1996) trap and brushed aside Meehan's (1997) charge of irredeemable whingeing.

NOTES

1. One of the most most telling illustrations of this is that Chancellor of the Exchequer Sir George Goschen (1888), when announcing the territorial allocation formula now bearing his name, referred only to the three countries of Scotland, Ireland and England (Heald, 1992).
2. Nairn (1981: 129) described the results of the Act of Union as '... a nationality which resigned statehood but preserved an extraordinary amount of the institutional and psychological baggage normally associated with independence – a decapitated nation state, as it were, rather than an ordinary 'assimilated' nationality'. Leruez (1983) elegantly captured the idea with his book title: *L'Ecosse: Une Nation Sans Etat*.
3. No firm criteria as to what is or is not 'acceptable' can be enunciated. A parallel is that ministers have to resign when they have lost the confidence of their colleagues, not when they have crossed some invisible line (Woodhouse, 1994).
4. This observation was made in his editorial comments on a draft version of Heald (1980).
5. The *Referendums (Scotland and Wales) Act 1997* provided for electors entitled to vote in local government elections in Scotland to be asked to indicate their assent to one of two opposing statements offered on two questions. On a 60.4% poll, voting on the first question (whether there should be a Scottish Parliament) was 74.3% (Yes) to 25.7% (No). Voting on the second question (whether that Parliament should have tax-varying powers) was 63.5% (Yes) to 36.5% (No). Because there were two separate ballot papers, the combinations chosen by voters are not known. However, results on each question were declared separately for the 32 local authority areas; there were Yes majorities in all 32 on the first question and in 30 (Dumfries and Galloway, and Orkney being the exceptions) on the second question. The referendum in Wales was held one week later on 18 September. On a 50.1% turnout, the voting was 50.3% (Yes) and 49.7% (No). The 22 local authority areas split 11:11, with Pembrokeshire (No) in the far south west being the sole exception to the geographical pattern of results (the east voting No and the west voting Yes).
6. There were tactical motives for voting for the third combination (e.g. someone favouring independence who wanted to see constitutional movement from the status quo and the creation of a Scottish Parliament without long-term credibility) or for the fourth combination (e.g. someone favouring the status quo or full integration who believed that the defeat of tax-varying powers in the referendum would improve the chances of defeating devolution in Parliament). Urging the fourth combination, Mowbray (1997) stated that '... we should have little difficulty defeating tax-raising powers. And without them, what is the point of having a parliament at all?'
7. Paradoxically, the trap which Alexander (1996) identified as confronting Scotland ensnared the devolution proposals for Wales, which had been caught up in Labour's pre-legislative referendum tactic to diffuse the tartan tax controversy.
8. This extended beyond the use of the tax-varying powers in the devolution scheme to innumerable imagined extensions to those powers, including those which had been explicitly ruled out.
9. The System 3 poll regularly published in the *Herald* showed the following percentage division into Yes: No: Don't Know on the second question: 53:28:19 (May); 56:26:18 (June); 54:27:19 (July); and 47:32:21 (August).
10. In response to the question 'Would he ever try to stop a Scottish Parliament from using its

tax powers?', he is reported as having said: 'The powers are like those of any local authority. Powers that are constitutionally there can be used, but the Scottish Labour Party has no plans to raise income tax and once the power is given, it's like any parish council, it's got the right to exercise it' (Penman, 1997). This controversy has attracted attention to the role of the 8,100–8,200 parish councils in England. These councils have responsibility for services such as cemeteries, crime prevention, swimming pools, entertainments and local halls, tourism and for the provision and maintenance of open spaces, bus shelters, parking places and public lavatories. In some areas, county councils have devolved budgets for certain of their functions to parish councils, thereby turning them into local purchasers of county council services. Parish councils are financed for their own functions by means of a precept on the district council. In 1997–98, the average Band D equivalent parish council precept stands at £8.82, compared with £688.98 for the total Band D equivalent council tax bill. Some of the larger parish councils also have significant income from fees and charges. An interesting sidelight is that capping powers do not extend to parish councils, which, in principle, levy whatever precept they wish. However, since their expenditure falls outside the Revenue Support Grant system, the whole precept falls directly upon the council taxpayers within the parish, who are themselves electors in parish council elections.

11. Public finance economists have drawn attention to the 'flypaper effect', namely that money tends to stick where it lands. This draws attention to the greater enthusiasm of sub-national governments for spending money they receive as grants rather than money they have to raise themselves (King, 1993).

12. There are ongoing legal arguments in Australia about the constitutionality of so-called quasi-excises: e.g. high volume-related licences issued by the state governments for the right to sell alcohol, the taxation of which is constitutionally the exclusive preserve of the Commonwealth.

13. An important qualification relates to cases where increases in a sub-national tax (e.g. council tax) or charge (e.g. public sector housing rent) would partly be met through higher benefit expenditure. The Scotland White Paper (Scottish Office, 1997c, para 7.24) explicitly warned that 'excessive' growth in local authority expenditure relative to England might be charged to the block grant. The Treasury's (1996a,b) estimate at the UK level is that about 20% of property tax increases would be benefit-financed. The second-round effects are more difficult to track; for example, the effects of higher council tax on the RPI would feed through to indexed benefits, and more expenditure on teachers' salaries would increase UK income tax receipts.

14. Borrowing by provincial governments, both for capital expenditure and to finance deficits, has been a significant factor in the growth of Canada's debt/GDP ratio.

15. More technically, the Marginal Cost of Public Funds (MCPF) will be lower when corporate and consumption taxes are levied by central governments than when levied by local governments. It should be noted that the MCPF of raising £1 will be higher than £1 because of two separate elements: the administrative and compliance costs; and the 'excess burden' arising from the distortion of firm and household market choices due to the tax wedge between the amount which one economic transactor pays and the other receives. The argument is that there will be economies of scale in central tax administration, and that harmonized tax rates will generate lower excess burden.

16. It is worth recalling the extent to which central government in the 1980s treated Revenue Support Grant to local authorities as a subsidy, rather than as a reflection of the differential assignment of expenditure functions and revenue sources.

17. The motivation for adopting the Barnett formula was to secure a better alignment between each country's expenditure and need relatives, not to bring convergence of per capita expenditure.Two of the probable reasons why this has not happened are that there have been significant changes in relative population, and there has been formula by-pass, the quantitative significance of which cannot be assessed from material in the public domain (Heald, 1992, 1994).

18. The nearest this became to being explicit was: 'It is not clear to us that the problems of fiscal dependency can be overcome' (Midwinter and McVicar, 1996a: 51); 'We do not see this as promoting more accountable government' (1996a: 51); and 'This is not a mix for enhancing

political accountability, but for a pattern of friction-based relationships over spending, which will further confuse responsibility in government' (1996: 51).

19. Midwinter and McVicar (1996a: 50) adversely compared 3% for the devolved Scottish Executive with 15% raised for local authorities by the council tax, without regard to the fact that a significant proportion of the denominator for the first calculation relates to the way the Public Expenditure Survey scores local government.

20. Housing, trading services and special funds are excluded.

21. It should be noted that council tax rebate grants represent 18.9% of council tax income, thereby reducing the proportion actually met by council taxpayers to 11.6%.

22. The exclusion of local government finance from the remit of the proposed Independent Commission on Local Government and the Scottish Parliament (Scottish Office, 1997d) has deservedly attracted severe criticism.

23. Issues of principle concerning the tax-varying power are covered in Heald and Geaughan (1996) and matters of detailed design and implementation are analysed in Heald and Geaughan (1997).

24. Because the tartan tax is restricted to the basic rate band, the maximum liability of an individual taxpayer would on 1997–98 tax schedules be capped at £660 (Heald and Geaughan, 1997).

25. Nevertheless, the Labour Party 1997 manifesto said that 'there are sound democratic reasons why, in principle, the business rate should be set locally, not nationally' (Labour Party, 1997: 34). There was, however, a commitment to 'make no change to the present system for determining the business rate without full consultation with business' (p.34). If policy for England were to move in this direction, a Scottish Parliament might index a Scottish unified rate to a weighted average of English rates. Even this approach might create some controversy if business rates in the English counties adjacent to the Scottish border were set below that weighted average. For a discussion of policy options, see Denny et al. (1995). A curious aspect of these debates is the emphasis which public statements place on tax rates, with much less attention paid to tax bills (which depend also on valuations which differ markedly between local authority areas).

26. The wording on personal tax rates used by Labour in the 1997 election survived the referendum campaign: namely, that the Prime Minister's promise covered the five years of the present Westminster Parliament and would therefore bind Labour members of a Scottish Parliament not to use the tax-varying power for the first two years (which would overlap).

27. The Barnett formula (10:5:85) of 1978 provided that increases in public expenditure in Scotland and in Wales for specific purposes within the territorial blocks would be determined according to the formula consequences of changes in equivalent English expenditure. A parallel formula allocated 2.75% of the change in equivalent GB expenditure to Northern Ireland. The formula was recalibrated in 1992 following the 1991 census: the new factors were set at 10.66:6.02:100.00, with Northern Ireland revised to 2.87% (Heald, 1994).

28. There are some variations in his proposals for Scottish representation at Westminster: 40 (McLean, 1995), 45 (McLean, 1997a), and 40 or 45 (McLean, 1997b). The Scotland White Paper (Scottish Office, 1997c, para 4.5) announced that a common population quota would in future boundary reviews be applied to Scotland and England, though the existing statutory requirements to give due weight to geographical considerations (which are more likely to be thought applicable in the Scottish highlands and islands) and local ties would still apply. (In the Scottish Constitutional Convention, the Labour Party had resisted a Liberal Democrat proposal to this effect.) There is no similar reduction envisaged for Wales (Welsh Office, 1997). Taken together, the White Papers indicated that executive devolution would hold no implications for Westminster representation, and that legislative devolution would bring proportionality. McLean (1995) advocated a devolution discount for both Scotland and Wales, which would reduce their representation below proportionality, citing a one-third discount applied to Northern Ireland under the *Government of Ireland Act 1920*.

29. The break-up of Czechoslavakia has been attributed to the desire of Czech politicians to evict Slovakia from the federation.

30. These numbers are crucially affected by the revaluation of an assumed 90% Scottish share of oil revenues over that period to 1996–97 prices. The contribution of 1983–84, 1984–85

and 1985–86 to the total surplus was £30.1 billion (Hall, 1997; Wilson, 1997; Wood, 1997).
31. On the basis of Scottish Office figures (1996, p.32), Scotland's GGBR was £8.2 billion in 1994–95 out of a UK GGBR of £47.9 billion (excluding privatization proceeds and North Sea oil revenues). On the basis of Waldegrave (1997a,b), Scotland's GGBR (assuming a GDP share of privatization proceeds and a 90% share of North Sea oil revenues) was £6.2 billion.
32. There will be an opportunity for the United Kingdom to import expertise from countries whose governmental systems it strongly influenced in the past. For example, the Commonwealth Grants Commission in Australia has been advising the Government of China on the structure of financial relationships between tiers of government.
33. There are technical factors reinforcing these political points. First, on the basis of a strict application of the Barnett formula, Scotland will always get a lower percentage increase due to the relationship between the base and the increment. Second, because the formula is driven by what happens in England, developments in England feed through to Scotland, Wales and Northern Ireland. For example, middle-class exit from inner London schools will in time mean less money through 'formula consequences'. Third, because of higher participation rates, whatever is decided in England about higher education funding and fees is likely to be more expensive in Scotland.

REFERENCES

Adonis, A. (1997), 'Breaking the Code on New Labour', *Observer*, 6 April.
Aitken, J. (1995), Speech to the *Scottish Council for Development and Industry*, 24 February, Gleneagles, mimeo.
Alexander, A. (1996) 'Under Starters Orders: Facing Competition in 1997 – Strategies for Success in the Next Round of CCT', Annual Seminar of the Scottish Association of Direct Leisure Organisations (Direct Services Division), Coylumbridge Hotel, Aviemore, 11 October, mimeo.
Alexander, A. (1997) 'Leisure Services: The Future', Keynote Session, Annual Conference of the Scottish Association of Directors of Leisure Service), Dunkeld, 26 August, mimeo.
Ballantyne, R. and P. MacMahon (1997), 'Bank Chief Sounds Home Rule Warning', *Scotsman*, 22 May.
Bell, D., S. Dow, D. King and N. Massie (1996), *Financing Devolution*, Hume Papers on Public Policy, Vol.4, No.2, Edinburgh: Edinburgh University Press.
Birrell, D. and A. Murie (1980), *Policy and Government in Northern Ireland: Lessons of Devolution*, Dublin: Gill and Macmillan.
Bloomfield, K. (1996), 'Devolution: Lessons from Northern Ireland?', *Political Quarterly*, Vol.67 (2), pp.135–40.
Blow, L., J. Hall and S. Smith (1996), *Financing Regional Government in Britain*, IFS Commentary No.54, London: Institute for Fiscal Studies.
Canavan, D. (1997), *Hansard*, 14 May, col.89.
Clarke, K. (1995), Speech to the *Focus on Scotland* Lunch, 24 March, Edinburgh: mimeo.
Cochrane, A. (1997), 'Law Lord Poses Tough Questions', *Scotsman*, 23 April.
Constitution Unit (1996), *Scotland's Parliament: Fundamentals for a New Scotland Act*, London: Constitution Unit.
Crick, B. (1995), 'Ambushes and Advances: The Scottish Act 1998', *Political Quarterly*, Vol.66 (4), pp.237–49.
Day, K.M. (1992) 'Interprovincial Migration and Local Public Goods', *Canadian Journal of Economics*, Vol.25, pp.123–44.
Denny, K., J. Hall and S. Smith (1995), *Options for Business Rate Reform*, London: Institute for Fiscal Studies.
Dinwoodie, R. (1997), 'Forsyth Raises £2.5bn Spectre', *Herald*, 30 April.
Donegan, L. (1997), 'Yes Vote Not Certain for Hesitant Scots', *Guardian*, 15 April.

Farquharson, K. (1995), 'Why the Labour Leadership Must Learn to Let Go', *Scotland on Sunday*, 17 December.

Fry, M. (1997), 'Scots Tories Must Put House in Order', *Herald*, 7 May.

Gay, O., B.W. Winetrobe and E. Wood (1995), *The Government of Scotland: Recent Proposals*, Research Paper 95/131, London: House of Commons Library.

Gibson, J.S. (1985), *The Thistle and the Crown: A History of the Scottish Office*, Edinburgh: HMSO.

Hall, J. (1997) 'SNP's Oil-fuelled Budget Slips Up on the Arithmetic', *Scotsman*, 18 April.

Heald, D.A. (1980), *Financing Devolution within the United Kingdom: A Study of the Lessons from Failure*, Research Monograph No.32, Centre for Research on Federal Financial Relations, Australian National University, Canberra: ANU Press.

Heald, D.A. (1990), *Financing a Scottish Parliament: Options for Debate*, Discussion Paper No.1, Glasgow: Scottish Foundation for Economic Research.

Heald, D.A. (1992), *Formula-based Territorial Public Expenditure in the United Kingdom*, Aberdeen Papers in Accountancy, Finance and Management W7, Aberdeen: Department of Accountancy, University of Aberdeen.

Heald, D.A. (1994), 'Territorial Public Expenditure in the United Kingdom', *Public Administration*, Vol.72, pp.147–75.

Heald, D.A. (1997), 'Controlling Public Expenditure', in D. Corry (ed.) *Public Expenditure: Effective Management and Control*, London: Dryden Press for the Institute for Public Policy Research, pp.167–91.

Heald, D.A. and N. Geaughan (1996), 'Financing a Scottish Parliament', in S. Tindale (ed.) *The State and the Nations: The Politics of Devolution*, London: Institute for Public Policy Research, pp.167–83.

Heald, D.A. and N. Geaughan (1997), 'The "Tartan Tax": Devolved Variation in Income Tax Rates', *British Tax Review*, No.5, pp.337–48.

Helms, L.J. (1985), 'The Effect of State and Local Taxes on Economic Growth: A Time Series–Cross Section Approach, *Review of Economics and Statistics*, Vol.67, pp.574–82.

Institute for Fiscal Studies (1996), 'Funding Regional Government', *IFS Update*, Winter 1996/Spring 1997, p.1.

Keating, M. (1997), 'What's Wrong with Asymmetrical Government?', Paper presented to conference on devolution, ECPR Standing Group on Regionalism, University of Northumbria, Newcastle upon Tyne, 20–22 February.

Kellas, J. (1989), *The Scottish Political System*, Fourth Edition, Cambridge: Cambridge University Press.

King, D. (1984), *Fiscal Tiers: The Economics of Multi-Level Government*, London: George Allen & Unwin.

King, D. (1993), 'Issues in Multi-Level Government', in P.M. Jackson (ed.) *Current Issues in Public Sector Economics*, Basingstoke: Macmillan.

Labour Party (1997), *New Labour Because Britain Deserves Better*, London: Labour Party.

Lawrence, R.J. (1965), *The Government of Northern Ireland: Public Finance and Public Services 1921–64*, Oxford: Clarendon Press.

Leruez, J. (1983), *L'Ecosse: Une Nation Sans Etat*, Lille: Presses Universitaires de Lille.

Lord President of the Council, Secretary of State for Scotland and Secretary of State for Wales (1975), *Our Changing Democracy: Devolution to Scotland and Wales*, Cmnd 6348, London: HMSO.

MacAskill, E. (1995), 'Passions Run High over Way Ahead: Lang Warning on Tax Cost of Devolution', *Scotsman*, 13 February.

McCormick, J. (1996), *The Green and the Tartan: Business Rates after Devolution*, London: Institute for Public Policy Research.

McGregor, P., J. Stevens, K. Swales and Y. Yin (1997), 'The Economics of the Tartan Tax', *Fraser of Allander Quarterly Economic Commentary*, Vol.22 (3), pp.72–85.

McLean, I. (1995), 'Are Scotland and Wales Over-represented in the House of Commons?' *Political Quarterly*, Vol.66, pp.250–68.

McLean, I. (1997a), 'Previous Convictions', *Prospect*, May, p.80.

McLean, I. (1997b), 'Yes, Yes! Begone with Scotland!', *New Statesman*, 22 August, pp.18–21.

McLean, I. (1997c), Interview on 'The World at One', BBC Radio 4, 12 September.

MacKay, D. (ed.) (1979), *Scotland: The Framework for Change*, Edinburgh: Paul Harris Publishing.

Mair, C. and M. McAteer (1997), 'Scotching the Myth: Analysing the Relations Between a Scottish Parliament and Westminster', *Scottish Affairs*, No.19, pp.1–13.

Martin, I., T. Condon, E. Quigley and S. Fraser (1997), 'Patriot Games', *Scotland on Sunday*, 31 August.

Meehan, E. (1997) 'Do Scots Have Confidence in Themselves?' (letter to the editor), *Scotland on Sunday*, 8 September.

Midwinter, A. and M. McVicar (1996a), 'Uncharted Waters? Problems of Financing Labour's Scottish Parliament', *Public Money & Management*, Vol.16 (2), pp.1–6.

Midwinter, A. and M. McVicar (1996b), 'The Devolution Proposals for Scotland: An Assessment and Critique', *Public Money & Management*, Vol.16 (4), pp.13–20.

Mitchell, J. (1992), 'Scottish Office Feels Need to Bolster Lang's Image', *Scotsman*, 28 July.

Mitchell, J. (1995), Paper for Meeting of Consultative Group on the Establishment of a Scottish Parliament, mimeo.

Mowbray, R. (1997), 'Letter to the Editor', *Scotsman*, 14 May.

Musgrave, R. (1997), 'Reconsidering the Fiscal Role of Government', *American Economic Review*, Vol.87 (2: Papers and Proceedings), pp.156–59.

Nairn, T. (1981), *The Break-up of Britain: Crisis and Neo-nationalism*, Second Edition, London: New Left Books.

Neil, A. (1997a), 'Sleep-walk to Devolution', *Scotsman*, 18 April.

Neil, A. (1997b), 'Is This the Best They Can Do?', *Scotsman*, 9 May.

Northern Ireland Office (1982), *Northern Ireland: A Framework for Devolution*, Cmnd 8541, London: HMSO.

Northern Ireland Office (1995), 'The Government's Proposals for Reform of the Government of Northern Ireland since 1979: Summary of Financial Arrangements', *House of Commons Library Deposited Paper Series 3, 1539*, mimeo.

Parker, A. (1997), 'Dorrell in Devolution Warning', *Scotsman*, 10 February.

Penman, J. (1997), 'Sovereignty Rests with Me as an English MP and That's the Way It Will Stay', *Scotsman*, 4 April.

Referendums (Scotland and Wales) Act 1997, Chapter 61, London: Stationery Office.

Rifkind, M. (1997), 'Why I Changed My Mind on Devolution', *Scotland on Sunday*, 31 August.

Scott, D. and P. MacMahon (1997), 'Officials Refuse to Back Forsyth on £2.5bn Threat', *Scotsman*, 1 May.

Scottish Constitutional Convention (1990), *Towards Scotland's Parliament*, Edinburgh: Scottish Constitutional Convention.

Scottish Constitutional Convention (1995), *Scotland's Parliament: Scotland's Right*, Edinburgh: Scottish Constitutional Convention.

Scottish Council Foundation (1997), *Scotland's Parliament: A Business Guide to Devolution*, Edinburgh: Scottish Council Foundation.

Scottish Office (1992), *Government Expenditure and Revenues in Scotland*, Edinburgh: Scottish Office.

Scottish Office (1995), *Government Expenditure and Revenue in Scotland, 1993–94*, Glasgow: Scottish Office.

Scottish Office (1996), *Government Expenditure and Revenue in Scotland, 1994–95*, Glasgow: Scottish Office.

Scottish Office (1997a), *Scottish Local Government Financial Statistics 1994–95*, Edinburgh: Office of National Statistics.

Scottish Office (1997b), *Serving Scotland's Needs: Departments of the Secretary of State for Scotland and the Forestry Commission*, Cm 3614, London: Stationery Office.

Scottish Office (1997c), *Scotland's Parliament*, Cm 3658, Edinburgh: Stationery Office.

Scottish Office (1997d), *Independent Commission on Local Government and the Scottish Parliament*, Edinburgh: Stationery Office.

Select Committee on Relations between Central and Local Government (1996), *'Rebuilding Trust'*, Volume I – Report, HL Paper 97, London: HMSO.

Stewart, G. (1997), 'Blair Has Lost Touch, says Forsyth', *Scotsman*, 7 April.

Treasury (1979), *Needs Assessment Study – Report*, London: HM Treasury.

Treasury (1996a), 'Memorandum by HM Treasury', in Select Committee on Relations between Central and Local Government, *'Rebuilding Trust'*, Volume I – Oral Evidence and Associated Memoranda, HL Paper 97-I, London: HMSO, pp.280–83.

Treasury (1996b), 'Supplementary Evidence from HM Treasury', in Select Committee on Relations between Central and Local Government, *'Rebuilding Trust'*, Volume I – Oral Evidence and Associated Memoranda, HL Paper 97-I, London: HMSO, pp.308–9.

Treasury (1997), *Public Expenditure: Statistical Analyses 1997–98*, Cm 3601, London: Stationery Office.

Waldegrave, W. (1997a), *Hansard*, 13 January, cols.25–6.

Waldegrave, W. (1997b), *Hansard*, 21 March, col.969.

Wallace, S. (1993), 'The Effects of State Personal Income Tax Differentials on Wages', *Regional Science and Urban Economics,* Vol.23, pp.611–28.

Welsh Office (1997), *A Voice for Wales: The Government's Proposals for a Welsh Assembly*, Cm 3718, London: Stationery Office.

Wilson, A. (1997), 'Stuck on the Starting Blocks – A Response to Mr Stevens' Comment on the SNP General Election Budget 1997', *Fraser of Allander Quarterly Economic Commentary*, Vol.22 (3), pp.57–67.

Wood, P. (1997), 'An Analysis of the SNP's 1997 Election Budget Proposals', *Fraser of Allander Quarterly Economic Commentary*, Vol.22 (3), pp.68–71.

Woodhouse, D. (1994), *Ministers and Parliament: Accountability in Theory and Practice*, Oxford: Clarendon Press.

Scottish Home Rule:
Radical Break or Pragmatic Adjustment?

LINDSAY PATERSON

Most supporters of a Scottish Parliament within the union like to claim that it will be able to deal radically with Scotland's social problems, and – in particular – will be able to diverge significantly from England where popular preferences seem to indicate that it ought to do so. Unionist opponents of the proposed parliament generally agree, but view the prospects of radical divergence as a reason not to have a parliament at all. Nationalist opponents, on the other hand, argue that a domestic parliament would be so constrained by the framework of the union as to represent no departure at all from the situation Scotland has faced for the last three centuries; such a parliament, they believe, would therefore be wholly ineffective as a means of social reform.

This contribution assesses these attitudes to the legislation that is likely to emerge after the referendum in September 1997. It argues three main propositions:

1. Scotland's position in the union – including its position this century – has always involved negotiation and compromise, and so has never been a matter of straightforward assimilation of Scotland to England. The unionist alarm at the prospects of divergence is misplaced, in that the divergence opened up by a domestic parliament would be no greater than the divergence which did in fact happen under the UK's system of government at least until the 1960s. For the same reason, the nationalist belief that no divergence is possible within the union ignores this history. Throughout the last three centuries, Scotland has developed its own autonomy in a variety of ways based mainly on the institutions of civil society.

2. The pressure for a Scottish Parliament since the 1960s has merely been the latest phase in the process of negotiation within the union. This current context, however, has four features which are unprecedented since the eighteenth century – divergence between Scottish and English voting patterns, a loss by the UK state of its previous capacity to tolerate territorial diversity, the declining economic effectiveness of the UK state generally, and the alternative broader framework of the European Union.

3. So a parliament is more likely to come about in this phase of the negotiated processes between Scotland and its neighbours than in any previous era. But the autonomy which such a parliament will represent will continue to be constrained by the wider context of both the UK and the EU. That autonomy might therefore not be much greater than was available informally to Scotland up till the middle of the twentieth century – real enough, but possibly not as much as recent electoral divergence between Scotland and England might seem to indicate as being necessary. The biggest impact that a parliament could have could, however, be in the reform it could undertake in Scottish policy making (towards more democratic openness) rather than in any radical break it could make with the fairly recent past.

SCOTTISH AUTONOMY IN THE TWENTIETH CENTURY

The starting point for an understanding of the twentieth-century state in Scotland lies as far back as the system of government which emerged from the union between the Scottish and English Parliaments in 1707.[1] The important point for our purposes is that the union was partial. In return for surrendering its parliament, Scotland kept control of the key agencies of an incipient civil society – a separate legal system, a system of local government that was beginning to assert its independence of the state, and a thoroughly independent and supremely self-confident presbyterian church.

These agencies then shaped the Scotland which emerged with the industrial revolution. Local government was reformed in 1832 in a largely successful attempt to modernize it for the new age. Equally influential thereafter was the emerging network of boards and committees which oversaw growing parts of state activities in Scotland – for example, education, the poor law, a rudimentary system of public health, and so on. These structures were given coherence by a continuing attachment to presbyterian philanthropy (undisturbed despite organizational schisms in the presbyterian church), by a strong preference for Liberal politics, and by the increasingly important edifice of Scots law. The legal system not only gave a philosophical shape to the regulations and practices of the local agencies. At the local level, it also supplied the unifying figure of the sheriff – primarily, but by no means merely, the local judge. The sheriff organized many of the boards and committees, and was an efficient means by which local issues were communicated to central government in Edinburgh. Nationally, the legal system also gave the closest that Scotland had to a central government, in the Faculty of Advocates, in the supreme courts of law, and in the Lord Advocate, the chief legal officer of the central state, whose main task was to articulate to London the preferences which came up through these networks, and who was usually charged with translating these into legislation wherever that was necessary.

The details of this governing system are not directly relevant to our discussion of the twentieth century. Two points matter for the legacy it left. It operated relatively independently of the London government, the UK state then being mainly concerned with foreign and imperial matters. In that sense, Scottish autonomy was at least as great as that of many small nations elsewhere in Europe: it resembled the governing systems of places that did have their own parliament (such as Finland and Norway) rather more than places which did not (such as Bohemia or Catalonia), where recurrent bouts of repression by an imperial state encroached on what remaining autonomy the local civil societies might have inherited. The solid bourgeois Scottish men who ran the system were well aware of the rather good bargain Scotland had: autonomy in domestic matters, and access through free trade and migration to the biggest empire the world had ever seen. For an economy based on trade, and for a middle class that had developed an excellent system of meritocratic education, these opportunities could hardly be rivalled by any alternative constitutional arrangements.

The other way in which the governing system of nineteenth-century Scotland matters for the present discussion is that it provided the context in which a more interventionist state grew in the twentieth century. To understand that process, the key point is the growth of a professional bureaucracy as the main arm of government, something that happened throughout the developed world. Poggi and others have called this system 'technocracy' – government by professionals (Poggi, 1978; Bell, 1976; Held, 1984; Keane, 1988; Kumar, 1978). It grew readily out of the nineteenth century settlement: it was easy for rule by lawyers and doctors to become government by civil servants and medical scientists.

There was not much that was peculiar about Scotland in this respect: as elsewhere, the welfare state grew as a response to mass democracy, and, as in many other places, it was shaped by a dominant social democratic party. In Scotland, however, the pragmatic dullness of technocracy responded not only to socialist agitation: it was equally a displacement of nationalist pressure for a separate Scottish legislature. The one agency served both purposes: a separate Scottish arm of the welfare-state bureaucracy, in and around the Scottish Office. Although founded as long ago as 1885, this body rose to become the embodiment of Scottish national government in the 1930s, shaped by the same forces of 'middle opinion' that also devised the technocratic ideas that underpinned the welfare state throughout the UK. Since then, the Scottish Office has grown to be in charge of most areas of social policy, the main exception being social security (Brown *et al.* 1996; Scottish Office, 1996).

In the absence of a Scottish Parliament, it might appear, of course, that a separate bureaucracy was not much of a political prize. But that is true only insofar as the liberal-democratic theory of the state is true, and political science has long taught us to be sceptical of its claims. Consider three other perspectives on the policy process, and what they have to say about the nature of Scottish government as it evolved with the welfare state. The first is pluralism (McLennan, 1989; Jordan and Richardson, 1987). If policy is made by the bargaining which goes on among interest groups, then Scottish policy has to be judged to have been made within Scotland to a very significant extent.

In Scottish education, for example, almost all these groups other than Parliament itself were Scottish rather than British, and indeed until the 1960s Parliament paid almost no attention (Paterson, 1997b). At the centre of the process was the Scottish Education Department; it was part of the Scottish Office and was overseen by the Secretary of State for Scotland, a member of the UK Cabinet. It supervised a dense network of committees, and maintained official and informal contacts with pressure groups, with representatives of local government, and with professional associations. McPherson and Raab (1988: 472) have described these as the 'policy community', the Scottish instance of British pluralism.

A similar point can be made about other aspects of the welfare state. In the unique system of child welfare which Scotland has developed since the late 1960s, the key agencies have been professional groups in Scotland (mainly of social workers and lawyers), rather than the political process of Westminster. As Murphy has commented in his history of Scottish social services, 'the White Paper [of 1966] represented a unique opportunity to influence social policy', and so the contents of the resulting Social Work (Scotland) Act of 1968 'were considerably influenced by social work lobbying'. The origins of the ideas lay in the Kilbrandon report of 1964, which itself articulated 'a clear general will for change'. The Scottish consensus – drawing on international thinking about child-centred welfare – was able to achieve a remarkably radical reform while divisions between social work and the magistrate courts in England produced stasis there (Murphy, 1992; Asquith, 1992).

Furthermore, insofar as undiluted pluralism is not a wholly satisfactory way of characterizing the process, the relative autonomy of the system can be seen to be all the more officially entrenched. For example, if we follow the corporatist critique of straightforward pluralism, we are led to see the Scottish Office as an official agency for coordinating Scottish pressure on the UK state – in fact, a nationalist agency, and not at all the unionist instrument which its nationalist critics allege.

For education, McPherson and Raab conclude that the Scottish system became increasingly corporatist in the 1960s, as the power of the Scottish

Office increased. The partnership they describe

> resembles corporatism in the exclusiveness of its relationships, in its assumption that mutual interests outweigh the partners' separate or conflicting interests, and in the sharing of authority (McPherson and Raab, 1988: 473).

This 'mutual interest' is another way of putting the sense of a Scottish national interest. The Scottish Office, represented politically by the Secretary of State, could become the national leader, especially in bargaining with the Treasury. For example, McPherson and Raab quote Bruce Millan (Secretary of State, 1976–79) as telling them that the Scottish Office was left to sort out by itself the consequences of changing patterns of expenditure. The scope for this autonomy increased from 1978 onwards when, in anticipation of the setting up of an elected Scottish Assembly, the Secretary of State was given power of vires over most of the Scottish Office's block grant from the Treasury. Lying behind Millan's comment is an unquestioned national framework, in which the Secretary of State speaks for Scotland and has the authority to decide what is in Scotland's best interests. If that convention was not acceptable within Scotland itself, then it would not work as a negotiating position around the Cabinet table (Levitt, 1992).

Likewise, in the debates about child welfare in the 1960s, the movement towards reform was helped by the active encouragement which came from the Scottish Office civil servants: they were, says Murphy, 'active initiators, encouragers, and facilitators', backed up by a strong commitment from the Secretary of State for Scotland, Willie Ross, and the junior minister in charge, Judith Hart. They fought and largely won the battles within the Labour Party: they were 'interested, active and powerful enough to carry through to fruition in their province of Scotland ideas which chimed with their party's aspirations, so far unachievable in the South' (Murphy, 1992: 136).

Furthermore, whatever the process by which national decisions are made – pluralism or corporatism or something else – there remains the large area of implementation, the means by which the national policies have an impact on everyday experience. As Hogwood and Gunn (1984) argue, 'perfect implementation is unattainable', because all policy proposals have to be modified in practice when placed in the hands of professionals such as teachers or social workers, and when faced with the complexity of society and of individuals.

In education, the arm of the Scottish Office which has most to do with implementation has been the inspectorate, and in that sense the Office has been able to keep some control of the process. But the inspectors have always themselves been educational professionals, and so their negotiation of practice with teachers has been shaped by a shared professional outlook. They have also had to deal with the local directors of education, also from the same professional background. Schools themselves, in any case, had a great deal of scope to devise their own ways of responding to national policies, although – because of the centralizing effects of the inspectorate and the Scottish Examination Board – they tended to follow a common pattern to a greater extent than did schools in England and Wales.

In child welfare, similarly, the now widespread acceptance of the system which was started in 1968 is due to its daily operation by social workers and by the new system of Children's Hearings, mostly away from the politicians' sight. As Asquith wrote on the twenty-first anniversary of the date at which the Act came fully into effect, 'the general acceptance of the Hearings as an appropriate forum for the making of decisions about children has been reflected in the absence of any vigorous or concerted arguments either in favour of its abolition or in rejection of the philosophy on which it is based'(Asquith, 1992: 157).

PRESSURE FOR CHANGE

Given this relative autonomy which Scotland enjoyed at least as recently as the 1960s, why has there been an increase in pressure for changing the system of Scottish government?

The first reason is electoral divergence. In 1955, the Conservative Party received around 50 per cent of the vote in both Scotland and England; by 1992, while it managed to attract 47 per cent in England, it had only 26 per cent in Scotland[2] (Brown et al., 1996: 146); even in its disaster of the 1997 general election, the Conservative Party retained 34 per cent of the vote in England but only 18 per cent in Scotland (*The Observer*, 4 May 1997) Its relative weakness in Scotland was most marked among two social groups in particular. It attracted just one third of the support of people in the Registrar General categories I and II (professionals and managers), in contrast to over one half in the rest of Britain up to 1992 (Brown et al., 1996: 147, 149). And it got only 18 per cent support among skilled-manual workers, the group which, in the Midlands of England, had been the bedrock of Thatcherism, and which still gave the Tories 40 per cent support in 1992 (Brown et al., 1996: 147, 149).

Several explanations have been offered of this relative decline of the Scottish Conservatives. Their lack of middle-class strength has been attributed to the attachment of the Scottish middle class to the state, whether for employment or for public services such as health and education (McCrone, 1992).

Also cited as reasons are the decline of indigenously owned Scottish industry, and the very low rate of self-employment. The working-class support which the Conservatives used to enjoy in west-central Scotland has been dissipated by the decline of religious motives in politics: the party's support used to be strong among the Protestant working class, but religion has become a matter of political indifference for most Scots, and is far less strongly associated with vote than is social class (Brown *et al.*, 1996: 148). Running through all the social groups, moreover, has been a sense that the Conservatives are an essentially English party which does not have Scotland's interests at heart: according to one poll conducted during the 1997 general election campaign, 73 per cent of all voters agreed that 'the Conservative Party is a mainly English party with little relevance to Scotland'; even 28 per cent of Conservative voters accepted this (ICM, 17 February 1997). The result of the election will have reinforced the English character of the Conservatives, insofar as they now have no MPs or MEPs at all in Scotland, and do not control any local authorities.

Although all the other parties have benefited from this Conservative decline, its simple fact has tended to reinforce a sense that Scotland is an essentially left-wing place. This has tended to induce the other three parties into increasingly nationalist rhetoric, insofar as the contrast in the English and Scottish majorities has seemed to point inexorably to the need for an elected Scottish forum that could reflect Scottish preferences.

Feeding the perception of the Conservatives as being anti-Scottish has been the second reason why pressure for constitutional change has become so insistent. It is widely felt that the UK state no longer tolerates the diversity which it earlier allowed or even fostered (as outlined earlier). Crick has argued that

> many of the old English Tories had a clear and politic sense of the diversity of the United Kingdom...Unlike the new breed of self-made men and women, they had some sense of history; and, unlike most socialists, a sense that discontinuities between sociology and govern-ment were possible, given political will and skill (Crick, 1991: 91).

In particular, Thatcher's distrust of the intermediate bodies of civil society was interpreted in Scotland as being anti-Scottish, in that Scottish autonomy had lain precisely in these spheres. For example, weakening local government was not, in Scotland, just a centralizing manoeuvre. It was also perceived as one that was hostile to Scottish autonomy and (potentially) distinctiveness.

The third reason for the pressures towards a Scottish Parliament has been a Scottish instance of a very general problem for the welfare states – the weakening of legitimacy that has followed on a decline in the effectiveness of the state at delivering welfare and prosperity. McCrone (1992) and also Kendrick (1983) have argued that the welfare-state nationalism which mattered in Scotland was Scottish rather than British. There emerged, in Scotland as in other nations, a belief that the purpose of the state was to serve the national interest. Successive waves of economic crisis (at least until the mid-1980s) or bouts of welfare-state contraction (from the 1970s onwards) have, therefore, been seen in Scotland as evidence that the state was no longer working in the interests of the nation. The fourth and final main reason for the pressures has been the European Union, relatively more popular in Scotland than in Wales or any region of England (Brown *et al.*, 1996: 161). Europe has seemed to offer an alternative external reference, a way of overcoming some of the first three complaints about the recent functioning of the UK state. Thus the broadly left-of-centre majority in the EU would be consistent with the Scottish majority; the European tradition of written constitutions and respect for subsidiarity would tend to strengthen Scotland's institutions; and the EU would provide an alternative market for Scottish produce. Moreover, insofar as several other EU states (most notably Spain) have been decentralizing their legislative structures, Scotland might be expected to benefit by analogy.

These four reasons why the constitutional debate has become so central to Scottish politics have tended to create a rhetoric of crisis. But, in response, the Conservative government in fact strengthened Scottish distinctiveness in policy, although usually in a manner that was much more centralized on the Scottish Office than would have been normal half a century ago. In education, for example, the arrangements for curricula, for assessment, for school management, and for accountability are different now in important ways from their English analogues, and – more significantly – are more different now than they were in 1979. Despite the rhetoric of opposition politicians, the Conservative government did not impede the current flourishing of Scottish cultural practices: insofar as it made the Scottish Arts Council autonomous of its English counterpart, and treated it in financial terms relatively more generously, it could be said that the Conservative government helped the diversity to develop. The Conservative Secretary of State, Michael Forsyth, was particularly active in promoting Gaelic culture and other aspects of the distinctive social life of the Highlands. And the Scottish Office continued to lobby, usually discreetly, for Scottish interests, sometimes producing departures in policy that were at least as radical as, say, the child welfare legislation of 1968. For example, the distinctive system of vocational education which the Office developed in the face of opposition from Lord Young's Manpower Services Commission in 1984 is now growing into the first attempt in Europe to unify academic and vocational course for the post-16 age group (Fairley and Paterson, 1991; Raffe, forthcoming; SOED, 1994). This reform, moreover, is being developed by a policy process that, for the Scottish Office, is unprecedented in its openness, involving several hundred local seminars attended by many thousand teachers and others.

Of course, one of the main reasons why the government and the Scottish Office have continued to promote Scottish distinctiveness is as an attempt to defuse the case for an elected parliament. In other words, the home rule campaigners may have had an important effect on Scottish politics even in the absence of a parliament. This would not be the first time this century or last in which home rule pressure has been met by pragmatic adjustment from the Scottish Office (Paterson, 1994). The question must then be asked whether a parliament would make much difference. Take the example of education just given: it is difficult to see what extra a parliament could do to reform the post-16 courses in ways that would both serve Scottish interests and also build on Scottish traditions and foster Scottish difference. The non-Conservative political parties differ from the Conservative government only over the timing of the reform, and not at all over its philosophy or over the highly consultative style with which the policy is being developed.

WHAT DIFFERENCE WOULD A DOMESTIC PARLIAMENT MAKE?

The UK in the middle of the twentieth century has been described as a quasi-federation. Livingston, for example, used it as a pre-eminent instance of a state which had the outward forms of being unitary, but which, in practice, respected the essentially federal character of the territory which it governed (Livingston, 1952). This was the twentieth-century version of that tolerance of diversity of which Crick wrote. The outcome, for Scotland, was a greater degree of freedom than the component parts of some federations enjoy. For example, Scottish education is much more different from English education than any of the education systems of the German Länder are from each other. Another example is the independence of Scots law: no federation in the world has one of its entities with an almost completely independent legal system; (although Quebec's is rather more independent than most, incorporating a distinctive civil code, it is still subject to the federal Supreme Court (Bumstead, 1992: 444–54; Dickinson and Young, 1993: 172, 244)). Insofar as the proposals for a domestic Scottish Parliament resemble a step towards a UK federation, it is difficult to see how they could give greater autonomy to Scotland than the country enjoyed in the middle of the century. That degree of independence might have been satisfactory then, because of the essentially shared political ideologies of the whole of Britain, and might continue to be acceptable while the Blair government continues to command majority support in England. But, with the memory of recent divergence still fresh, it could be that the rules that have to constrain the component parts of a federation simply could not tolerate Scottish separateness. So, for good or ill, the domestic parliament would be propelled towards seeking full independence.

There are two replies to that which could be made by those people who support domestic autonomy as a valuable goal in its own right (rather than as a step towards independence). The first is to reiterate the points about pluralism and implementation which were made earlier. If the formulation of the details of policy matters, and if implementation matters even more, then the fact that the parliaments of the German Länder have control mainly of such details leaves them with a significant role in shaping the social policy for their regions.

Imagine for a moment that a Scottish Assembly had been set up by the 1974–79 Labour government, that it had been dominated by the Scottish Labour Party, and that Westminster had been dominated (as in reality) by the Conservatives. Part of what would have counted as the expression of the assembly's autonomy would have been the ways it interpreted for Scotland some policy pressures that were being felt across Britain. It, too, would probably have embarked on the kinds of school examination reforms which are already under way, modifying them at the margins by some extra money, and possibly by some form of bursary to encourage people aged 16–18 to stay in full-time education. Likewise, in economic development, it, too would probably have devolved powers to local bodies and would have tied development to training, just as the Conservative government did, and in contrast to what has happened in England (Fairley, 1996). The main difference might have been that the local bodies would have had some statutory representation from elected local authorities and trades unions.

The point, in other words, is that there would have been some details over which the assembly could have had control which could have made a real difference to the way that policy developed. There would also have been a small number of highly salient issues on which the assembly and Westminster would have disagreed fundamentally, and in which the Assembly would have had autonomy. The most notable example would have been the poll tax, which would certainly not have been introduced in Scotland (McCrone, 1991). But in many important areas, the policy that would have emerged with an assembly would not have been fundamentally more different from English policy than policy is at the moment.

The second reply to the complaint that a domestic parliament would be severely circumscribed is that, if the people of Scotland settle for home rule rather than full independence, then that will be partly because their policy preferences are, in fact, not as different from those of England as is sometimes claimed. The party-political divergence exaggerates the ideological differences, which are really rather slight (Brown *et al.,* 1996: 156–62).

As the 1997 general election shows in retrospect, England differed from Scotland and Wales up to 1992 not in its fundamental social values and political beliefs, but over whether the unreformed Labour Party could be trusted to run the economy. Even the Conservative Party in government noticed this: after all, the poll tax was abolished soon after its unpopularity throughout Britain became evident. Given this broad popular agreement, the Scots seem to want their policies to differ in emphasis and detail, not in basic philosophy. Consider, for example, the changes which have taken place in public sector styles of management. Although the more aggressive forms of 'new managerialism' have often been labelled as Thatcherite in Scotland, we can find analogous though more emollient versions being applied by local authorities controlled by all three non-Conservative parties throughout Scotland (Fairley and Paterson, 1995). We can also find some enthusiasm for at least some of the managerial reforms in the health service, even from people who would not identify themselves with the New Right philosophy that allegedly inspired them (Williamson, 1992). If the political distinctiveness which Scotland wants can be measured by these matters of emphasis rather than by fundamental differences of philosophy, then the constrained autonomy which a domestic parliament would have might be perfectly satisfactory to the majority.

This, after all, is probably a major reason why previous waves of home rule support this century have not led to a parliament.[3] For example, when Labour support for self-government fizzled out in the 1930s and 1940s, it was largely because that party and its supporters settled for a different way of implementing the welfare state (through the Scottish Office) rather than a fundamentally different approach to it. In secondary education, for example, they chose after 1945 a different balance within a system of selective schools, rather than a rejection of selection altogether. In health, they chose a system which integrated the general practitioners more fully into the rest of the service, rather than a radically different model that might have placed an emphasis on prevention rather than cure. And, in housing, they chose to build more and more council houses, rather than pursue the completely different approach of housing co-operatives. These are precisely the kinds of nuances in which we might expect a domestic parliament to be interested.

If that was all, then there might be reason to wonder what all the fuss is about. When unionist opponents of home rule allege all sorts of things about the wild excesses that a Scottish Parliament will get up to, they are not basing their analysis on the experience of any domestic legislature in the world.

But there is, finally, one area where a substantial difference might be feasible, and that is in the style of policy making itself.[4] The movement for self-government in Scotland has been quite strongly influenced by recent thinking on the Left in Britain – thinking which places an emphasis on renewing citizenship and civil society as the basis for more participation and more openness.[5] (But although it has been influenced by that thinking, Scotland has not, in fact, made much of an impact on it: new ideas on civil society have tended to come from England, where Scottish constitutional radicalism is exaggerated in a way that can be embarrassing to those of us who observe it from close up.)

In some respects this strand of the home rule programme goes back to the 1960s, when the late John P.Mackintosh and others argued that a main reason for setting up an elected Scottish Assembly was to subject the bureaucracy of the Scottish Office to public and democratic scrutiny.[6] The current proposals for a Scottish Parliament have inherited some of this radicalism. For example, the Constitutional Convention which drew up the scheme that is the basis of the Labour government's proposals advocated that the parliament would have powerful committees that would have a professional staff and the right to initiate legislation as well as a right to scrutinize the executive. They also proposed that the parliament be required to consult more thoroughly before legislation was devised. Working conditions were to be more consistent with the members' leading a family life. Perhaps most radical of all was the proposal on the electoral system. It was to be proportional with respect both to party and gender. In the event, the agreement between the Liberal Democrats and Labour allowed for elections to be conducted on a version of the Additional Member System, and stipulated that the two parties would ensure that they each had equal numbers of men and women elected (by whatever means the parties separately chose, the Liberal Democrats being opposed to statutory interference in parties' internal decision making).

Such changes would instantly have some very noticeable effects on the style of Scottish politics: even if the SNP and the Conservatives did not join in the agreement on gender, about 30 per cent of the members of the parliament would be women, moving Scotland from one of the lowest proportions in Europe to one of the highest (Brown et al., 1996: 163–88). The party proportionality would end Labour's hegemony, and would start to restore the Conservatives' legitimacy. In Scotland, the Tories have been grossly underrepresented under first-past-the-post, most spectacularly in 1997 when they won no seats at all for 18 per cent of the vote. Following from these changes, and from any requirements to engage in the kinds of consultation which the Convention adumbrates, there might begin to be a renewal of civil society of the type which the reformist Left throughout the UK now advocates.

That is all somewhat speculative. What matters to the present discussion is that, with the exception of setting the party-proportionality of the electoral system, all these issues would be well within the powers of the proposed domestic parliament. Getting an electoral system that is proportional for the parties is part of the Labour government's proposals, and so will probably be put in place. So there is a realistic prospect that the proposed domestic parliament could have a real effect on the civic culture of Scotland: at its best, it could become something of a laboratory for a range of radical ideas on citizenship, perhaps rather as Oregon has done in the United States.

The reason why there might be this scope for a domestic Scottish Parliament to make a difference is that, in a sense, renewing civil society is as much about the processes of policy as were the examples of substantive areas given earlier (the distinctive Scottish details of education, economic development, and so on). The new ideas about democracy are about how policy is made and implemented, not about its content. What then happens when the new participants come up against the substantive constraints on the parliament is unpredictable. The advocates of independence would, presumably, argue that it will be precisely at that point that a popular shift towards supporting separate statehood will happen. But equally possible is that a more open democracy will in fact lead to a much broader appreciation of the reasons why a Scottish Parliament has to be constrained if the benefits of a union with England are to be maintained. In that sense, a domestic parliament with that kind of open political process could serve to re-legitimate the union in a much more thorough way than the Scottish Office could ever do. Slightly ironically, the more distinctively radical the parliament was in its policy-making styles, the more it could popularly entrench realistic support for the union.

NOTES

1. This section draws heavily on Section 2 of Paterson, 1997a. For further expansion of the argument, see Brown, McCrone, and Paterson, 1996; Fry, 1987; Harvie, 1998; Keating, 1996; Kellas, 1984; McCrone, 1992; Nairn, 1981; and Paterson, 1994.
2. These and all subsequent statistics on Scottish electoral behaviour and political attitudes were drawn from the British and Scottish Election Studies (apart from the 1997 figures, which come from opinion polls as specified).
3. As well as the sources cited in note 1, see also Mitchell (1996)
4. See also the papers by Alice Brown and by James Mitchell in the present volume.
5. The general debate can be found in, for example, Hirst, 1996. The Scottish reactions are discussed by Brown et al., 1996 and by Paterson, 1997a.
6. See, for example, Mackintosh (1969).

REFERENCES

Asquith, S. (1992) 'Coming of Age: 21 Years of the Children's Hearings System', in L. Paterson and D. McCrone (eds), *Scottish Government Yearbook* (Edinburgh: Unit for the Study of Government in Scotland) pp.157–72.

Bell, D. (1976) *The Coming of Post-Industrial Society*(Harmondsworth: Penguin).

Brown, A., D. McCrone, and L. Paterson (1996) *Politics and Society in Scotland* (London: Macmillan).

Bumstead, B.M. (1992) *The Peoples of Canada: A Post-Federation History* (Oxford: Oxford University Press).

Crick, B. (1991)'The English and the British', in B. Crick (ed.) *National Identities* (Oxford: Blackwell (special issue of *The Political Quarterly*) pp.90–104.

Dickinson, J.A., and B. Young (1993) *A Short History of Quebec* (Toronto: Copp Clark Pitman).

Fairley, J. and L. Paterson (1991) 'The Reform of Vocational Education and Training in Scotland', *Scottish Educational Review*, Vol.23, pp.68–77.

Fairley, J. and L. Paterson (1995) 'Scottish Education and the New Managerialism', *Scottish Educational Review*, Vol.27, pp.13–36.

Fairley, J. (1996) 'Scotland's New Local Authority and Economic Development', Scottish Affairs, No.15 (Spring), pp.101–22..

Fry, M. (1987) *Patronage and Principle* (Aberdeen University Press).

Harvie, C. (1998) *No Gods and Precious Few Heroes*, 3rd Edn (Edinburgh: Edinburgh University Press; 1st Edn Edward Arnold, 1981).

Held, D. (1984) 'Central Perspectives on the Modern State', in G. McLennan, D. Held, and S. Hall (eds), *The Idea of the Modern State* (Milton Keynes: Open University Press), pp.29–79.

Hirst, P. (ed.)(1996) *Reinventing Democracy* (special issue of *The Political Quarterly*) (Oxford: Blackwell).

Hogwood, B.W. and L.A. Gunn (1984) *Policy Analysis for the Real World* (Oxford University Press).

ICM for *The Scotsman*, 17 February 1997.

Jordan, A.G. and J.J. Richardson (1987) *British Politics and the Policy Process*(London: Unwin Hyman).

Keane, J. (1988) 'Despotism and Democracy', in J. Keane (ed.), *Civil Society and the State* (London: Verso), pp.35–71.

Keating, M. (1996) *Nations Against the State* (London: Macmillan).

Kellas, J. (1984)*The Scottish Political System* (Cambridge University Press).

Kendrick, S. (1983) *Social Change and Nationalism in Modern Scotland*, PhD Thesis, Edinburgh University.

Kumar, K. (1978) *Prophecy and Progress* (Harmondsworth: Penguin).

Levitt, I. (1992) *The Scottish Office, 1919–1959* (Edinburgh: Scottish History Society).

Livingston, W.S. (1952)'A Note on the Nature of Federalism', *Political Science Quarterly*, Vol.67, pp.81–95.

Mackintosh, J.P. (1969) *The Devolution of Power* (Harmondsworth: Penguin).

McCrone, D. (1991) '"Excessive and Unreasonable": The Politics of the Poll Tax in Scotland', *International Journal of Urban and Regional Research*, Vol.15, pp.443–52.

McCrone, D. (1992) *Understanding Scotland* (London: Routledge).

McLennan, G. (1989) *Marxism, Pluralism and Beyond* (Cambridge: Polity).

McPherson, A. and C.D. Raab (1988) *Governing Education* (Edinburgh University Press).

Mitchell, J. (1996 *Strategies for Self Government* (Edinburgh: Polygon).

Murphy, J. (1992) *British Social Services: The Scottish Dimension* (Edinburgh: Scottish Academic Press).

Nairn, T. (1981) *The Break-Up of Britain* (London: Verso).

The Observer, 4 May 1997.

Paterson, L. (1994) *The Autonomy of Modern Scotland* (Edinburgh University Press).

Paterson, L. (1997a) 'Scottish Autonomy and the Future of the Welfare State', *Scottish Affairs*, No.19, Spring, 55–73.

Paterson, L. (1997b) 'Policy-making in Scottish Education: A Case of Pragmatic Nationalism', in P. Munn and M. Clark (eds), *Education in* Scotland (London: Routledge) pp.138–55.

Poggi, G. (1978) *The Development of the Modern State* (London: Hutchinson).

Raffe, D. 'The Scottish Experience of Reform: From Action Plan to Higher Still', in A. Hodgson and K. Spours (eds), *Dearing and Beyond: 14–19 Qualifications, Frameworks and Systems* (London: Kogan Page), forthcoming.

Scottish Office (1996) *Government Expenditure and Revenue in Scotland.* (Edinburgh: HMSO).

Scottish Office Education Department (1994) *Higher Still: Opportunity for All* (Edinburgh: Scottish Office).

Williamson, P. (1992) 'Management Reform of the NHS in Scotland: English Plans, Scottish Interpretation?', in L. Paterson and D. McCrone (eds), *Scottish Government Yearbook* (Edinburgh: Unit for the Study of Government in Scotland), pp.190–205.

What Could a
Scottish Parliament Do?

JAMES MITCHELL

Discussions of the powers of the proposed Scottish Parliament often begin and end with a definition of its competencies. However, a number of considerations are required to ascertain the real scope of any Scottish parliament, its autonomy and its powers. A distinction between power and responsibility needs to be drawn at the outset of any discussion. To devolve responsibilities without power is the devolution of penury (Meny and Wright, 1985: 7). The centre in various systems of government have often devolved difficult decisions to local parliaments and tiers of government. The 'new federalism' under Reagan in the United States was a classic example of this. Reagan declared support for the restoration of American federalism. In practice this involved devolving responsibilities to the states and halting many of the federal government's subsidies to the states (McKay, 1985). The key to any understanding of the extent to which powers or simply responsibilities are being devolved is finance. The grant structure rather than tax levying powers of the Scottish Parliament will be crucial in this respect (see contribution by Heald).

In this analysis a number of other considerations are explored: first the legal definition of powers; second, Westminster's 'over-ride' powers, which will set important parameters within which a Scottish Parliament may operate; third, different types of policy and the prospects for autonomy in each type of policy; fourth, interdependence; and finally, the dynamic nature of institutional development.

This contribution considers what a Scottish Parliament could do by focusing on these considerations rather than on specific policy areas. An underlying assumption here is that any attempt to consider what a Scottish Parliament might do must begin by considering these matters. Another underlying theme is that much of the devolution debate has been unduly influenced by black letter legal terminology. Concern with 'entrenchment' as a legal right has meant that less importance has been attached to notions such as authority and legitimacy. An implicit argument here is that lack of legal entrenchment will prove less important than ensuring that the Scottish Parliament gains authority and legitimacy. The autonomy of the parliament will be entrenched in the sense that its competencies and very existence will depend less on any clause in the founding legislation than in its subsequent perceived success or failure. In addition, it is not possible to define powers discretely to each 'level' of government.

THE LEGAL DEFINITION OF DEVOLVED COMPETENCIES

The Kilbrandon Commission on the Constitution stated in its report in 1973 that there were two possible ways of defining the matters to be devolved to regional assemblies - either by listing the matters upon which the assemblies will be able to legislate, leaving the residue to Parliament, or by listing the matters on which only Parliament will be able to legislate, leaving the assemblies with the residue (Royal Commission on the Constitution, 1969–73 para. 738). The Government of Ireland Act, 1920 had provided for a bicameral parliament for Northern Ireland and an all-Ireland Parliament. It gave the Northern Ireland Assembly powers to make laws for 'peace, order and good government'. There were three classes of responsibilities. First, there were excepted matters which would be retained by Westminster. Second, there were reserved matters, some of which had been intended for transfer to the Council of Ireland. Third, there were all other matters which were to be transferred to the Assembly. In the event, the all-Ireland Parliament forum did not come into being and the reserved and excepted matters were, in large measure, retained at Westminster (see Appendix I for list of 'reserved' and 'excepted' matters).

The 1920 Act was complex and long, going into detail on a number of key points. Nevertheless, little attention was paid to the precise responsibilities, particularly economic responsibilities, which the Assembly was to be given largely because Northern Ireland was 'not brought into existence for financial or economic reasons. There were economic interests to be protected but few or none to be advanced.' (Mansergh, 1972: 245). This is significant in that the nature of the demand ensured that emphasis was placed on the parliament as an institutional symbol and means of creating a Northern Ireland polity rather than as a policy-making body or legislature. Its policy-making role developed after its establishment.

The Scotland Act, 1978 allocated responsibilities using the other method. Those matters not referred to in the legislation were to be retained at Westminster. The Scotland Act, 1978 was also a very long piece of legislation due to the detail involved in defining devolved responsibilities and the controls and safeguards built into it to maintain a large measure of control from London (Bradley and Christie, 1979: 51). It failed to provide a clear allocation of responsibilities conforming to any discernible rationale. New legislation would have been required for even minor alterations in its responsibilities. A related matter was how any adjudication of disputes would occur given the absence of any obvious principle to guide adjudicators. Complicating matters further, the Act also devolved executive powers to the Assembly without legislative powers (Bogdanor, 1978: 169–71; Cornford, 1996: 41–2).

As the Act was never implemented, the extent to which problems could have been dealt with through informal means was never tested. It is probable that relations between Scotland and Westminster would have been fraught with difficulty. The pressures for the establishment of the Scottish Assembly were centrifugal whereas in the case of Northern Ireland they were centripetal and thus could have had a direct impact on relations between Edinburgh and London. The Scotland Bill proposed by the Labour Party in 1987 also listed the matters which would come within the competence of the proposed assembly but also listed those matters which would come within the Scottish executive's competence but without its legislative competence as well as those matters not within the powers of the assembly.

One of the claims some supporters of the Constitutional Convention made was that their scheme was better than the Scotland Act, 1978 because it proposed more extensive competencies. In fact, there was far less detail available to make such a claim with great confidence. The Convention argued that defining powers to be retained by Westminster and devolving all else might be appropriate in the context of devolution throughout the UK but it was 'more practical to have the prospective powers of the Scottish Parliament identified positively' (Bradley and Christie, 1979: 63). A list of functions was identified where issues of responsibility are 'not so clear cut and where further consideration must be given to the issues and implications arising before a conclusion can be reached as to whether these should be the responsibilities of the Scottish Parliament, should be exercised jointly with Westminster, or indeed should remain with Westminster' (Bradley and Christie, 1979: 65) (see Appendix II–III). A number of additional responsibilities were proposed extending the scope of the Scottish Parliament compared with the 1978 Act: the administration of social security; the universities; electricity generation and the terms and conditions of availability of energy to the consumer; forestry; industrial development; land use and planning; vocational training and re-training.

The Labour Government's White Paper (The Scottish Office, 1997, Cm.3658) accepted the proposal made by the independent think-tank the Constitution Unit in its report on Scottish devolution that the devolution legislation should list the reserved powers rather than the transferred powers. The Constitution Unit argued that defining powers to be reserved 'would have changed the premise of the interdepartmental negotiations and might have introduced some principle into the allocation of powers other than simple horse-trading' (The Constitution Unit, 1996: 32). In its White

Paper, the government listed both matters which would be devolved and those reserved and noted that devolved matters which were not in the 1978 Act included economic development, financial and other assistance to industry, training, forestry, certain transport matters, the police and prosecution system (Cm.3658, para.2.2). More significantly, given the intention to define powers retained in the legislation, were those matters which the White Paper listed would be retained (Appendix IV).

The discussion of economic and industrial powers and responsibilities is important. In the case of Scottish devolution, this has proved far more important than was the case with the establishment of the Northern Ireland Assembly. In contrast to the Northern Ireland Assembly, the motivation for supporting Scottish devolution is concerned with satisfying what Kellas refers to as people's 'psychic incomes' but also, to a large degree, with satisfying their financial and material incomes (Kellas, 1991: 66–7). The extent of autonomy in this respect is likely to be important in determining subsequent events. If the hypothesis is correct that Scottish support for constitutional change is based to a large degree on defending and extending those institutions and policies largely associated with the welfare state (the 'state' to which Scots have been consistently loyal over the post-war period), then it will be the outputs in these areas which will determine the future course of politics. More importance should therefore be attached to these powers in the case of the Scottish Parliament now than would have been the case in the past and was the case with Northern Ireland.

THE 'OVER-RIDE' POWERS AND THE FUTURE OF THE SECRETARY OF STATE

The Government of Ireland Act, 1920 provided for 'over-ride powers', ie the power of Westminster to veto decisions taken by Stormont.[1] Westminster retained its sovereign power in and over Northern Ireland (Government of Ireland Act, 1920, Sections 6(2) and 75). Bills passed in Stormont had to be submitted to the Governor with the Northern Ireland Attorney General certifying that the powers of Stormont had not been exceeded (Section 12(2)). There were also powers for the referral of disputes to the Judicial Committee of the Privy Council. However, these provisions were weakened in practice early on.

The House of Commons Speaker ruled in 1923 that no question could be asked there on 'transferred matters'. In 1922, Royal Assent was given to a Bill abolishing proportional representation in local government, despite the Governor reserving the Bill (Hadfield, 1992: 3). The British government faced the prospect of the Government in Northern Ireland resigning, followed by a general election there. In effect, Northern Ireland was raising the stakes substantially which would, in all probability, have meant that direct rule from London would have been necessary or that the Northern Ireland legislation abolishing proportional representation should be accepted. Winston Churchill, as Colonial Secretary, told the Southern Irish government, which lobbied against the change, that to veto the 1922 Bill could create a 'precedent limiting for the future of Dominion Parliaments' (quoted in Hadfield, 1989: 50).

The failure to veto the act abolishing proportional representation was highly significant in setting the sectarian tone of Northern Ireland's politics for the next 50 years. In addition, the parameters of autonomy were set far more widely than the 1920 Act had suggested.[2] The episode 'unequivocally dictated the course of the relationship that was to develop over the ensuing decades between Westminster and Stormont'.[3] The prospect of 'over-ride' powers being used was raised on one further occasion. In 1970 the Governor was petitioned to intervene over the Public Order (Amendment) Bill (NI) – enacted to counter the (non-violent) civil rights movement – but failed to do so after consulting the Home Office in London.

The lessons drawn from the Stormont case cannot easily be applied to any prospective Scottish Parliament. The issues on which intervention is conceivable are unlikely to be those of sectarianism but rather matters deemed to have direct consequences for the rest of the state or designed to push out the parameters of autonomy. On the one hand, Westminster can probably be assured that there will always be an alternative party of government in Scotland, unlike the situation in Northern Ireland, should the Scottish Parliament decide to dissolve itself and fight an election, thus removing one of the problems Westminster faced if it had chosen to over-ride Stormont in its early years. On the other hand, the centrifugal tendencies which will have brought the parliament into being will always have to be considered in any attempt to intervene.

There was much debate on the role of the Secretary of State for Scotland under Labour's devolution proposals in the 1970s. John Mackintosh argued in response to proposals set out in the White Paper *Our Changing Democracy, Devolution to Scotland and Wales* for the abolition of the office. The 1978 Act went beyond the power which central government had in its relations with local government in the event of the latter acting *intra vires*. Mackintosh identified six functions and powers which would be performed by the Secretary of State in relation to devolution as proposed:

- As a UK Cabinet Minister
- 'Wet nurse functions'[4]
- 'Vice regal functions' or 'continuity functions'[5]
- 'Veto' functions or the 'disallowed' functions[6]

- As channel for all communications with the EEC
- As chief adviser to UK government on all aspects of Scottish affairs. (Mackintosh, 1976: 6–16).

As a Cabinet Minister, the Scottish Secretary currently represents Scotland's interests in Cabinet meeting and Cabinet Committee meetings. The abolition of the post would necessitate some alternative means of feeding Scottish opinion into Whitehall. The 'wet nurse' and 'vice regal' functions were, Mackintosh felt, most easily reallocated. The 'veto' functions were described by Mackintosh as of the 'one-man House of Lords' sort. Not only Assembly legislation but executive action could be interfered with by the Secretary of State with the consent of Parliament (Mackintosh, 1976: 11). Dealings with the EU have become far more important over the last 20 years. Mackintosh maintained that the Scottish Secretary 'probably knows less about the EEC than any other British Cabinet Minister and it would make more sense if the Scottish government, when it had to deal, say, with Fisheries, dealt with the Fisheries section of the UK delegation at Brussels' (Mackintosh, 1976: 14). The Scottish Secretary's involvement in EU matters has since grown, though there is still strength in the argument that 'putting all the connections through the Secretary of State is clumsy and serves to over-emphasise his position' (Mackintosh, 1976: 14). As chief adviser to the UK government on all aspects of Scottish affairs under the devolution proposals of the 1970s, the Scottish Secretary would continue to perform the main function given to the office at its inception in 1885 – as chief spokesman for the Scots. In essence, Mackintosh concluded that the retention of the Office of Secretary of State would cause conflict.

In its 1997 White Paper, the Labour Government saw a continuing role for the Secretary of State for Scotland after the establishment of a Scottish Parliament. It was less as someone to over-ride the Scottish Assembly, as anticipated in the 1978 Act, and more to promote 'communication between the Scottish Parliament and Executive and between the UK Parliament and government on matters of mutual interest; and on representing Scottish interest in reserved areas' (Cm.3658, Para.4.12). The tone of the White Paper and the debate had changed between the 1970s and 1997. The emphasis on mechanisms to over-ride the Scottish Parliament had diminished suggesting it would have greater autonomy in practice.

TYPES OF POLICIES

The categorization of policy types identified by Ted Lowi in a classic review article published in 1964 is a useful framework for considering what a Scottish Parliament could do (Lowi, 1964). These types were those in the distributive arena, the redistributive arena and the regulatory arena. In addition, though not strictly speaking a policy, the process of policy-making is important and can have a significant impact on what emerges.

Redistributive policies involve redistribution between classes of people. Examples of these types of policies include taxation and social security policies. Distributive policies are those policies which involve handouts to groups rather than individuals. This would include grants to farmers, to local authorities. Regulatory types of policies are those involving public control over private activities in the public interest such as consumer and environmental protection. These are, of course, ideal-types. Some policies will be difficult to categorize. By process is meant the procedures established to make decisions from agenda setting to implementation. It is important, for example, to recognize that distributive policies, especially over time, may have redistributive consequences.

Whatever changes occur in the foreseeable future, there is unlikely to be any dramatic change in Britain's economic performance. Governments at every level will have to operate within strict financial limits. This has implications for policy types. Whoever is in power, it is unlikely that there will be much change in redistributive policies. Taxation and social security, benefits and pensions payments will be outwith the control of the Scottish Parliament except to an extremely limited extent.

There will be scope for change in terms of distributive policies. Unless there is a dramatic change in public revenues available, then change will be limited. The Scottish Parliament's scope will be limited by prior commitments. Much of its budget will already be spoken for. The budgetary process is incremental. Previous years' commitments and standing commitments account for much of the budget: increased expenditure in one area will only be achieved at another's expense unless the total allocation is increased. There will be some scope for change, but this will have an opportunity cost. Once a distributive type policy is established it is notoriously difficult to get rid of it. Policies often create interests and pressure groups around them rather than vice versa. The strength of the agricultural lobby is explained largely by the substantial agricultural support policies which exist. The farming lobby exists to protect these. So again we should not expect any dramatic change in the short term.

But there will be scope for some change. It is worth remembering, because Labour were last in power 18 years ago, that under Labour certain types of local authority tend to benefit more in grant settlements than they do under the Tories. Changes in formula will over time have a cumulative impact. The Scottish Parliament will be able to do what George Younger claimed to be doing when he was Scottish Secretary in the early 1980s and

use its powers of virement to re-allocate funds. Younger told the Scottish
Affairs Select Committee in 1982 that, compared with changes his Cabinet
colleagues made to programmes, he had 'allocated rather less to transport
and housing and rather more to education and law and order than they did'.
(H.C. 413, 1982: 44, para.10). Such changes will probably have to take
place slowly to avoid financial disruptions and undermine financial
planning but there will be scope for setting new priorities.

   Regulatory politics have become increasingly important in European
Union politics and indeed in European states. This is perhaps one of the
biggest changes we have witnessed over the last two decades. It is not that
the state has been 'rolled back', rather it is that the state has been
transformed. It is less dirigiste (less emphasis on public ownership,
planning and centralized administration), and more regulatory. The
European Union discovered the merits of regulatory politics and has offered
the Commission a cheap and effective way of increasing its scope of
activities. The EU's budget is less than four per cent of central government
spending of member states but it has cut out an important role for itself.
Environmental regulations in particular have grown in number and
significance, despite budgetary crises and economic difficulties. Of course
the key point about European directives is that the EU Commission does not
itself implement them – that is left to other levels of government. As
Majone, one of the leading scholars of regulatory politics, has noted:

> The financial resources of the community go, for the most part, to the
> Common Agricultural Policy and to a handful of distributive
> programmes. The remaining resources are insufficient to support
> large-scale initiatives in areas such as industrial policy, energy,
> research, or technological innovation. Given this constraint, the only
> way for the Commission to increase its role is to expand the scope of
> its regulatory activities (Majone, 1994: 87).

Regulatory politics necessarily involves multi-level governance, at least if
the individual is seen as a level of government. There is considerable scope
in this area for the activities of the Scottish Parliament.

   Perhaps the greatest changes will take place in the processes of policy-
making. Policy-making will likely become more open than at present if only
because the parliament, from which decisions will derive their legitimacy,
will be elected. The role of legislatures in policy-making is not as
straightforward as might be imagined. Richardson and Jordan questioned
whether the House of Commons 'contributes more to the policy process or
to the tourist trade' (Jordan and Richardson, 1987: 57). Nonetheless, the
legitimizing function of parliament and the prospect of opening up the
system of policy-making is enhanced with the existence of a Scottish

Parliament. A more proportional system will be used in elections and the issue of gender equality is now firmly on the agenda, suggesting that a more representative type of politics will emerge (see Brown's chapter in this collection). The prospect of issues getting on to the political agenda through the opening up of the policy-making process offers some long-term opportunities. In much the same way that the European Parliament set out to increase its power and influence, the Scottish Parliament might succeed in altering the agenda of debate which, in turn, will have an impact on the policies it pursues.

In essence, the prospects of the parliament being able to pursue redistributive policies will be extremely limited at least in the immediate future. It will have greater scope in the field of distributive policies especially over time to cut out a distinct role for itself. It is in the fields of regulatory policies that imaginative policies could emerge which will ensure that the parliament makes a considerable difference. In addition, the manner of policy-making will change and could change considerably. Perhaps most significant will be the long-term impact of changes in the style of policy-making on the kinds of policies which emerge. The challenge before the Scottish Parliament, as all legislatures, will be to cut out a role for itself, some autonomy, without having to spend considerable additional sums of money.

INTERDEPENDENCE AND MULTI-LEVEL GOVERNANCE

One conception of federalism sees it as the territorial separation of powers in which each layer of government is allocated discrete functions. An alternative conception sees it as a system of territorial government laying stress on the links between the different levels of government, as an interdependent system of government. The contrasting analogies are of federalism as a layered cake and federalism as a marble cake. The latter is a more accurate analogy in understanding federalism or devolution. In addition, there has been a 'paradigm shift from a world of states, modelled after the ideal of the nation-state developed at the beginning of the modern epoch in the seventeenth century and increased interstate linkages of a constitutional federal character' (Elazar, 1996: 417). All of this amounts to the importance of interdependence or, perhaps more accurately, the strong inter-relationship between different levels of government.

Inevitably, there are indeterminate areas and changes in the political and economic context which will alter the balance of responsibilities and powers of each level of government. The relationship between Stormont and London approximated more to the layered cake analogy for most of Stormont's existence than is likely to be the case with regard to the Scottish

Parliament and London. Indeed, the exceptional extent of autonomy which was given to Stormont was ultimately its undoing. This was an unusual case of separation of powers, akin to the US Federal government's relationship with the Southern states up to the 1950s.

The Scotland Act, 1978 was never implemented so that the relationship remained theoretical. Much attention was paid to how the Edinburgh Assembly would relate to London. Probably more attention to detail was paid than was required, as discussed above. The existence of the European Union, covering much that was traditionally seen as domestic politics adds to the complexity of the picture today. The multi-level nature of governance which will emerge – local government, Edinburgh, London and Brussels – will not simply be a hierarchy of levels of government. In some areas, each level will develop a fair degree of autonomy. In others, some direct links will be developed between individual levels while more complex, triadic relationships will emerge. In some areas each of the four levels may have or will develop some competence. The nexus of relationships will be complex and dynamic.

Local government will have a particularly close relationship with Edinburgh especially when it comes to the distribution of grants and regulatory politics. Local government's relationship with London is likely to diminish, if only because much that constitutes central–local relations will involve relations between the Scottish Office and local government. The 'centre' in this relationship is somewhat ambiguous: at times London will be the centre but, from a local government perspective, Edinburgh will be the centre. In a number of areas the Scottish Parliament will pass laws and local government will be expected to administer and implement these. But equally, there will be decisions taken in Brussels and London affecting local government. This will leave considerable scope for the 'street level bureaucrats' (Lipsky, 1980) at local level to influence matters. There will inevitably be some conflict between these levels, as between each level in any democratic polity, but one change which can be anticipated is that the political complexion of the Scottish Parliament and local government will not be so widely at variance as was the case with the Scottish Office and local government in the 1980s. This should make for more consensual politics.

Increasing contact between local government and the European Union has been noted in recent years. There have been a number of features to the 'Europeanisation' of local government (Goldsmith, 1993: 683–99). The Audit Commission report on local authorities and the EU identified three main ways in which Europe affects local authorities:

- Euro-regulation imposes unavoidable obligations to implement, enforce

and monitor EU legislation;
- European economic integration creates new opportunities for (and pressures on) the local economic base; and
- Euro-funds offer potential support for the local economy and for a range of local authority projects (Audit Commission, 1991: 7).

Keogh has argued that within a short space of time in the late 1980s and early 1990s, Scottish local government 'embraced' the European Community. The structures of local government have taken account of the EU, with new posts, committees and departments established to deal with European affairs (Keogh, 1996).

The Scottish Parliament's relationship with London is likely to be similar in some respects to local government's relationship with London. The key aspect of this will be financial. The allocation of grant to the Scottish Parliament will make the relationship extremely important. Much debate has focused on the financial relations between London and Edinburgh in the event of devolution, and much of this assumes some dramatic turn of events. In fact, Scotland has been treated as a distinct financial entity throughout the history of Britain. From the development of the earliest state subventions to local polities with education grants in the early nineteenth century, Scotland has had be treated as a separate entity. The development of separate Local Taxation Accounts for the constituent nations of the United Kingdom ensured the continuance of this territorial aspect of public finances in Britain into the twentieth century.

What potentially will be new is the partners involved in negotiating part of Scotland's share of public expenditure. Instead of the rather mysterious system that currently prevails, a more open system is likely to emerge. As the current system involves the Scottish Office fairly indirectly, largely as the recipient of awards decided elsewhere in Whitehall, it is conceivable that there will be little change. The likelihood is, however, that the Scottish Parliament will result in greater openness, and one of the key questions which will emerge will be the extent to which a democratically-elected institution will prove more or less successful than the Scottish Office. This should not be over-stated. Other important factors will play their part in the determination of Scottish public expenditure levels. Not least of these is the increasing salience of territorial levels of public expenditure in Britain which has arisen even without constitutional change. The alteration of the formula which was instituted after the 1992 election demonstrates that change in Scotland's share of public expenditure is a matter which is not tied exclusively to constitutional change. The pressures for changes to Scotland's disadvantage have been building up for some years and the coincidence of such changes with the establishment of a Scottish Parliament should not necessarily be linked.

The London–Edinburgh relationship will also be significant in a vast range of other areas. There will be areas in which London remains the legislature while executive functions are given to Edinburgh.[7] In most important respects, London will remain in charge of economic affairs. Fiscal policy will be determined in London and this will limit the autonomy of the Scottish Parliament and have considerable impact on the activities of the Scottish Parliament. In many areas there is likely to be dual responsibility. Just as greater consensus can be expected between the Scottish Parliament and local government, more conflict, or at least, more openness in existing conflict, will be evident in relations between London and Edinburgh. However, this is far from exceptional in any system of government with more than one level. The level of conflict will differ across the range of issues and competencies dealt with jointly.

The Edinburgh–Brussels link has proved one of the most difficult areas for the Constitutional Convention and Labour Party. The Scotland Act, 1978 was quite clear in stating that EC matters would remain the prerogative of Westminster but since then the European dimension and its links to the Scottish Question have become more salient. In particular, the Scottish National Party's policy of 'independence in Europe' has provoked a need among devolutionists for some kind of response.

The White Paper suggests that the Scottish executive should 'learn from best practice in those member states with strong regional government and adapt it to the needs of Scotland and the UK' (Cm 3658 1997, para.5.3). But most significantly, it proposes that in 'appropriate cases, Scottish Ministers could speak for the UK in Councils [of Ministers] (Cm 3658 1997, para.5.6). The phrase 'where appropriate' is important as this allows for a variety of possibilities but the likeliest outcome would be that Scottish Ministers would represent the UK on very few occasions, most likely on fishing policy. Nonetheless, there is a commitment to involve Scottish Ministers and officials in the formulation of UK policy positions on all devolved matters. This may prove difficult at times but reflects the inter-dependent nature of multi-level governance.

The same problems afflict the Convention as have had to be confronted by local government in the UK and other sub-state levels of government elsewhere in Europe. Even in Germany, with one of the most developed systems of sub-state levels of government in the form of the 16 Länder, this issue has proved extremely difficult. The Länder discovered that the constitutional requirement that foreign (including EU) affairs be dealt with by the Federal government meant that issues that were competencies given to the Länder in the German Basic Law, which were increasingly dealt with at the European level, were being drawn out of their remit. The Federal government was able, through its prerogative for European affairs, to engage in what were constitutionally the competencies of the Länder. The increasing role of the EU in areas such as the environment create new challenges for sub-state government throughout the EU. A real danger exists of competencies given to Scottish Parliament being lost through the process of European integration without some direct involvement by the Scottish Parliament in EU affairs. The current situation in which local authorities can work together or individually to lobby the various EU institutions would seem the most likely model for the Scottish Parliament. Its competencies are likely to be affected in similar areas as local government has been. For this reason the relations between London and Brussels cannot be ignored as they will have an impact on the work of the Scottish Parliament. Decisions made in the intergovernmental Council of Ministers will have an impact on a wide range of competencies of the Scottish Parliament. It is in these areas that the Scottish Parliament may find itself excluded.

EU structural funds will involve each level. Local government's role has included implementation but also increasingly – and often in conjunction with Edinburgh (the Scottish Office in the past and the Scottish Parliament in the future) and London – bidding for grants and lobbying the Commission. London's role within the Council of Ministers will remain central to the whole process determining in large measure the overall package agreed for the structural funds. The Commission has managed to cut out an increased role for itself in the structural funds. However, as we have seen over the period since the establishment in 1975 of the European Regional Development Fund (ERDF), the nature of the relationships can change (Marks, 1993).

The nexus of relations will be not only complex but dynamic. Relations between the parliament and other levels will change depending on the issue being addressed and the context. The nature of the relationship will depend on the relative power of each level which in turn will be determined by the resources available in each case.

What is clear is that the different types of policies discussed above must be seen as operating to a greater or lesser extent within a multi-level framework. Redistributive policies will remain largely the prerogative of London, though increasingly constraints will be imposed by Brussels as the movement towards a common European currency occurs. In the field of distributive policies the key dimensions will be the relationships between London and Edinburgh and between Edinburgh and local government. Indeed, the latter relationship will largely be dependent on the former. The distribution of grants to local government will be determined largely by the settlement won by the Scottish Parliament from London. Other distributive policies of the Scottish Parliament will also impinge on local government so far as this is a zero sum game.

Regulatory politics have become increasingly important for the European Commission and it is with this type of policy the Scottish Parliament may seek to emulate the Commission in cutting out a fairly independent role for itself. Nonetheless, many regulations emanating from Brussels, and of course from London, will have an impact on the work of the Scottish Parliament. In certain areas, the Scottish Parliament, along with Scottish local authorities, will find itself implementing regulations and directives decided upon elsewhere. Multi-level politics will mean a greater degree of interdependence than is probably appreciated by those engaged in the devolution debate. The degree of autonomy of the parliament will depend not only on the types of policies but also the changing context and the particular issue under discussion.

CONCLUSION: A DYNAMIC POLITY

The dynamic nature of constitutional development means that whatever legislation is passed, further developments are certain. New contexts, new pressures and the learning process will all ensure further change. The early years will likely see informal rules and standard operating procedures develop which will, to some degree, set parameters within which further change occurs. Experience, expectations and context will all be important.

The experience that will be important will not only be that of the working of the Scottish Parliament but also of Westminster. Perceptions of responsibility, culpability and credit will be important. If it is perceived that London is failing either through the use of its own powers or through interfering in the affairs of the Scottish Parliament, then this will affect the course of events. The expectations of the Scottish people in the 1880s when a Secretary of State for Scotland was being proposed were described by Prime Minister Lord Salisbury as 'approaching the arch-angelic' (quoted Hanham, 1965). Expectations may prove an important dynamic in the development of the parliament. But perhaps more important will be the expectations Scots will have of London. Devolution is about reforming the state as a whole and it will be the state as a whole which will be judged. If the perceived failure of Britain lies behind the demand for Scottish constitutional change, then it might be expected that perceived continued failure will result in increased demands. Even though many matters will be the joint responsibility of both London and Edinburgh, this may not be how it appears to the Scottish public. Again, a lesson can be drawn from the history of the Scottish Office. The Gilmour report on Scottish central administration noted that the Scottish people looked to the Scottish Office for answers even when the office had no statutorily defined responsibility (Report of the Committee on Scottish Administration, 1937, Cmd.5563: 10, para.37). Whether London or Edinburgh is blamed or credited with the success or failure of devolution will probably be a major determinant of future constitutional development. The role of political leadership will also prove important. Opportunities and limitations can be identified but at the end of the day, skilful politicians and officials can overcome difficulties while less skilled actors can fail to take advantage of opportunities.

An attempt to assess what a Scottish Parliament could do may start by looking at the list of competencies but as in studying any polity there must be a recognition that constitutions are merely frameworks within which politics occur and policies develop. Some attention needs to be paid to the interdependence of modern government, what is meant by a policy and the dynamic inherent in constitutional and political development. The real powers of the Scottish Parliament may prove more or less than what is suggested in the government's White Paper. The true scope of autonomy will ultimately depend on what Scots make of the institutions available to them.

NOTES

1. 'Stormont' is used here though the actual location of the Northern Ireland Assembly was not at Stormont until 1932.
2. Patrick Buckland, *The Factory of Grievances: Devolved Government in Northern Ireland* Dublin, Gill and Macmillan, 1979, Ch.12.
3. Brigid Hadfield, *The Constitution of Northern Ireland Belfast*, SLS, 1989, p.51.
4. Fixing and running elections for the Assembly; arranging date, time and place of first meeting; initially arranging the pay and allowances of Members of Assembly; publishing its standing orders and fixing the number of Ministers and their assistants.
5. To invite someone after the election to form a Government and formally appoint him/her as chief executive if able to secure a vote of confidence; formally ratifies changes in personnel of Scottish government at request of chief executive (Scottish Prime Minister); power to appoint a caretaker Government if Government loses its majority and attempt to replace chief executive.
6. Adjudicating on whether legislation is *ultra vires* and requesting Assembly to remove offending sections; general power to declare a Bill as unacceptable on policy grounds and with consent of Parliament to have measure overruled; to take over and undertake executive acts of chief executive or the Scottish government.
7. Cm 3658, July 1997 para.2.7 lists these as the administration of EU structural funds; powers and duties in relation to electricity supply and civil nuclear emergency planning; the determination of certain public sector pension schemes; an appropriate oversight role in relation to all Scottish passenger rail services; administration of freight facilities and track access grants; applications to the EU for designation of lifeline air services' powers; powers to issue policy and financial directions to National Lottery distributors in Scotland; designation of casino areas; and the setting of gaming hours and certain licence fees; Justices of the Peace and General Commissioners of Income Tax; and some Crown, church and ceremonial matters.

REFERENCES

Bogdanor, Vernon (1979), *Devolution* (Oxford: Oxford University Press).
Bradley, A.W. Christie, D.J. (1979*), The Scotland Act, 1978* (Edinburgh: W. Green and Son/Sweet and Maxwell).
Buckland, Patrick (1979), *The Factory of Grievances: Devolved Government in Northern Ireland* (Dublin: Gill and Macmillan).
Cornford, James (1996), 'Constitutional reform in the UK' in Stephan Tindale (ed.) *The State and the Nations* (London: IPPR).
Elazar, D. (1996), 'From Statism to Federalism – A Paradigm Shift', *International Political Science Review*, Vol.17.
Goldsmith, Mike (1993), 'The Europeanisation of Local Government', *Urban Studies*,Vol.30, pp.683–99.
Government of Ireland Act, 1920.
Hadfield, Brigid, (1992), *The Constitution of Northern Ireland* (Belfast: SLS).
Hanham (1965), 'The Creation of the Scottish Office, 1881–87', *Judicial Review*, pp.205–44.
House of Commons Paper 413, (1982) Select Committee on Scottish Affairs, Minutes of Evidence.
Jordan, A.G. and J.J. Richardson (1987), *British Politics and Policy Processes* (London: Allan and Unwin).
Kellas, James (1991) *The Politics of Nationalism and Ethnicity* (Basingstoke: Macmillan).
Keogh, Marion (1996), 'The Europeanisation of Scottish Local Government', in Danica Fink Hafner and Terry Cox (eds), *Into Europe? Perspectives from Britain and Slovenia* (Ljubljana: Scientific Library, Faculty of Social Sciences), pp.315–35.
Lipsky, Martin (1980), *Street Level Bureaucracy* (New York: Russell Sage).
Lowi, Theodore, J. (1964), 'American Business, Public Policy, Case Studies, and Political Theory', *World Politics*, Vol.16, No.4, 1964.
Mackintosh, J.P. (1976) 'The Power of the Secretary of State', *New Edinburg Review*, February 1976, No.31.
Majone, G. (1994), 'The Rise of the Regulatory State in Europe', *West European Politics*, Vol.17.
Mansergh, Nicolas, *The Unresolved Question: The Anglo-Irish Settlement and Its Undoing 1912–72*, (London: Yale Unversity Press).
Marks, Gary (1993), 'Structural Policy and Multilevel Governance in the EC', in Alan Cafruny and Glenda Rosenthal (eds), *The State of the European Community: The Maastricht Debates and Beyond*, Vol.2 (Harlow, Essex: Longman), pp.391–4.
McKay, David (1985), 'Theory and Practise in Public Policy: The Case of the New Federalism', *Political Studies*, June 1985.
Meny, Yves and Vincent Wright (1985), 'General Introduction' in Meny and Wright (eds.), *Centre–Periphery Relations In Western Europe* (London: George Allen and Unwin).
Royal Commission on the Constitution (1969–73), (Kilbrandon) *Report*, HMSO.
The Constitution Unit (1996), Scotland's Parliament Constitution Unit.
The Scottish Office (1997) *Scotland's Parliament* Cm.3658 July 1997.

APPENDIX I

'Reserved' and 'excepted' matters in the Government of Ireland Act, 1920

Matters relating to the Crown
Making war and peace
The armed services
Foreign and Commonwealth relations
Elections to the Parliament at Westminster
Dignities and titles
Treason
Aliens and naturalization
Trade with places outside Northern Ireland
Merchant shipping
Wireless telegraphy
Aerial navigation
Coinage
Trademarks
Copyrights and patents
The Supreme Court of Judicature of Northern Ireland
The postal services
Customs and excise
Income tax
Tax on profits

APPENDIX II

Functions identified as those which should certainly come within the responsibilities of a Scottish Parliament
(*Towards a Scottish Parliament* consultative document, October 1989)

1. All matters relating to the Health Service.
2. Social welfare, including children and adoption.
3. All aspects of Education, including the universities and cultural and recreational activities (libraries, museums, art galleries etc.).
4. All aspects of Housing.
5. All aspects of Local Government.
6. All aspects of Land Use and Planning.
7. All aspects of Pollution (possibly excepting motor vehicles, aircraft, and dumping at sea outwith inland waters).
8. Coastal erosion and the flooding of land.
9. Matters related to the development and conservation of the countryside.
10. Water supply and inland waterways.
11. The Fire Service and fire precautions.
12. The development of Tourism.
13. Ancient monuments and historic buildings.
14. Transport.
15. Terms and conditions of availability of Energy to the consumer.
16. Vocational training and re-training.
17. Provision, improvement and maintenance of roads.
18. Provision, improvement and maintenance of harbours etc.
19. Forestry matters.
20. Agriculture.

21. All aspects of fisheries policy.
22. Registration of births, deaths, marriages and adoption.
23. The legal system and profession.
24. Tribunals and enquiries related to all functions of the parliament.
25. Civil Law, with the exception of some areas of commercial law, including industrial relations.
26. The Police.
27. Crime, excluding deportation, extradition and some other areas.
28. Public records.
29. A range of economic powers (including the administration of regional development incentives and the attraction of overseas investment).

APPENDIX III

Areas where further consideration was to be given regarding level of responsibility
(*Towards a Scottish Parliament* consultative document, October 1989)

1. Social security (although this would carry the clear implication that there might be different levels of social security payments in Scotland).
2. Certain aspects of Energy and Economic Policy.
3. European Community matters.
4. Oil (and oil revenues).
5. Company Law and Competition Policy.
6. Control of Drugs and Infectious Diseases.
7. The Prison Service.

APPENDIX IV

Matters to be retained by Westminster
('Scotland's Parliament' white paper, July 1997)

The constitution of the United Kingdom
UK foreign policy
UK defence and national security
The protection of borders and certain matters subject to border controls
The stability of the UK's fiscal, economic and monetary system
Common markets for UK goods and services
Employment legislation
Social security policy and administration
Regulation of certain professions
Transport safety and regulation
Certain other matters presently subject to UK or GB regulation or operation.

Reactive Capital: The Scottish Business Community and Devolution

PETER LYNCH

Over the last two decades, opinion polls in Scotland have consistently demonstrated a public consensus in favour of the establishment of a Scottish Parliament. However, throughout this period the Scottish business community stood outside this consensus. For example, business was a strong opponent of the establishment of a Scottish Assembly in the 1970s and was active in the *Scotland Says No* campaign at the 1979 devolution referendum (Bochel, Denver and Macartney, 1981). While major political and economic organizations such as the trades unions and local government became supportive of devolution, business scepticism about the merits of constitutional change persisted. An opinion poll in 1991 discovered that 54 per cent of Scottish business supported the constitutional status quo, 26 per cent favoured a Scottish Assembly without tax-raising powers and only 10 per cent favoured a tax-raising parliament in Edinburgh (Keating, 1996: 198). In 1996, another poll indicated that business remained hostile to devolution, with 63 per cent of business leaders opposed to devolution and only 16 per cent in favour.[1] Such evidence would seem to present business as an implacable opponent of devolution. However, business interest in devolution has been sporadic, as any survey of business magazines and the financial pages of the Scottish press would demonstrate. While Scottish business was never a proponent of devolution, it cannot be argued that business was unequivocally opposed to constitutional change and existed as a 'veto group' over devolution as polls suggested.

The aim of this contribution is twofold. First, it will seek to outline business attitudes to constitutional change in Scotland. Whereas it is often possible to determine business responses to economic and commercial issues in public policy (Grant, 1987), territorial politics is a more abstract area in which to examine the role of capital and business pressure group activity. The study therefore seeks to examine the pattern of business responses to Scottish devolution through the medium of Scottish business interest associations (BIAs). Second, this contribution will analyse business as an actor in the devolution debate, through assessing business concerns about devolution and whether it was able to have any impact on the devolution measures proposed by the Labour government. Particular attention will be paid to the role of business in developing a strategy of market-building in Scotland, which shapes its approach to state-building, and its role and policy preferences as an actor in territorial politics (Coleman and Jacek, 1989).

BUSINESS AND TERRITORIAL POLITICS

The business community is an important actor in Scottish political and commercial life. There are a number of distinct Scottish business interest associations (BIAs) which have developed as a result of distinctive Scottish economic interests, the existence of Scottish government institutions (Grant, 1989) and the creation of regional units of UK-wide business associations such as the Confederation of British Industry (CBI Scotland) and Institute of Directors. These organizations have adopted the traditional representational function of pressure groups but have also developed a role in territorial politics through their concerns with market-building and state-building (Coleman and Jacek, 1989). In terms of market-building, regional BIAs face two alternative choices: to play an integrative role within the national economy or attempt to sustain or develop a distinctive regional economy. Thus business pressure groups can seek to create 'a highly integrated national economy where no significant cultural, regional or economic barriers exist to the expansion of markets within the national territory' (Coleman and Jacek, 1989: 3) or attempt to develop a balkanized, regionally-centred economy in which economic, political and cultural barriers to trade are maintained to the region's advantage. Regional BIAs also have a role as instigators or insulators in state-building. They could instigate political centralization through supporting centralized government structures and uniform policies across territory, integrating the region into national decisionmaking and building ties between regional BIAs to establish national networks and institutions. Conversely, regional BIAs could seek to insulate the region from central government through supporting regional autonomy, resisting central government control and supporting regional political and economic differentiation (Coleman and Jacek, 1989).

The notions of market-building and state-building are central to business attitudes to territorial politics in Scotland. Scottish BIAs are committed to the maintenance of the UK single market and the retention of a level playing field for Scottish companies which do business in England: a reality which meant that Scottish BIAs often favoured political centralization. In some circumstances, devolution has been viewed as a threat to such market-building. However, business is sensitive to the decentralist aspect of state-building, particularly because of public support for devolution. Business certainly cannot be seen as unequivocally centralist in its attitude to state-building as it exhibits sympathies towards greater administrative devolution and to the creation of a Scottish Parliament on the 1978 model (Scottish Chamber of Commerce, 1995). Where business becomes more hostile to devolution is when it involves taxation powers that could disturb the level playing field of the UK economy. However, in recent years, business has been keen to avoid taking a political stance over devolution. As a result, business attitudes to devolution tended towards public neutrality and private dialogue over the details of constitutional change rather than public criticism. As will become clear here, business has increasingly viewed devolution as an inevitable development, but one which would involve bargaining and negotiation between government and pressure groups (Richardson and Jordan, 1979). Thus, while not supporters of devolution, Scottish BIAs have sought to avoid alienating pro-devolution forces in Scotland, in order to maintain a position as a major interest which must be consulted over the devolution package.

REACTIVE CAPITAL: BUSINESS AND DEVOLUTION

Devolution is not a new issue for the Scottish business community, but it has been an issue in which business has had a reactive rather than an active role. CBI Scotland, was originally involved in discussions over devolution during the consultations that comprised the Royal Commission on the Constitution in 1970. Then, CBI Scotland stated that it could find no disadvantages from the establishment of a Scottish Assembly, yet no advantages either. The CBI's main concern was that devolution would add unnecessarily to the complexities and cost of government (CBI Scotland, 1970). However, despite such an anodyne view, Scottish business came out of its shell to support the *Scotland Says No* campaign at the 1979 devolution referendum. *Scotland Says No* was directed by an official seconded from Glasgow Chamber of Commerce who ran the campaign from the Coats Paton office in Glasgow (Bochel, Denver and Macartney, 1981: 30). Scottish business leaders such as Lord Weir, Peter Balfour of Scottish and Newcastle, Gerard Elliot of Christian Salveson, David Nickson of Collins and Eric Yarrow of Yarrow's shipbuilders all played an active role in the *No* campaign (Young, 1995: 48). The campaign had around £100,000 in its war chest, of which 80 per cent was provided by business. The extent to which business bankrolled the organization and BIAs played a networking role in promoting the No campaign would seem to indicate the level of importance that some members of the business community gave to preventing the emergence of a Scottish Assembly. However, it was only a small section of the business community which actively opposed devolution in 1979, often those most closely allied with the Conservatives. The majority of businesses were not involved in the referendum or the devolution debate.

Business concerns about devolution in the 1970s were largely influenced by fairly set political and economic assumptions. The political assumption was that any devolved assembly would be controlled by an interventionist Labour Party. The economic assumption was that the assembly would seek to maximize its powers of economic intervention (though these were actually very slight in the Scotland Act 1978) to constrain the free market. This scenario of a left-wing, interventionist Labour assembly remains influential today. The intention to provide a Scottish Parliament with tax-raising powers in the current devolution debate (Scottish Constitutional Convention, 1995) was therefore seen as the most pressing problem for business. Negative expectations of a Scottish Parliament with tax-raising powers are widely held within the business community. The Scottish division of the Institute of Directors stated that its members were 'apprehensive about potential financial and regulatory policies ... the apprehensions were based on the likely expectations of Scots voters who for 40 years have voted for increased government expenditure. This can only mean either raising extra revenues or increasing frustration with UK Treasury control of government funds available to Scotland.'[2] Such apprehensions led several businesses to publicly oppose constitutional change during the 1992 general election campaign, though they dropped their opposition in 1997.

In contrast to the trade unions, local government, the churches and a range of other social organizations, business was not involved in the Scottish Constitutional Convention – the cross-party organization which met from 1989 to 1995 to design a package of measures for a devolved Scottish Parliament (Lynch, 1996). Non-participation meant that business had little direct influence on the current devolution proposals. From 1989 to 1990, the only participating business organization was the National Federation of Self-employed and Small Business (Scottish section). The Scottish Council of Development and Industry and Dundee and Tayside Chamber of Commerce were involved in the Convention as observers, but took no part in debates (Scottish Constitutional Convention, 1990: 20). Each of these business organizations retained the same level of involvement in the Convention in 1995, joined by an observer from the Forum for Private Business and a representative from the Law Society of Scotland/Faculty of Advocates (Scottish Constitutional Convention, 1995: 35). More significant business pressure groups such as the Institute of Directors, CBI Scotland, Scotch Whisky Association and Scottish Financial Enterprise all avoided the Convention and played no part in its public discussions.

The only significant role for business in the Convention was when the Convention's executive launched a series of consultations over its proposals to gain support and neutralize opposition to devolution.[3] Meetings between business and the Convention and political parties did occur, but it was difficult to determine whether the Convention's scheme for devolution was influenced by business. The biggest issue of concern to business – tax-raising powers – remained an integral part of the Convention package, though other Scottish Parliament responsibilities disappeared in mysterious circumstances. The ability to take companies into public ownership was included in the Convention's 1990 proposals but had disappeared by 1995 as had the proposal to create a specific Scottish Monopolies and Mergers Commission. However, in many areas neither the Convention nor the political parties adopted clear policy positions and the Convention's scheme largely consisted of broad principles rather than detailed legislation. The overall result was to leave many gaps to be filled in by Westminster and Whitehall, and a range of policy uncertainties and lobbying opportunities for Scottish business interest associations. Following the election of the new Labour government in 1997, business organizations had a number of consultations over the devolution legislation. The government's devolution Minister, Henry McLeish, held meetings with CBI Scotland, the Scottish Chambers of Commerce and the Federation of Small Businesses, an opportunity for constructive discussion over the details of devolution and for Labour to offer reassurance to business over its devolution plans (*Scotland on Sunday*, 1 June 1997).

BUSINESS CONCERNS ABOUT DEVOLUTION

Scottish business concerns about devolution revolve around four main issues: taxation levels under devolution, the impact of devolution on inward investment, the effect of devolution on Scotland's existing role in the United Kingdom and the bureaucratic and regulatory impact of devolution. As indicated above, the market-building preferences of Scottish business mean that it is most keen to avoid disruption to the level playing field of the UK market. The centrality of the UK market to Scottish business makes this the dominant concern which is often the motivating force behind more specific policy concerns related to issues such as taxation levels and regulatory policy.

Taxation, and its impact on business costs, has been the most prominent issue of concern to business in Scotland in relation to devolution. Indeed, business has become overly fixated on the taxation issue.[4] This situation resulted from the proposal to give the Scottish Parliament the power to vary income tax by +/–3p (Scottish Constitutional Constitutional, 1995). This taxation power was seen to damage the commercial level playing field because of its potential to place additional costs on Scottish business which would make it uncompetitive with other parts of the UK. Thus any increase in Scottish income tax would have an adverse effect on wage demands in Scotland and make it more difficult to recruit staff from England (CBI Scotland, 1996). Business was also concerned with the mechanics of providing the Scottish Parliament with tax-varying powers when the power to set overall tax levels remained at Westminster.[5] There was also uncertainty over the application of tax powers, with concern that it could be applied to individual income tax, tax on individual savings, income earned from fund management by Scottish financial institutions, income tax on non-residents of Scotland working in Scotland and companies paying the small companies rate of corporation tax, which is linked to income tax (CBI Scotland, 1996: 10). Scotland's financial sector was also concerned about tax on savings and the prospect of a Scottish Parliament being able to levy withholding tax on investments (Scottish Financial Enterprise, 1992a: 4–5).

Business was also concerned about the impact of devolution on levels of local taxation. Scottish business often complained of paying markedly higher local taxes than other parts of the UK, which made Scottish business less competitive with English firms. The Conservative government's solution to this problem was the institution of the Uniform Business Rate (UBR), which was set by central not local government and was gradually phased in to produce a level playing field for local business taxation in Scotland that was similar to levels in England. The main concern of business was that the UBR would be abandoned and power to set local business rates handed back to Scottish local authorities through devolution: a position Labour would adopt to sell devolution to its local authorities in Scotland. Labour's policy response was to allow local authorities to set business rates, but to keep rates at the same level of increase as domestic council taxes (*The Herald*, 8 November 1996: 1): a clear attempt to find a middle way between the interests of local government and business. However, after devolution, it will be the Scottish Parliament that assumes responsibility for business rates, with the potential for considerable changes in policy.

The business community has also been concerned about the impact of devolution on inward investment, fixated by the image of a left-wing interventionist parliament which will raise personal and business taxes and make Scotland unattractive as an investment location. However, as is often the case with the devolution issue, concerns about inward investment have been exaggerated to suit political ends. The former director of the government's Scottish inward investment operation remarked of the devolution plans that 'it is difficult to convincingly argue that these proposals constitute a level of uncertainty for international companies operating in Scotland which in any way matches the shifts of technological advantage, market demand and exchange rate volatility already handled by them on an ongoing basis' (Hood, 1995: 3). Thus devolution is seen as a relatively minor issue for inward investors. The more important considerations for inward investors – both current and prospective – are issues such as EU enlargement to Eastern Europe and economic and monetary union. The negative impact of devolution on inward investment also seems to be negligible in real life. There have recently been a number of substantial inward investments into Scotland by Chunghwa and First Direct at a time when a Labour government and a Scottish Parliament were highly likely, and more inward investors chose to locate in Scotland after Labour was elected in 1997.[6]

Business has also expressed concern about the maintenance of Scotland's share of UK public expenditure under devolution. There is a belief within the business community, backed by government analysis, that Scotland receives a significantly larger proportion of UK public spending than the UK average and the average for England (Scottish Office, 1996). Devolution is seen to threaten the existing Barnett formula under which Scotland gains 10/85s of identifiable UK public expenditure (even though it was instituted because of devolution in the 1970s), with an assumption that the Treasury and Westminster will expect Scotland to reduce its spending or fund its own expenditure to comply with UK averages. Business has also been concerned about devolution damaging the image of Scottish companies in England. This situation would come about if devolution was perceived to give Scotland an unfair advantage within the UK: its own parliament and ability to make legislation separately from Westminster, yet able to play a decisive role in the Commons because of the over-representation of Scottish MPs and unwilling to end Scotland's disproportionate share of UK public expenditure (Scottish Financial Enterprise, 1992b). The political uncertainty created by devolution has also been of concern to business, with the assumption that devolution would not be a closed-ended process, but one likely to lead to independence which would threaten the integrity of the UK market and pose serious problems for Scottish companies operating in UK markets (Scottish Financial Enterprise, 1992b: 2).

Business is traditionally concerned to prevent government bureaucracy and regulation adding unnecessary costs to company activities and devolution is problematic in this context. However, the reorganization of local government in Scotland in 1995, to create a single tier of local government, has taken the steam out of some of the concerns about over-regulation. What remains is concern over the powers of a Scottish Parliament and how the parliament will seek to perform its functions. For example, Scottish financial institutions do not want a Scottish Parliament to have regulatory or legislative functions in employment and trade union law, commercial law, taxation, supervision of financial services or standards and reporting requirements (Scottish Financial Enterprise, 1992b: 6.). They also rejected the creation of a Scottish Monopolies and Mergers Commission, viewing it as an institution which would become a political football to protect takeovers and mergers within Scotland. However, such proposals were not included in the 1995 package of measures of the Constitutional Convention: a reflection of private dialogue between the business community and supporters of devolution.

SCOTTISH BUSINESS INTEREST ASSOCIATIONS AND DEVOLUTION

Signs of business opposition to devolution have usually dominated media coverage of the issue. However, as the following survey of attitudes to devolution will demonstrate, Scottish business interest associations have a much more complex, ambiguous and changing set of attitudes towards the constitutional issue which belie simple depiction. What is clear is that business support for devolution has been very slight. Pro-devolutionists did have some brief success in establishing *Business Says Yes* as a lobbying group in support of constitutional change in the early 1990s, but the group lasted only a few years and had little impact. More recently, a prominent businessman, Nigel Smith, the managing director of a Glasgow engineering firm, came to prominence. Smith was instrumental in establishing *Scotland Forward*, a non-party home rule group to galvanize business and public support for the *Yes* campaign at the devolution referendum. However, generally business has avoided public expressions of support for change. This lack of vocal business support for devolution made it relatively easy for opponents of constitutional change to claim that business opposed devolution, even though many business organizations were neutral or apathetic about devolution.

CBI Scotland has adopted a high profile in recent years, a development connected to the likelihood of the establishment of a Scottish Parliament. CBI Scotland sought to influence the political parties and public agencies in Scotland through the publication of a number of reports intended to galvanize support for economic development, such as *Manufacturing Matters* (CBI Scotland, 1994), *The Scottish Business Agenda* (CBI Scotland, 1995) and *Scottish Manufacturing – A Shared Vision* (CBI Scotland, 1997). However, the CBI's third report *The Challenge for Government in Scotland* (CBI Scotland, 1996) was a more partisan affair. CBI Scotland had been under considerable pressure to condemn Labour's devolution plans from Conservative supporters inside and outside the CBI's Scottish Council. There was some dismay within Conservative circles that the CBI was taking an evenhanded approach to constitutional change when its membership and interests were seen to rest with the Union and the constitutional status quo.[7] However, the CBI was in a difficult position similar to other Scottish BIAs: adopting a high-profile and quasi-partisan stance against devolution was not clever politics when Labour was likely to win the election and establish a Scottish Parliament. The type of oppositional stance sought by Conservatives could have wrecked the CBI's prospects of a constructive relationship with the incoming government and the new parliament.

The medium through which CBI Scotland adopted a formal position on devolution was to publish a report on its aims for the Scottish economy and pose 39 specific questions to the political parties to judge their views on the future government of Scotland (CBI Scotland, 1996). The 39 questions ranged over areas such as education and training, transport and communications, the promotion of enterprise and government structure. The economic and constitutional components of the 39 questions were the largest and most detailed and included questions relating to the maintenance of the Barnett formula, targets for inflation and economic growth, the borrowing powers for a Scottish Parliament, the reduction of the costs of central and local government, the maintenance of a level playing field between the Scottish and UK economies, the minimization of business costs and regulations and arrangements for taxation under a Scottish Parliament (CBI Scotland, 1996: 8–10). These issues prompted the CBI to oppose devolution and support the constitutional status quo. This was clearly a boon for the Tories and a blow to Labour. However, as shall be seen below, the CBI was the only business interest association unequivocally hostile to devolution, though its director, Ian Macmillan, pledged to maintain a non-partisan stance during the election campaign (*Scotland on Sunday*, 16 February 1997) – a pledge which was upheld during and after the election.

The view of the Scottish Division of the Institute of Directors (IoD) gives a fair indication of contemporary business views about a Scottish Parliament. Though coming out in opposition to devolution, through a survey of 600 members, the IoD advocated a more qualified position towards change. The organization recognized some benefits from devolution, such as the economic benefits to Edinburgh of a Scottish Parliament, improved policymaking in distinctive areas such as education and the likelihood of legislation being enacted more quickly through devolution. The major problem for the IoD in Scotland was the tax-raising element to the devolution proposals (and its effects on the business community) and the retention of Scotland's share of public expenditure. However, the IoD took a cautious approach to political opposition to devolution. The IoD's Scottish director, Donald Hardie, stated that 'it would be wrong for us to enter into a political campaign when we have members who, if not supporters, lean towards Labour's policy.' (*The Scotsman*, 21 March 1996). Significantly, the IoD remained aloof from the constitutional debate after 1996 and its qualified opposition to devolution brought no campaigning or publicity.

The Scottish Chambers of Commerce did not adopt a formal position on devolution, but its survey of members generated some interesting findings about business opinion on constitutional change. The Chamber's survey offered four choices to business: more government decentralization to Scotland (administrative devolution), devolution without taxation powers; devolution with tax powers; and independence. The Chamber received 650 responses from its members and the exercise provided some interesting results (see Table 1). The principal finding was that business found taxation powers too hard to swallow. While business was neutral or enthusiastic about more administrative devolution or the establishment of a Scottish Parliament on the 1978 scheme, support for change fell away when confronted with taxation powers and independence (*The Journal*, December 1995: 315). Similarly, when confronted with the effects of the different types of devolution on their operating costs, turnover and company development, most firms viewed decentralization and non-tax devolution as the preferable options. Seventy per cent of firms thought that decentralization and non-tax devolution would have no effect on turnover or operating costs, while 66 per cent thought they would have no effect on company development. In contrast, 67 per cent of the same firms thought that they would face higher operating costs from tax-raising devolution and independence, mirrored by 48 per cent thinking that company development would be affected and 33 per cent thinking that turnover would suffer (Scottish Chambers of Commerce, 1995).

TABLE 1
CONSTITUTIONAL VIEWS OF MEMBERS OF SCOTTISH
CHAMBERS OF COMMERCE

Constitutional option	Better/same for business (%)	Worse for business (%)
Decentralization	88	12
Devolution without tax	65	35
Devolution with tax	31	69
Independence	26	74

Source: Scottish Chambers of Commerce, Constitutional Canvass (1995).

Perhaps the most significant thing about the Chambers of Commerce survey was that it indicated a considerable change in attitudes from the previous survey conducted in 1991. Then, 67 per cent of Chamber members supported the constitutional status quo, with only 28 per cent favouring the establishment of a Scottish Parliament (*The Herald*, 17 November 1995). Therefore, the balance of opinion seems to have shifted towards accepting the creation of a Scottish Parliament, albeit one that does not have tax-raising powers.

Small business in Scotland has been quite supportive of constitutional change, and the Scottish division of the National Federation of Small Businesses took a positive view of constitutional change. The attitudes of the organization's membership in Scotland provided a very mixed view of devolution and its effects. Opinion on devolution was finely balanced within the small business community, with 37 per cent favouring devolution and 38 per cent opposed. In addition, 24 per cent of small businesses interviewed had no strong feelings for or against devolution (*The Herald*, 9 May 1996). These figures contrasted markedly with large firms questioned in the same survey who opposed devolution by 63 per cent to 18 per cent in favour, with 19 per cent neutral about its impact. However, what was more encouraging for supporters of devolution was that the small business sector took a fairly neutral view of the impact of devolution in a number of areas (see Table 2), with the feeling that change would not have a negative effect on business and a perception that a Scottish Parliament would have positive effects on inward investment and employment in Scotland.

TABLE 2
CONSTITUTIONAL VIEWS OF MEMBERS OF SMALL BUSINESS SECTOR

Impact of devolution	Positive (%)	No difference (%)	Negative (%)	Don't Know (%)
On Scottish economy	33	19	41	7
On Scottish businesses	37	22	35	6
On inward investment	60	15	18	7
Employment	43	23	29	5
Your own business	23	51	21	5

Source: System 3, *The Herald*, 9 May 1996.

Scottish Financial Enterprise, the promotional organization of the large Scottish financial sector, has been more concerned with market-building in the global economy and the promotion of Scottish financial services in Eastern Europe and Far Eastern markets than constitutional change. A review of the organization's newsletter to members from 1992–7 (*SFE News*) revealed very few occasions in which devolution was mentioned, particularly in contrast to EU directives, the single currency and various international promotional initiatives. However, the organization was not inactive over devolution: the former SFE chairman and a range of senior institutional representatives held meetings with Labour shadow ministers over devolution and a range of economic issues such as corporate taxation and financial regulation (Scottish Financial Enterprise, 1996: 3). Such lobbying continued after the 1997 general election with the new Labour government.

THE DEVOLUTION REFERENDUM

Though business kept its head down over constitutional issues in advance of the 1997 general election, the referendum on 11 September 1997 to establish a Scottish Parliament with tax-raising powers provided an additional opportunity for business to voice its support or opposition to devolution. Business interest associations and individual business leaders took part in the devolution debate in advance of the referendum, with very mixed results. The issue of tax-raising powers dominated business concerns during the devolution campaign, though most business associations preferred to voice concern at the tax powers and their implications, rather than involve themselves in debates about the principle of devolution itself. The Labour government and the political parties supportive of constitutional change – Labour, Liberal Democrats and the Scottish National Party – all made efforts to reassure the business community about the nature of the devolution package, with Labour Ministers seeking to play down the impact of tax-raising powers and deal with business fears that devolution would involve tax changes that would damage the economic level playing field of the British economy and undermine business competitiveness. The government held a series of meetings with Scottish business-interest associations between the publication of the devolution White Paper (Scottish Office, 1997) and the referendum.

A number of prominent businessmen did intervene in the devolution campaign, most notably and controversially the Governor of the Bank of Scotland, Bruce Patullo, who spoke out against tax-raising powers (*The Herald*, 22 August, 1997). Patullo's intervention was controversial because it was a personal opinion which gained great publicity, but it was not the official position of the Bank itself, which remained neutral. Criticism of Patullo's position by the three parties campaigning for a double *Yes* vote at the referendum was also extremely vociferous and probably had the impact of deterring other business figures from participating in the debate. There is also an indication that the Scottish Secretary, Donald Dewar, put pressure on business leaders in Scotland to stay out of the debate, and that some pro-devolution organizations put commercial pressure on the Bank of Scotland to refrain from the debate (*Scotland on Sunday*, 7 September 1997). Individual businessmen and businesses tended not to adopt positions on devolution and tax-raising powers, though some did put their head above the parapet to express an opinion. Such interventions came on both sides of the devolution issue, with business leaders both supportive of the government's plans for Scottish devolution and also opposed in some cases. Overall, there seems to have been no discernible pattern to such interventions.

CBI Scotland was the most prominent business association which debated the devolution issue during the referendum campaign and appeared to come close to adopting a policy of opposition to devolution. The organization gave very mixed signals about devolution, with its position wavering between neutrality and outright opposition. However, when it came to the crunch, the CBI council and membership was divided, with some members wanting the CBI to unequivocally oppose devolution and tax-raising powers while others wished to avoid adopting such a highly political position when the organization was still divided itself on the devolution issue. CBI Scotland certainly had the opportunity to come out of the closet and oppose devolution as the campaign reached a climax, as the organization had scheduled meetings for its devolution working party and Scottish council in the last week of the referendum campaign. However, CBI Scotland decided against declaring its opposition to the devolution plans (*The Herald*, 8 September 1997), which removed one of the final political cards available to the *No* campaign group, *Think Twice*, which found itself claiming that business was opposed to devolution but unable to cite the example of any Scottish business interest association which had actually declared itself opposed to devolution. There was also discontent within some sections of the business community about the CBI's intervention during the referendum. It emerged that Scottish business interest associations had established a 'gentleman's agreement' not to intervene in the devolution debate in advance of the referendum – an agreement broken by the CBI.[8]

The Scottish Chambers of Commerce also commissioned fresh opinion polls among the business community to determine business attitudes to constitutional change, building on early surveys quoted above in 1995. Such polling, taken during the referendum campaign itself, demonstrated a hardening of attitudes towards devolution and tax-raising powers among the business community (*Scotland on Sunday*, 7 September 1997). However, despite the efforts of the *No* campaigners, such polling evidence only reinforced business efforts to restate their case about taxation and the uniform business rate. It did not lead businesses to come out against devolution.

Overall, with a few exceptions among individual business chiefs, there was a consensus that the business community should not get involved in the constitutional debate beyond expressing concern about issues such as tax powers, inward investment and the uniform business rate. Clearly, business organizations could have taken a firm stand on the tax question and on the principle of devolution itself. However, pragmatically, they chose not to adopt a political role, both because of internal divisions, shifting attitudes and fear of being out of step with public opinion. Realistically, business could see that a Scottish Parliament had widespread public support and business would have to develop a constructive relationship with the new parliament once it was established. Such pragmatism definitely deprived the *No* campaigners of one of their best weapons. Given the convincing nature of the referendum result, with 74.3 per cent favouring a Scottish Parliament and 63.5 per cent favouring tax-varying powers, business pragmatism was justified.

FACING THE FUTURE: BUSINESS UNDER DEVOLUTION

The Scottish business community had a number of opportunities to participate in the shaping of a Scottish Parliament. Though business remained aloof from the Constitutional Convention, it did take steps to make its views known to the Convention, the political parties and the Labour government. To its credit, business sought to deal with devolution in a pragmatic manner, which was always wise given the strength of public opinion in favour of constitutional change and the likelihood that Labour would win the 1997 general election and move quickly to establish a Scottish Parliament. Thus there was not merely a need for a constructive dialogue between business and the parties/government over devolution, but a recognition that a devolved parliament would be established which business would need to work with in policy areas such as economic development policy, transport, land use planning, environmental policy, education and training (Smith, 1996: 9). The business community and Scottish BIAs are certain to become heavily involved with the parliament and its policy activities. Overall, this process will generate two types of scenarios: conflict scenarios and consensus scenarios.

Conflict scenarios are likely to come about if the new Scottish government adopts an interventionist approach to economic policy and seeks to exploit its economic and tax powers. There is likely to be pressure from local government, public sector areas such as education and health, in addition to the trades unions to exploit the parliament's economic powers to the full, particularly to raise extra funds for public services. Business will seek a non-interventionist Scottish Parliament which does not greatly involve itself in commercial life and does not raise taxes. However, the extent to which a Scottish Parliament undermines the market-building preference of business is questionable. First, there is the fact that the economic powers of a Scottish Parliament are likely to be constrained, both by the devolution legislation itself and by the limited economic ambitions of the New Labour project (Mitchell, 1996). Put simply, the type of interventionism that business fears will follow from devolution, is firmly off of the Labour agenda and likely to remain so. Second, expansive market-building strategies and regulatory policies are more the preserve of the British government and the European Union than a Scottish Parliament. Business may discover that the parliament has little control over such policy areas, but is prepared to support business demands in some areas in pursuit of some perceived Scottish economic interest. Though tax/redistribution has the potential to be the overarching policy conflict for business, individual conflicts will arise in numerous policy areas such as transport and the environment, though here conflict may occur with other socio-economic organizations through the medium of the Scottish Parliament, rather than with the parliament itself.

Alternatively, there is also the potential for consensus scenarios on specific policy areas. Sections of the business community, such as CBI Scotland, have made common cause with the Scottish Trades Union Congress and local authorities in Scotland over some of the key issues in economic development and training policy (CBI Scotland, 1994, 1995). While business and other economic actors such as the unions may be in conflict over some aspects of devolution policy and the economic powers of a Scottish Parliament, they also share some common ground which will also come to the fore after the parliament is established. There is the clear potential for Scottish business to participate more coherently in building a regional economy in partnership with the Scottish Parliament and local authorities. Thus the business community will have a number of opportunities to establish 'growth coalitions' in support of economic development with other economic actors.

CONCLUSION

While business was never a supporter of devolution, it became reluctant to act as an opponent of a Scottish Parliament. Though clearly sceptical of the benefits of devolution, Scottish business sought to deal pragmatically with the issue through entering bilateral negotiations over devolution policy with the Constitutional Convention and the Labour government. Business did so in the knowledge that although devolution was inevitable, business could play a role in limiting some aspects of devolution policy, particularly in the field of taxation. The preference of Scottish business for open markets and a level playing field has guided business attitudes to devolution, even though business views of devolution softened. The impact business has had on the devolution issue has been twofold. First, it made the taxation question a real issue both before and during the referendum campaign. Second, its private and public dialogue with the government over tax meant that the tax powers were highly restricted. Of course, not all sections of the business community viewed devolution negatively. Some sectors of the business community will stand to gain from devolution – such as the media, legal services, the hotel and catering business and the property industry. The Scottish business community is heavily sectoral, and business scepticism about devolution is not shared across the entire business community.

What business lacked most over the devolution issue was a positive agenda. Business lobbying over devolution was monopolized by taxation and by the negative agenda of removing tax powers from the devolution scheme or limiting their usage. Business responses to devolution were therefore almost completely reactive and somewhat unimaginative. At a time when many British business leaders adopted a more active role in public policy, Scottish business remained conservative and inactive. Significantly, Scottish business appeared completely unable to view devolution as a 'political opportunity structure', which it could benefit from. Despite the fact that business is likely to be viewed as an ally of a Scottish Parliament in key areas such as training, economic development, tourism and trade policy, and that the main political parties, local authorities and trades unions have all stressed the need for public–private partnerships for a decade or more, Scottish business seems stuck in a time warp, unable to view devolution as an opportunity to develop a more dynamic Scottish economy and promote and protect Scottish business in the global marketplace. Business attitudes therefore seem set to remain defensive after devolution has occurred, rather than develop more active pressure group strategies to compete with other socio-economic interests.

NOTES

1. Poll of senior executives of top 500 companies in Scotland. *The Herald*, 22 April 1996.
2. Scottish Division of IoD, 'The likely implications for business if there were to be a Scottish Parliament', press release, 21 March 1996.
3. The Convention proposed to hold meetings with the CBI, Scottish Council for Development and Industry, Scottish Association of Chambers of Commerce and the Federation of Small Business. *Preparing for Change*, Executive Committee report to Scottish Constitutional Convention (Edinburgh, 1994).
4. Significantly, business has become fixated on the income tax varying powers of the parliament, and ignored taxation powers which could assist business such as selective tax breaks for investment and development. *Scotland on Sunday*, 15 June 1997.

5. Lex Gold, Director of Scottish Chambers of Commerce, *The Scotsman*, 13 March 1996.
6. The Royal Bank of Scotland/Tesco call centre to be established in Glasgow and the Award PLC investment in Livingstone are the most recent examples.
7. Senior members of the CBI, undoubtedly also Conservatives, were unhappy with the CBI's pre-1996 neutrality on constitutional change and wished it to adopt an unequivocally hostile stance. *The Herald*, 7 December 1995.
8. The Federation of Small Businesses revealed this agreement in *The Scotsman* 8 September 1997 and complained that the CBI's efforts led to 'a business versus the people campaign on devolution....that can only damage Scottish business and its partnership with the wider community'.

REFERENCES

Bochel, John, David Denver and Allan Macartney (eds), (1981) *The Referendum Experience: Scotland 1979* (Aberdeen: Aberdeen University Press)
CBI Scotland (1970) 'Memorandum Submitted by the Scottish Council of the CBI', Minutes of Evidence, Royal Commission on the Constitution, 5 May 1970.
CBI Scotland (1994) *Manufacturing Matters* (Glasgow: CBI).
CBI Scotland (1995) *The Scottish Business Agenda* (Glasgow CBI).
CBI Scotland (1996) *The Challenge for Government in Scotland* (Glasgow CBI).
CBI Scotland (1997) *Scottish Manufacturing – A Shared Vision* (Glasgow: CBI).
Coleman, William and Henry Jacek (1989) 'Capitalists, Collective Action and Regionalism', in Coleman and Jacek (eds), *Regionalism, Business Interests and Public Policy* (London: Sage).
Grant, Wyn (1987) *Business and Politics in Britain* (London Macmillan).
Grant, Wyn (1989) 'The Regional Organisation of Business Interests and Public Policy in the United Kingdom', in W. Coleman and H. Jacek (eds), *Regionalism, Business Interests and Public Policy* (London: Sage).
Hood, Neil (1995) 'Inward Investment and Scottish devolution: Towards a Balanced View', Scottish International Business Unit, Working Paper 95/6, University of Strathclyde.
Keating, Michael (1996) *Nations against the State* (London: Macmillan).
Lynch, Peter (1996) 'The Scottish Constitutional Convention, 1992–5', *Scottish Affairs*, No.15, Spring, pp.1–16.
Mitchell, James (1996) 'From Unitary State to Union State: Labour's Changing View of the United Kingdom and its Implications', *Regional Studies*, Vol.30.6, pp.607–11.
Richardson, J. and A.G. Jordan (1979) *Governing Under Pressure* (Oxford: Blackwell).
Scottish Chambers of Commerce (1995*) Constitutional Canvass: Canvassing Business Opinions* (Edinburgh: Maclay, Murray and Spens).
Scottish Constitutional Convention (1990) *Towards Scotland's Parliament* (Edinburgh).
Scottish Constitutional Convention (1995) *Scotland's Parliament, Scotland's Right* (Edinburgh).
Scottish Financial Enterprise*, Devolution: Views of Scottish Financial Institutions* (Edinburgh: Scottish Financial Enterprise).
Scottish Financial Enterprise (1992) *Devolution II: Views of Scottish Financial Institutions* (Edinburgh: Scottish Financial Enterprise).
Scottish Financial Enterprise (1996) *Annual Report 1995* (Edinburgh: Scottish Financial Enterprise).
Scottish Office (1996*) Government Expenditure and Revenue in Scotland 1994-1995* (Glasgow: Scottish Office).
Scottish Office (1997) *Scotland's Parliament* (Edinburgh: HMSO).
Smith, Nigel (1996) 'The Business Case for Devolution', *Scottish Affairs*, No.16, Summer, pp.7-17.
Young, Alf (1995) 'How Business Views the Prospect of Home Rule', *Parliamentary Brief*, March.

Deepening Democracy:
Women and the Scottish Parliament

ALICE BROWN

One of the striking features of the current debate on home rule in Scotland that contrasts with the devolution debate in the 1970s is the inclusion of a significant gender dimension. This dimension relates both to the way in which women political activists have become involved in the debate and to the fact that equality of representation in a Scottish Parliament has been pushed up the political agenda in an unprecedented way. The explanations for this shift can be found in developments both within and outside Scotland. They include wider campaigns by women across the world for greater equality and for improved representation in political institutions and public bodies[1] and the specific aspects of the campaign for constitutional change in Scotland which are grounded in the arguments for creating a new form of democratic political system and legislature.

The support for constitutional change in Scotland gathered force during the administrations of the Conservative government in the 1980s and 1990s. In the run-up to the 1997 general election, all the major political parties, with the exception of the Conservative Party, stated their commitment to the establishment of a Scottish Parliament – the Scottish Labour Party and the Scottish Liberal Democrats favouring a devolved parliament within the UK, along the lines advocated in the final report of the Scottish Constitutional Convention (1995) and the Scottish National Party (1995) arguing instead for an independent parliament within the European Union. The case for a Scottish Parliament contains within it a critique of the Westminster style of government and of an electoral system that has consistently returned a party to power with just over 40 per cent of the popular vote. The argument had particular resonance in Scotland, where support for the then party of government, the Conservative Party, fell from a peak of over 50 per cent in the 1950s to 25 per cent in the 1992 general election and just 11 per cent in the 1995 elections for the new shadow local authorities, fuelling claims of a 'democratic deficit' in Scotland. The British system of government is charged by its critics with being undemocratic, unrepresentative, inaccessible, highly centralized and secretive. A claim has been made for the establishment of a parliament in Scotland which is run on fundamentally different lines from Westminster, which has a more proportional and representative electoral system and which engenders a new democratic political culture (Scottish Constitutional Convention, 1990).

As the campaign for a Scottish Parliament has developed, women political activists in Scotland have entered the debate to make their own specific claim for improving democracy and for the equal representation of women within the new legislature. In sharing the general critique of the Westminster parliament and style of government, they have added a further criticism of the existence of a predominantly male political culture which they perceive as hostile to the participation of women in politics. They see the setting up of a new parliament as a unique opportunity for radical change and the chance to have an institution in which women can participate equally, contributing to new democratic practices and procedures that they hope will fundamentally alter the political culture of politics in Scotland.

This contribution outlines the way in which women have become involved in the politics and discourse of constitutional reform and have made their claim to play an equal part in the future governance of Scotland. Women political activists from the political parties, trade unions, local government, the voluntary sector and a broad range of organizations and women's groups have seized the political opportunity opened up by the constitutional debate in order to make their own proposals for deepening democracy. They have networked and formed coalitions and alliances around their shared objective of improving the representation of women. They hold similar perceptions and experience of a political system that has failed to deliver equality and to be responsive to the needs of women and others, articulating instead their desire for a different type of parliament and politics in Scotland.[2]

THE CONTEXT

Key factors influencing the constitutional debate are the decline in electoral support for the Conservative Party in Scotland and the unwillingness of the party leadership during the 1980s and 1990s to concede the case for significant constitutional reform. Electoral support for the Conservative Party in Scotland has been in decline since the mid-1950s, reaching a low level at the 1987 general election when the party gained only 10 of the 72 parliamentary seats in Scotland and just 24 per cent of the vote. With no change in policies that had proved to be unpopular in Scotland and the persistence of the Prime Minister of the time, Margaret Thatcher, and other Cabinet ministers in criticizing the Scots for their 'dependency culture', support for the Conservatives in Scotland continued to deteriorate. In the run-up to the 1992 general election, commentators predicted a humiliating defeat for the Conservative Party in Scotland with the loss of more parliamentary seats. Against these expectations, the party returned 11 MPs to the House of Commons and enjoyed a short-lived increase in their share of the vote (Bochel and Denver, 1992; Mitchell, 1992; Paterson, Brown and McCrone, 1992). The 1997 general election was to prove disastrous for the Conservative Party as they lost every parliamentary seat in Scotland when their vote collapsed to 17.5 per cent. Such a wipe-out had not been predicted (Brown, 1997).

Within this broader picture, the number of women MPs from Scottish constituencies has remained relatively low. At the general election in 1992, the number rose to five women from a total of 72 Scottish MPs, a representation rate of less than seven per cent. However, the same number of women were elected at the general elections in 1959 and 1964, demonstrating that little progress had been made for women's representation in the intervening years.[3] Following two by-elections in 1994 and 1995, Helen Liddell was elected to represent the Labour Party in Monklands East and Roseanna Cunningham to represent the SNP in Perth and Kinross. This brought the total number of women MPs to seven, a representation rate of just under 9.7 per cent. This all-time record was broken by the return of 12 women MPs at the 1997 general election, 9 from the Labour Party, two from the SNP and one from the Liberal Democrats, increasing the representation rate to 16.6 per cent.

At local government level, the Conservative Party has also experienced a fall in electoral support. Following plans to re-organize local government in Scotland from a two tier to a unitary system, elections were held for the new shadow authorities in April 1995, with the new unitary authorities taking control in April 1996. At these elections the Conservative Party gained just 11 per cent of the vote and failed to win control of any of the 32 new local authorities. The elections did not result in a significant improvement in the representation of women to the new councils. Although the participation of women in local government is greater than at central government level, the representation rate rose marginally to 22.35 per cent, an increase of some half a per cent on the 1992 district council elections (Bochel and Denver, 1995; Brown, 1996). The failure of the parties to select significantly more women for election did not go unnoticed by those women campaigning for equality in the Scottish Parliament.[4]

The pattern of low electoral support for the Conservative Party in Scotland and low representation of women politicians is repeated at the level of the European Parliament. At the European Elections in 1994, the Conservative Party failed to win any of the eight vacant seats, and, against the trend in most other European countries, the number of women MEPs fell from two to one (Bochel and Denver, 1994).

It is within this electoral and political context that the campaign for constitutional change in Scotland has taken place. The campaign has involved a number of groups and organizations including the Campaign for a Scottish Assembly (CSA) which was formed in 1979 following the setbacks in proposals for devolution at that time, as a cross- and non-party body established to campaign for and co-ordinate the pressure for constitutional reform. Following the so-called 'doomsday scenario' in 1987, a phrase coined by opponents of the government to describe the situation where the collapse of electoral support in Scotland coincided with the return of a Conservative majority government to Westminster, the movement for constitutional reform intensified (Lawson, 1988). In response to the re-election of a third Thatcher government, the CSA published a document, *A Claim of Right for Scotland,* in 1988 in which it supported the sovereign right of the Scottish people to govern themselves. It recommended the establishment of a Scottish Constitutional Convention as a forum for discussing the future government of Scotland.

A Scottish Constitutional Convention was created and held its first meeting early in 1989 at which it adopted the *Claim of Right* document and its three key proposals: first, to draw up and agree a scheme for a Scottish Parliament; second, to mobilize Scottish opinion and ensure the approval of the Scottish people for the scheme; and third, to assert the right of the Scottish people to secure the implementation of the scheme (Scottish Constitutional Convention, 1990). Membership of the Convention included representatives from the Scottish Labour Party, the Scottish Liberal Democrats, the Scottish Trades Union Congress (STUC), the CSA (later to change its name to the Campaign for a Scottish Parliament, CSP), and others from Scottish local government, the churches, small political parties and other civic organizations including the Scottish Convention of Women (SCOW). After attending the first meeting, the Scottish National Party decided to withdraw from the Convention and opposed plans for a devolved parliament, advocating instead an independent Scottish Parliament within the European Union. Officially declaring its opposition to constitutional change, the Conservative Party in Scotland was not represented in the Convention, although some well-known members of the party voiced their support for some form of devolved power.

Despite the non-participation of two of the main political parties in Scotland, the *Scottish Constitutional Convention* represented a broad alliance of Scottish institutions and organizations in favour of the establishment of a devolved Scottish Parliament. The case for a parliament was based on the view that Scotland was suffering a 'democratic deficit' in that the Conservative Party did not have a mandate to rule and impose policies on a Scottish electorate while it had minority electoral support in Scotland. As a result, criticisms of the first-past-the-post electoral system increased while support for some form of proportional representation grew and the political system was charged with being undemocratic and unrepresentative. Other attacks on the Westminster style of government surrounded its highly centralized decision-making, secrecy and lack of accessibility and accountability, as well as other practical considerations such as the hours of meetings and the geographical location of Parliament. According to the Convention, such conditions were not conducive to modern, open and effective government and democracy, and operated against the participation and recruitment of a wider spectrum of the Scottish population, to the particular disadvantage of women. The Convention began its work by establishing working groups which had the task of drawing up options for the future government of Scotland. A Women's Issues Group was formed as a result of pressure from women activists and from men in the Convention who gave their support to increasing the representation of women.

WOMEN'S ROLE IN THE CONSTITUTIONAL DEBATE

In contrast to the devolution campaigns in the 1970s, women political activists in Scotland formed a broad alliance in support of a Scottish Parliament and have been successful in placing the issue of gender balance in representation in the new parliament high on the political agenda. Catriona Levy (1992) notes that the feminist journal, *MsPrint* reported that the women's movement ignored the referendum or saw it as irrelevant. Others feared that a parliament in Scotland could be a backward step for women, with Westminster providing an opportunity for more progressive social policies (Breitenbach, 1990). Yet by the late 1980s, women recognized that they had to be involved in the preliminary stages of the discussions surrounding the proposed Scottish Parliament to ensure that the key decisions were not taken by men and that the needs and priorities of women were not marginalized. One of the immediate responses by some women activists was to form A Woman's Claim of Right Group, partially as a response to the composition of the newly established Scottish Constitutional Convention which was predominantly (90 per cent) male: 'Once again, major proposals and decisions affecting the life and well-being of Scottish people would be made with women being significantly under-represented' (A Woman's Claim of Right Group (eds), 1991: 1). The group published a separate document entitled, *A Woman's Claim of Right in Scotland,* which was submitted to the Women's Issues Group of the Convention,[5] in which they put forward their proposals for improving the representation of women stating that 'as few elements of the male "pub culture" should be allowed to surround the operation of the Assembly as is humanly possible' (Women's Claim of Right, 1989: 5).

When the Convention published its first report in 1990, *Towards Scotland's Parliament,* the efforts of the women activists were very much reflected in the document. The Convention noted the 'failure of the British political system to face the issue of women's representation', and in stating that the Scottish Parliament offered the 'opportunity for a new start' it committed itself to the 'principle of equal representation' (Scottish Constitutional Convention, 1990: 12). Two additional groups were then established by the Convention to undertake more detailed work on parliamentary procedures and the electoral system. The recommendations of these groups also reflected an awareness of the gender dimension. Recognizing that many women are politically active in their communities rather than at the political elite level, the procedures group considered ways in which the new parliament could be more accessible and accountable to all members of the community. It outlined plans for meetings of parliamentary committees to be held in communities affected by proposed policy changes and ways in which women's and other groups could be involved in initiating legislation and giving evidence to these committees. The removal of practical barriers to women's participation were also agreed. It was proposed that the parliament should meet at times compatible with family life and that carer and travel allowances should be provided. Similarly, the group responsible for proposing an electoral system for the parliament were asked to consider a scheme which would result in a truly representative assembly based on certain principles including gender equality: 'that it ensures, or at least takes effective positive action to bring about, equal representation of men and women, and encourages fair representation of ethnic and other minority groups' (Scottish Constitutional Convention, 1992).

Although there was wide acceptance of the view that women are under-represented in political elites and that steps needed to be taken to redress the gender imbalance, there was no consensus on the mechanism for ensuring gender equality. It was at the point of agreeing a precise mechanism that the ideological differences between the women in the different parties emerged. For example, the Scottish Labour Party's official policy was statutory 50:50, a policy that had originally been developed by the women's committee of the STUC. It was argued that the easiest and fairest way to achieve the objective of equal representation was to have a man and a woman member of parliament for each constituency in Scotland. It was further argued that, given the failure of voluntarism in the past, the scheme should be statutory so that all political parties would have the opportunity to field both a female and male candidate for each of Scotland's 72 constituencies. This scheme was opposed by the Scottish Liberal Democrats, on the grounds that it was being adopted by the Labour Party as a way of avoiding a more proportional electoral system and crucially on democratic grounds. It was contended that it was inherently undemocratic to 'force' political parties to select and the electorate to choose a man and a woman and in addition that it was not the place of the state to interfere with the democratic process within political parties themselves.

Another area of contention between the parties was the disagreement on the precise electoral system to be adopted in the new parliament. The Liberal Democrats advocated the use of the Single Transferable Vote system with modifications. For its part, the Scottish Labour Party had some difficulty in persuading some of its members of the advantages of changing to a proportional electoral system. After all, given the strong support for the Labour Party in Scotland, they had much to gain by retaining the first-past-the-post elections in a four-party system.

In spite of these differences, the broad consensus for change and pressure to create a more democratic and representative parliament kept the Convention discussions alive. It is widely acknowledged that the active participation of women in the Convention's Working Groups was crucial in ensuring that the issue of equal representation stayed on the agenda. In attempting to reach a compromise between the main political parties in the Convention on an agreed scheme, there was always the danger that the objective of equal representation would be sacrificed, particularly as the mechanism for achieving equity was a key area of contention between the main players. As one woman activist commented: 'Their (the men's) agenda was different and we had to keep raising the issue. Although some men on the Electoral Reform Group were supportive and sympathetic to our demands, we doubt whether they would have pursued the issue. We were the ones who had to argue the case again and again.'

Prior to the 1992 general election a compromise was reached and the Scottish Constitutional Convention issued its agreed proposals for a Scottish Parliament which included acceptance of an Additional Member System (AMS) for elections and a statutory obligation on parties to put forward an equal number of men and women candidates.[6] The debate surrounding gender balance went beyond the two main parties in the Convention. The fact that the Convention members had addressed the issue and had made commitments to ensure equal representation almost inevitably meant that the other two main political parties in Scotland, the SNP and the Conservative Party, were forced to respond. As Hayes and McAllister (1996) argue, the political representation of women became one of the key and divisive issues among the Scottish political parties at the 1992 general election and 'women's representation as well as constitutional reform were heavily influenced both by party ideology and political pragmatism'.

THE OPPORTUNITIES FOR WOMEN IN A SCOTTISH PARLIAMENT

Following the re-election of the Conservative government in 1992 which meant that proposals for a Scottish Parliament with gender balance were not going to be realized in the immediate future, campaign groups were formed to keep the constitutional question alive, including *Common Cause*, *Scotland United* and *Democracy for Scotland*. In spite of political difficulties, the Scottish Constitutional Convention remained in existence, setting up a Scottish Constitutional Commission in 1993 to examine the issues left unresolved prior to the general election and to make specific recommendations regarding gender balance with regard to the electoral system for a Scottish Parliament. In the same year the *Coalition for Scottish Democracy* was formed, bringing together many political activists in the different pressure groups and political parties with a view to establishing a Civic Assembly.[7] Women activists were involved in all of these organizations. In addition, the women's movement in Scotland maintained political pressure on the political parties and trade unions by forming the *Scottish Women's Co-ordination Group* with representatives from the main women's groups in Scotland, the CSP and the churches. Its main function was to ensure that the recruitment of women in a Scottish Parliament was kept high on the political agenda.

After taking oral evidence and written submissions from a wide range of individuals, groups and organizations in Scotland, the Commission delivered its report to the Convention in 1994 (Scottish Constitutional Convention, 1994). The Commission recommended a Scottish Parliament comprised of 112 members elected on the Additional Member System with 72 constituency members elected on a first-past-the-post basis using the existing Westminster parliamentary constituencies and an additional 40 members elected on a proportional basis from party lists using the eight European constituencies. To achieve greater gender balance, the Commission recommended a voluntary scheme in which parties should be asked to meet a target of at least 40 per cent representation of women in the parliament taking into account both the constituency and list seats under the AMS electoral system. It recommended further that the target should be achieved within five years of the setting up of a Scottish Parliament with targets being set for the fair representation of minority ethnic groups. To encourage more women to stand as parliamentary candidates, recommendations were made for the removal of social, economic and other barriers to women's participation.

The Commission's proposal were not well received. Those women activists who had campaigned long and hard for a firm and statutory commitment to gender equality for the first Scottish Parliament and for

50:50, saw the 40 per cent voluntary target as a weak substitute. Others who had advocated a more voluntary approach were also dissatisfied with the Commission's recommendations. It was at this point that the campaign for gender equality took unexpected turn. The Scottish Women's Co-ordination Group facilitated talks between women within the two main political parties in the Convention – Labour and Liberal Democrats – to see if there was a way of resolving their differences and finding an alternative solution to that proposed by the Scottish Constitutional Commission.

The women involved accepted that it was vital to begin with a parliament of equal representation, in recognition that it is much more difficult to reform a political institution once it is well established and parliamentary seats are already occupied. In spite of their political differences and reflecting the importance they attached to the issue, they sought a compromise which built on their shared objective to break the mould of under-representation. They agreed a scheme for the first Scottish Parliament that would satisfy their different perspectives and drew up an Electoral Contract for consideration by the executives and conferences of the Labour Party and Liberal Democrats. On the understanding that the Electoral Contract would pertain only to the first elections of the Scottish Parliament, the parties agreed to endorse the principle that there should be an equal number of men and women MSPs and to approve the selection and fielding of an equal number of male and female candidates, the fair distribution of female candidates in winnable seats, and the use of the AMS system in a parliament large enough to facilitate effective democratic and representative government (Brown, 1995). Within this scheme the parties were free to find their own mechanism for fulfilling their commitment to gender balance recognizing their different electoral positions in Scottish politics.[8]

The proposals for gender balance recommended by the Commission in 1994 had not been the only factor to cause discontent. The size of the parliament with 112 members was argued to be insufficient to allow the type of proportionality and representation that had been envisaged. The Scottish Liberal Democrats stated that they were only willing to accept the Electoral Contract if the minimum number of Scottish MSPs was 145. In another unexpected turn, the leaders of the Scottish Labour Party and the Liberal Democrats announced plans in September of 1995 for a parliament of 129 members (73[9] to be elected on the constituency side by FPTP and the other 56 on the additional member list with seven members from each of the eight European constituencies). After some opposition from the STUC and other organizations, not least from within the two political parties themselves, agreement was reached and the Scottish Constitutional Convention endorsed the proposal. The agreement on the size of parliament and provisions for gender equality were then written into the final scheme drawn up by the Convention and launched on St Andrew's Day 1995 (Scottish Constitutional Convention, 1995).[10]

Having agreed to a smaller parliament, the possibility of operating the 50:50 scheme as originally planned was not open to the Scottish Labour Party. A 50:50 constituency balance plus a top-up for proportionality would necessitate a parliament of around 200 members, far in excess of the 129 agreed with their Convention partners. Women within the party were anxious that the commitment to equality should not be diluted, and the Women's Caucus Group which had been formed following the 1992 general election took a particularly radical stance on the issue. The party then considered operating all-women short-lists in selection of candidates, a policy that had been adopted at the British level to improve women's representation at Westminster (Lovenduski, 1994; Norris, 1993).[11] When the Industrial Tribunal ruled against the use of all-women short-lists at the end of 1995, this presented a problem not only for the party in Britain but for the plans in Scotland, especially as the leadership of the party made the decision not to challenge the ruling just prior to a general election. Another option being consider by the Scottish Labour Party is that of twinning or pairing constituencies.[12] It is likely that the Liberal Democrats will use the top-up list on the additional member electoral system to redress any gender imbalance and will adopt other promotional strategies such as training and encouraging women to stand as candidates and support constituencies in selecting women. The precise mechanism to be adopted by the parties has still to be announced.

There have been significant political developments since the publication of the SCC report in 1995 including the controversy that followed Labour's decision in 1996 to introduce a referendum on constitutional change and not least the general election campaign in 1997. In this climate the debate on gender balance was somewhat overshadowed. However, it has re-emerged as a result of the positive reaction to the increase in the number of women MPs elected to the House of Commons[13] and in the context of the new government's plans for constitutional reform. Immediately after the election, the government announced a referendum in Scotland on 11 September 1997, in which 'Voters will be asked whether they agree that there should be a Scottish Parliament and whether they agree that such a Parliament should have powers to vary tax' (Scottish Office, 1997: 34). The women activists joined in the broad-based campaign for a Yes/Yes vote organized by Scotland FORward, holding a conference immediately after the general election at which the new Minister for Women, Henry McLeish, gave a keynote address.

A LEARNING EXPERIENCE?

It could be argued that the 1980s and 1990s have been something of a learning experience for political activists in Scotland as they have worked together to achieve constitutional change. The campaign has not been confined to the political parties and has involved a broad range of civic organizations and groups such as the Civic Assembly, the Campaign for a Scottish Parliament, Charter 88, Scottish Education and Action for Development (SEAD) and the Women's Co-ordination Group. They have played their part in widening and deepening democratic participation. As discussed above, the involvement of women has been an important aspect of this process. A number of factors can help explain why women activists have decided that constitutional reform is such a crucial political issue.

First, one can draw on political developments in the 1980s and 1990s which help to explain why women activists appear to have changed their political strategy since the devolution debate of the 1970s. The factors that might provide such an insight have been discussed elsewhere (Brown, McCrone and Paterson, 1996), and they include the impact of Thatcherism in Scotland and on women in particular; the experience gained by women through working within political parties, trade unions and local government during the period; women's growing frustration with the slow pace of change for women within the Westminster Parliament; the dislike articulated by women for the hostile and adversarial way in which they consider politics is conducted and the belief that women themselves have to be involved directly in making plans for the Scottish Parliament in order to ensure that their voices are heard.

Second, the constitutional campaign in Scotland and women's direct involvement in it has impacted on the level of awareness of the under-representation of women from the existing legislature. Participation in the debate has led to questions being asked about the reasons for the relative exclusion of women from political recruitment to parliament, a problem common to women in all the political parties in Scotland and in comparisons being drawn with women in other legislatures.[14] The experience of women in Europe, the United States and other countries such as Australia, has been charted and lessons drawn.[15] An interview survey of women political activists in Scotland carried out in 1993/4 helped to identify their views on legislative recruitment and their perceptions of the reasons for the low representation of women in political office.[16]

Third, in spite of their differences of view on the mechanisms for increasing the number of women in a Scottish Parliament, women activists in Scotland have campaigned together in support of the principle of equal representation and have transcended some of the boundaries that have existed between different feminist strategies. Traditionally, the claim for equal representation was assumed to be the preserve of liberal feminists, being rejected by socialist-Marxist feminists on the grounds that it would do little to change the nature of capitalist society, and by radical feminists who preferred to put their energies into autonomous women's groups and to bring such issues as domestic violence on to the political agenda. With growing recognition that these strategies are not necessarily in conflict, there has been a coming together of women from different perspectives with the aim of getting more women into key decision-making bodies, including Parliament – a trend that is not confined to Scotland or the UK. Getting women in is not seen just as an end in itself but as a means of achieving other objectives such as enhancing the political life and culture of the country and delivering resources and policies which will help women in the community.[17]

     In Scotland, this coming together of women within political parties, trade unions and local government with other women in women's groups, the voluntary sector and organizations around a common agenda has helped strengthen the campaign for a more democratic and woman-friendly Scottish Parliament. They have also been mobilized by their belief that a Scottish Parliament where half the members are women will be 'different' and will deliver not only a more representative and democratic system of government but also one which encourages the participation of women and others in the community and which delivers the type of policies which people in Scotland want.

     The strategic importance of the new parliament was reflected in the interviews with the women political activists. Their vision of a parliament which is located in Scotland, has equal numbers of men and women, a more proportional electoral system, hours and meeting times compatible with family life, payment of carer allowances and which is more accessible and accountable to Scottish society, has acted as a strong mobilizing force in their campaigns. Women across the party divide hold strong perceptions that significantly more women in parliament will make a substantial 'difference' to political life in Scotland. The view was expressed that women would bring their specific life experiences and expertise to the job and would alter the style and behaviour of political debate. Phrases such as 'women are more consensual', 'women are less confrontational and better at getting things done', 'women have a much more open and sharing approach' or 'with more women the whole political ethos would change' were often used.

     There was also general agreement between the women activists that politics is the poorer for the absence of women. With more women politicians, not only would the parliament operate more effectively but society in general would be improved. They justified this view on the grounds that there would be different policy priorities more directed at those in need in society and also different perspectives on the same policies.

These views could appear at first sight to be essentialist and to endorse theories of biological determinism that have been rejected by some feminists. Also they could be interpreted as logically inconsistent in that the women activists are arguing both for equality and difference. However, feminist theory has developed to incorporate the desire to achieve both equality and assert women's difference from men and the differences between women and to move away from rather narrow debates surrounding so-called 'women's issues'.[18] For example, Deborah Rhode argues that women are both the same and different but that the salient issue is not difference per se but the consequences of addressing it in particular social and historical circumstances. She puts forward the view that women's political strategies must rest on feminist principles and not feminine stereotypes: 'The issues of greatest concern to women are not simply "women's issues". Although the feminist agenda incorporates values traditionally associated with women, the stakes in its realization are ones that both sexes share' (Rhode, 1995: 158).

CONCLUSION

'Until recently no feminist in her right mind would have thought liberal democracy could deliver the goods.'   [Phillips, 1994: 195)]

The above quotation from Anne Phillips is a useful reminder that campaigning for gender equality in liberal democracies has not always been a political strategy advocated by feminists. In Scotland, a broad consensus now exists that increasing the representation of women is one way to ensure a more equal and democratic society (Breitenbach, 1995). The 'constitutional question' facilitated a discourse around issues of democracy, representation, proportionality and accountability. It also opened up an opportunity for women to enter the debate and make their specific claims for a parliament which reflected their priorities. As Catriona Burness (1995) has argued, women's representation is now intrinsically linked with wider campaigns for devolution and improved democratic participation.

Inevitably, the raising of demands for equal representation within the new Scottish Parliament has led to an examination of the policies of the political parties on gender equality and the asking of the question, 'How democratic and representative are the parties themselves?' Although women form almost half of the membership of the political parties in Scotland, they are significantly under-represented in the top posts. Women activists are increasingly aware that the political parties themselves have to change if women are to play an equal part in political life in Scotland. Women across the party divide support the view that the political culture in Scotland is predominantly male, a culture that needs to alter if more women are to become involved in the party and political system. Drawing on the experience of women in the Scandinavian countries in particular, women activists argue that a 'critical mass'[19] of women in a new Scottish Parliament will help engender a new political culture.

The government's White Paper on devolution endorses the Scottish Constitutional Convention's proposals for a parliament with 129 MSPs elected on a version of the Additional Member System. In posing the question of who will be eligible for selection and election to the Scottish Parliament, the government state that they are 'keen to see people with standing in their communities and who represent the widest possible range of interests in Scotland putting themselves forward for election. In particular the government attach great importance to equal opportunities for all – including women, members of ethnic minorities and disabled people'. The government urges 'all political parties offering candidates for election to the Scottish Parliament to have this in mind in their internal candidate selection processes' (Scottish Office, 1997).

On reflection, it is perhaps surprising that women have managed to make so much progress on the question of gender balance, although it would be difficult for those advocating the case for improving democracy to deny, at least publicly, the right of women to have an equal share in the future governance of Scotland. Writing in 1994, Tom Nairn noted that the 'elders (in the Labour Party) are still trying to depict all this as just a passing fad. They could not be more mistaken. The famous obstacles of which so much is made (not enough "suitable" women, unfair to some men, interminable time needed, etc.) are really chaff in the wind.' The proposals for gender balance can be argued to be one of the most radical aspects of the plans for constitutional change. However, the opposition to such plans should not be under-estimated. In moving towards a more proportional electoral system in which the Labour Party is unlikely to have an overall majority in the new parliament, the competition for constituency seats and places on the additional top-up lists will be intense. In such a climate, advocates of gender balance will have to work hard to ensure that the commitments to equality made by the political parties are met.

With the overwhelming Yes vote in the referendum of 11 September 1997, it seems likely that a parliament will be established by the year 2000 as planned by the government. Selection of candidates for seats and for the top-up lists will begin in 1998 with the first elections for the parliament being held in 1999. It will not be long, therefore, before we can judge whether women have achieved their goal of gender balance in Scotland's first parliament since 1707. The greatest fear of women activists is that they will have campaigned long and hard for a new democratic institution but that it will be dominated by old politics.

NOTES

1. One of the key outcomes of the United Nations Fourth World Conference on Women held in Beijing in 1995 was the demand for a significant improvement in the representation of women in decision-making bodies. It was also one of the three elements of the submission by Scottish women to Beijing, the other two being the elimination of poverty and violence against women (Scottish Women's Co-ordination Group, 1995).
2. Much of the material that follows is necessarily descriptive and draws on accounts to be found in Brown, 1996 and Brown, McCrone and Paterson, 1996, chapter 8.
3. It has been possible for women to stand for election since 1918. From 1918 to 1997 a total of just 28 women have represented Scottish constituencies at Westminster.
4. For example, Engender, the women's research and campaigning organization, held a press conference publicizing the election results and the effect on women's representation. They also published a survey of the impact of local government reform on women in the Gender Audit 1996 (Engender, 1996).
5. The group published a book of the same time in 1991 (Woman's Claim of Right Group (eds), 1991).
6. This statutory obligation did not imply a complete acceptance of the 50:50 proposal and the wording of the document was kept somewhat vague. The mechanism for ensuring equal representation was not spelled out. Following the 1992 general election,the Convention established a Scottish Constitutional Commission to take the issues forward. At this stage the Scottish Liberal Democrats noted their intention to withdraw from the 'statutory' clause in the Convention's document published in 1992.
7. The Civic Assembly held its first meeting in 1995 and operated the principle of gender balance by requesting the groups participating in the forum to ensure that they sent equal number of female and male representatives.
8. Given the difference in electoral support for the two parties in Scotland, it is estimated that Labour will obtain most of its parliamentary seats through the constituency side of the elections, while the Liberal Democrats will have to rely more heavily on the top-up list. The compromise meant that the parties could take this into account in drawing up their own particular mechanism for meeting their side of the Electoral Contract.
9. The increase from 72 to 73 constituencies resulted from the Boundary Commission's decision to divide the constituency of Orkney and Shetland.
10. The SNP and the Conservative Party re-stated their own plans on the same day. The SNP's proposals include a commitment to 'guarantee geographical and gender balance in SNP representation' by using the party lists. They propose a single chamber, with 200 members; 144 members are to be elected by the alternative vote system (two from each constituency) and 56 selected from party lists under the additional member system (SNP, 1995). The Conservative Party made their case for protecting the Union.
11. All women short-lists were to operate in fifty per cent of the winnable vacant seats for the 1997 general election. Consensus meetings were held within the party to identify the constituencies that would select a woman candidate from an all-woman short-list. Norris (1993) reminds us that although this sounds like a very radical policy, given the low turnover of MPs at any given election the actual increase in women MPs is likely to be more modest than many anticipate.
12. Under this proposal, women and men will be invited to stand as candidates for a pair of twinned constituency seats. The woman who receives the most votes from the list of women

candidates will be selected for one seat and the man who receives the most votes from the male list will be selected for the other.

13. A record number of 160 women were elected as MPs at the 1997 general election – 102 Labour, 14 Conservatives, 2 Liberal Democrats and 2 SNP – a representation rate of 18.2%. The Scottish figures are 9 Labour, 1 Liberal Democrat and 2 SNP (16.6% representation rate).

14. Parallels can be drawn with the politicization of women in the civil rights movement in the United States in the 1960s.

15. The Scandinavian countries in particular, with representation rates of around 40% women, attracted interest.

16. This survey was conducted by Alice Brown with the support of research grants from the Leverhulme Trust and the ESRC.

17. For a discussion on the consensus built around representation and other issues, see Breitenbach, 1995.

18. See, for example, the contributions in Bock and James, 1995.

19. A 'critical mass' is said to exist when there is around 25–30% representation of women.

REFERENCES

Bochel, John and David Denver (1992), 'The 1992 General Election in Scotland', in *Scottish Affairs*, 1.

Bochel, John and David Denver (1995), 'The Elections for the Shadow Local Authorities', in *Scottish Affairs,* 13.

Bock, Gisella and Susan James (eds) (1992), *Beyond the Quality and Difference* (London: Routledge).

Breitenbach, Esther (1990), 'Sisters Are Doing It for Themselves: The Women's Movement in Scotland', in A. Brown and D. McCrone *The Scottish Government Yearbook 1990*, Unit for the Study of Government in Scotland, University of Edinburgh.

Breitenbach, Esther (1995), 'The Women's Movement in Scotland in the 1990s', *New Waverley Papers*, Department of Politics, University of Edinburgh.

Brown, Alice (1995), 'The Scotswoman's Parliament', in *Parliamentary Brief*, April.

Brown, Alice (1996), 'Women and Politics in Scotland', in *Parliamentary Affairs*, Vol.49, No.1.

Brown, Alice (1997), 'The 1997 General Election in Scotland: Paving the Way for a Scottish Parliament?', in *Parliamentary Affairs*, Vol.50, No.4, September.

Brown, Alice, David McCrone and Lindsay Paterson, (1996), *Politics and Society in Scotland* (Macmillan).

Brown, Alice and Yvonne Galligan (1993), 'Changing the Political Agenda for Women in the Republic of Ireland and in Scotland', *West European Politics*, Vol.16, No.2.

Burness, Cartiona (1995), in *Parliamentary Brief*, March.

Crick, Bernard and David Miller (1991), *Standing Orders for a Scottish Parliament* (Edinburgh: John Wheatley Centre).

Crick, Bernard and Miller, David (1995), *To Make the Parliament of Scotland a Model for Democracy,* (Edinburgh: John Wheatley Centre).

Denver, David (1994), 'The 1994 European Elections in Scotland', in *Scottish Affairs*, 9.

Engender (1996), *Gender Audit*, Edinburgh.

Hayes, Bernadette and Ian McAllister (1996), 'Political Outcomes, Women's Legislative Rights and Devolution in Scotland', in D. Broughton, D. Farrell, D. Denver and C. Rallings, *British Elections and Parties Yearbook 1995* (London: Frank Cass).

Lawson, Alan (1988), 'Mair nor a rauch wind blawin', in David McCrone and Alice Brown, *The Scottish Government Yearbook*, Unit for the Study of Government in Scotland, Edinburgh.

Levy, Catriona (1992), 'A Woman's Place? The Future Scottish Parliament', in L. Paterson and D. McCrone, *The Scottish Government Yearbook 1992*, Unit for the Study of Government in Scotland, Edinburgh.

Lovenduski, Joni (1994), 'Will Quotas Make Women More Woman-Friendly', in *Renewal*, Vol.2, No.1, January.

Lovenduski, Joni and Pippa Norris (eds) (1993), *Gender and Party Politics* (London: Sage).

Mitchell, James (1992), 'The 1992 Election in Scotland in Context', in *Parliamentary Affairs*, Vol.45, No.4.

Nairn, Tom (1994), 'Gender Goes Top of the Agenda', *The Scotsman*, 28 December.

Norris, Pippa (1993), 'Slow Progress for Women MPs', in *Parliamentary Brief*, November/December.

Norris, Pippa and Joni Lovenduski (1995), *Political Recruitment: Gender, Race and Class in the British Parliament*, (Cambridge: Cambridge University Press).

Paterson, Lindsay, Alice Brown, and David McCrone (1992), 'Constitutional Crisis: The Causes and Consequences of the 1992 Scottish General Election Result', in *Parliamentary Affairs*, Vol.45, No.4.

Phillips, Anne (1994), 'The Representation of Women', in *The Polity Reader in Gender Studies* (Cambridge).

Rhode, Deborah (1995), 'The Politics of Paradigms: Gender Difference and Gender Disadvantage', in Gisella Bock and Susan James, *Beyond Equality and Difference* (London: Routledge).

Scottish Constitutional Commission (1994), *Further Steps: Towards a Scheme for Scotland's Parliament*, Cosla, Edinburgh, October.

Scottish Constitutional Convention (1990), *Towards Scotland's Parliament*, Cosla, Edinburgh, November.

Scottish Constitutional Convention (1992), *Electoral System for Scottish Parliament*, Cosla, Edinburgh, February.

Scottish Constitutional Convention (1995), *Scotland's Parliament, Scotland's Right*, Cosla, Edinburgh, November.

Scottish National Party (1995), *Programme for Government*, Edinburgh.

Scottish Office (1997), *Scotland's Parliament*, Cm.3658, July.

Scottish Women's Co-ordination Group (1995), *Report and Recommendations to the UN 4th World Conference on Women, Beijing 1995*.

Woman's Claim of Right Group (1989), *Submission to Scottish Constitutional Convention*.

Woman's Claim of Right Group (eds) (1991), *A Woman's Claim of Right in Scotland*, Polygon, Edinburgh.

The Devolution Debate in Wales during the Major Governments: The Politics of a Developing Union State?

JONATHAN BRADBURY

Following the 1992 British General Election, debate about the constitutional framework for the government of Wales re-emerged to command levels of interest not seen since the 1970s. The Conservative Major governments promoted a traditional approach which asserted rule according to laws determined in the Westminster Parliament and implemented through the Welsh Office. In response to the campaign for devolution, which they steadfastly opposed, they sought to improve the distinctive aspects of Welsh government, for example, by reforming the Welsh Grand Committee. In contrast, the Labour Party revived its case for devolution, resulting in proposals for a Welsh Assembly in 1995, revised further in 1996 and early 1997. The gist of these proposals was that while primary legislative and fiscal responsibility would stay at Westminster, the assembly would take over the executive responsibilities of the Welsh Office. The Labour Party committed itself to holding a referendum and to legislating for an assembly within a year of taking office. Both parties presented their approach as the one best able to facilitate good government, serve economic interests and sustain the stability of Wales' place in the British state, while damning the other's approach for threatening precisely the opposite.

Interest in this debate focused on the question of whether it was a re-run of that held in the 1970s, which would probably lead to a similar outcome in which the constitutional status quo prevailed, or whether there was a new politics of Welsh devolution. A key analytical framework within which this question can be addressed derives from the work of Rokkan and Urwin, who conceptualized the possibility of states being defined as union states as opposed to unitary states. They defined the distinction thus:

> The unitary state, built up around one unambiguous political centre, enjoys economic dominance and pursues a more or less undeviating policy of administrative standardization. All areas of the state are treated alike and all institutions are directly under the control of the centre. The union state is not the result of straightforward dynastic conquest. Incorporation of at least parts of its territory has been achieved through personal dynastic union, for example by treaty,

marriage or inheritance. Integration is less than perfect. While administrative standardization prevails over most of the territory, the consequences of personal union entails the survival in some areas of pre-union rights and institutional infrastructures which preserve some degree of regional autonomy and serve as agencies of indigenous elite recruitment (Rokkan and Urwin, 1982)

Britain has generally been seen as a unitary state, its constitution built upon the concept of parliamentary sovereignty. However, state development has embraced distinctive treatment of Northern Ireland, Scotland and Wales without apparently contravening parliamentary sovereignty. Such treatment has included special forms of parliamentary representation, administrative devolution and approaches to public finance. Even though not based uniformly on the consequences of personal union, one could argue that this treatment, in that it embodies a recognition of territorial rights, regional autonomy and the need for special forms of co-operation, represents the development of a union state tradition in British politics. Equally, one could argue that it would be an extension of the conception of Britain as a union state to have political devolution. Indeed, given the threat that devolution poses to the credibility of the concept of parliamentary sovereignty, which is central to the view of Britain as a unitary state, it has become a conventional argument to suggest that only if Britain is conceived of as a union state does devolution make sense (Constitution Unit, 1996). The experience of Northern Ireland in the period of the Stormont Parliament represented just such an exercise of taking the need for distinctive treatment as far as devolution. Satisficing solutions of constitutional problems were found which amounted to seeing Britain as a union state to sustain state stability, primarily because the situation dictated the desirability of devolution and the political will existed to make it work. It should be noted, however, that Urwin (1982) himself argued that Northern Ireland was a special case and not a precedent for Scotland and Wales where the lack of civil disorder did not warrant the risk to the integrity of the state that devolution involved.

Mitchell (1995, 1996) has sought to apply this analytical framework specifically to debates about Scottish government during the Major era. He has argued that the development of Scottish government from the eighteenth century was strongly influenced by the notion of pre-union rights, and that distinctive governing arrangements were developed out of respect for this tradition. After 1979, however, Conservative governments applied policy without reference to local views, abused and questioned conventions of parliamentary representation and sought to diminish public expenditure. The strength of the union state tradition was reflected in the growing unpopularity of Conservative governments and the emergence of a new campaign of dissent, arguably stronger than in the 1970s. It was as a result of this that initiatives to reassert respect for special treatment were devised in 1993 and 1995 but such moves came too late to win back the trust of the Scottish electorate (Mitchell, 1995; Bradbury, 1997). Mitchell's (1996) analysis of the Labour Party approach in the 1990s suggests that in fact the experience of Conservative government opened up the case for developing the application of the union state tradition to embrace political devolution. While Labour clearly argued for devolution, as they did in the 1970s as a way of countering the SNP electoral threat, the case was also put on the more principled grounds of cementing Scottish autonomy against an overbearing centre. This underpinned notions of talking about the Scottish right, the usage of the term 'parliament' and extensions of proposed legislative and fiscal powers from those conceived in the 1970s. Of course, Mitchell remained critical of Labour policy and cautious about whether the public would back it in a referendum. Overall, however, he suggested that constitutional debate during the Major era revealed the importance of the union state tradition to views of British state legitimacy in Scotland and suggested a new development in that tradition from the preservation of existing distinctive treatment to political devolution. Mitchell's answer to Urwin's doubts about state stability was to suggest that any failure to sustain a new position for Scotland in the British state would represent not the consequences of devolution but the consequences of the failure of Britain itself.

This contribution extends the application of the union state approach to a consideration of the constitutional debate which also emerged in Wales during the Major era. Some analysts' arguments support the view that historically Wales developed a strongly rooted union state tradition underpinning distinctive treatment; that Conservative governments after 1979 both acknowledged that distinctiveness and so abused it as to generate a strong movement in favour of political devolution as the only means by which Welsh political rights could be maintained; and that New Labour had a unique opportunity to promote devolution on more robust grounds (see for example Osmond, 1995; Gamble, 1994). The focus here is on providing a more sceptical perspective and generating further argument rather than hoping to provide the last word. The first section considers the historical background and argues that the British state as a union state developed on a more questionable and limited basis in relation to Wales than in Scotland. The following section assesses Conservative governments after 1979 and argues that they fairly consistently governed Wales in a manner which significantly contravened the expectations of a union state model. Indeed during the Major era they did much to intensify this approach in comparison with that adopted in Scotland. The final section then considers the background of the devolution debate in the 1970s and in comparison assesses the pressures for change in the early to mid 1990s and the approach taken by the Labour Party. This reveals that while there were greater pressures for devolution there were still grave doubts about whether it could conclusively command support and argues that the Labour Party, while having a greater commitment to devolution in the 1990s, made few changes to its 1970s approach. Labour did not appear to be able to embrace an approach that was not still strongly influenced by the need to sustain parliamentary sovereignty and central power. Consequently proposals for devolution were not couched in the language of autonomy and did not entertain the legislative or fiscal devolution considered for Scotland. On this basis it would seem apparent that the influence of union state thinking on the constitutional framework for Welsh government was much weaker than was the case for Scotland. Similarly, it can be concluded, by the time of the 1997 Election at least, that the case for the 1990s devolution debate in Wales embodying the politics of a significant stage in the development of Britain as a union state remained much weaker than that constructed by Mitchell for Scotland. Assumptions about Britain as a unitary state still preyed heavily on participants' minds.

WALES IN THE UNION

The basic foundation of the government of Wales is the formal Act of Union in 1536, by which it was determined that Wales should be treated as part of a common political, administrative and legal system with England. During the twentieth century, however, both major parties in office developed a Welsh aspect to government which suggested special treatment. Such distinctiveness included over-representation in the House of Commons from 1922 of between 15 and 20 per cent more seats than would have been the case had the English ratio of voters to seats been followed. It also covered the development of parliamentary conventions governing the passage of specifically Welsh legislation on the few occasions upon which it occurred; the creation of the Welsh Grand Committee in 1960, becoming a standing committee in 1969; and the creation of the Welsh affairs select committee in 1979. Distinctive treatment also included measures of administrative devolution. These began after 1945 and culminated in the creation of the Welsh Office and a Cabinet post of Secretary of State for Wales in 1964. Such developments were intended to ensure that government policy was made in sympathy with the special demands of the Welsh. Finally, government as a whole was more than proportionately dedicated to Wales, as reflected in the relatively high per capita public expenditure levels in the post-1945 era.

This is a significant catalogue of concessions to Welsh interests and it has become convenient for some analysts to bundle them together as evidence of a Welsh arena of politics which provides the basis to move towards devolution (see Osmond, 1995). Implicitly this suggests the coherent development of a union state tradition in Welsh politics, understood both in Westminster and Wales. It is, however, highly questionable whether this is the case. Three issues need emphasis to make this point. First, it can be argued that none of Wales' distinctive treatment flows from an agreed notion of pre-union rights. A reading of Welsh political and administrative history shows neither agreement over pre-union rights nor the development of institutional infrastructures which could underpin common agreed assertions of rights either in Wales or between Wales and Westminster (Bogdanor, 1979; Foulkes et al., 1983). Wales was essentially assimilated into England, leaving no separate civic institutions which could really underpin future ideas of self-government to the same extent as in Scotland. Indeed, from the late nineteenth century Wales came to be dominated by the Anglo-Welshness of south-east Wales, as well as the politics of class and the Labour Party. Welshness until the 1960s was primarily expressed in terms of cultural defence in relation to such matters as religious non-conformism and language.

Second, distinctive treatment is generally of a twentieth century vintage and can be interpreted as resulting as much from contingent factors as from any respect for special Welsh rights. For example, special parliamentary arrangements were not purely specific responses to a Welsh grievance; rather they tended to follow the observation of Scottish precedent and were implemented only after a significant time lag. Higher per capita public expenditure resulted largely from the chance fact that the Welsh economy for much of the century was based on coal and steel and that after 1945 these were nationalized industries. Finally, the push for administrative devolution appeared very closely related to explicit recognition of British relative decline and the promotion of regional policy throughout the UK to try and arrest the situation. Only on a few occasions such as in the 1960s over the water issue were Welsh interests broadly politicized.

Third, the Welsh dimension to government was much more limited than for Scotland. As a result of there being no Welsh law, no House of Commons standing committees were established. The lack of autonomy of Welsh civic culture, reflected in the weakness of the Welsh press compared to the well-read Scottish daily newspapers, meant that such institutions as the Welsh Grand Committee failed to excite the interest of either politicians or public. The Welsh Office, while a significant measure in absolute terms, has relatively been a much smaller department of state than the Scottish Office.

Overall, as both Birch (1989) and Griffiths (1996) argue, it is important to emphasize the high level of integration with regard to England, economically, culturally and politically, and the lower level of deference to the distinctive treatment of Wales that was needed than was the case in Scotland. On this basis one might argue that the development of the British state in relation to Wales has been relatively less influenced by explicit respect of a union state tradition and relatively more by the underlying respect for Britain as a unitary state revised by various ad hoc developments and chance circumstances. This is an important argument when one comes to consider the devolution debate in the early 1990s. The lack of a strong basis of distinctive arrangements for Wales in a union state tradition, even if only implicitly understood, suggested the vulnerability of those arrangements to changing contingent circumstances; they were vulnerable to contravention. Further, the weakness of the tradition implied inevitably that there was a questionable basis for moving towards political devolution. Just as Scottish history provided opportunities for advocates of constitutional reform Welsh history trapped them, leaving the case of Welsh rights still to be conclusively made.

CONSERVATIVE GOVERNMENTS AFTER 1979 AND WELSH GOVERNMENT

In the devolution debate of the 1970s the Conservative Party stood in favour of a continuation of the form of government for Wales which had evolved during the century. The Conservatives did make one further novel development while in office during the 1970s, which was to reorganize local government in 1972, thus giving a uniform two-tier structure, in the process refurbishing and strengthening the county tier. This local government regionalism was offered as a development of autonomy in the government of Wales which was entirely in keeping with past patterns of distinctive treatment and therefore as a desirable alternative to devolution (Foulkes *et al.*, 1983; Mclean 1995; Sharpe, 1993). There are also some grounds for arguing that after 1979 Conservative governments maintained an approach that showed special sympathy to Welsh interests. Generally, the practices of administrative devolution and higher per capita public expenditure, also now influenced by the application of the Barnett formula, were not dismantled. Moreover, the Walker-Hunt era (1987–93) sustained at least some notion of Wales being governed in sympathy with its particular characteristics. Both Walker and Hunt were obviously non-Thatcherites, placing an emphasis on the need for a more interventionist economic development strategy focused on inward investment and the need to address issues of social concern. A number of regional development initiatives were started, including the building of the second Severn bridge, the dualling of the A55 in North Wales, the work of the Cardiff Bay Development Corporation and the Valleys Initiative. Walker also presided over the establishment of the Welsh Language Board (Walker, 1991; Gamble, 1994).

However, evidence more generally supports the view that Conservative governments showed profound disrespect for notions of distinctive treatment. First, there was abuse of the special mechanisms of parliamentary representation. For example, the bill preceding the 1994 Welsh Local Government Act was introduced first in the House of Lords and in its passage through the House of Commons Standing Order 86, which states that the committee stage of any bill relating exclusively to Wales should include all members representing Welsh constituencies, was suspended because the government realized it would be defeated in committee if it was so constituted. The bill was passed in the face of widespread Welsh opposition. Similarly, parliamentary procedures governing the select committee on Welsh Affairs were changed to suit the government. In 1979 the Conservatives won 13 seats in Wales and filled their six places on the 11-person committee easily. By 1995, however, after losses of seats and with some members serving as ministers, only two of the six Conservative members on the committee represented Welsh constituencies.

Second, there was a contradiction of the conventions governing administrative devolution. In particular, it had been the practice that the Secretary of State would be an MP sitting for a Welsh constituency, so that they would be able in some form to be accountable to the Welsh electorate. Following the 1987 Election four consecutive secretaries of state were appointed who were MPs sitting for English constituencies: Peter Walker, David Hunt, John Redwood and William Hague. Third, dissent emerged from English Conservative MPs at the levels of Welsh public expenditure. Welsh questions in the House of Commons frequently became the scene for noisy debates upon this issue. Finally, the Conservative governments of the 1980s and 1990s showed a blatant reluctance to accept the legitimacy of locally elected representatives and abandoned the local government regionalism of the 1970s. This was done by first removing many powers from local government and then reducing local government to one tier. In the place of local government arose appointed quangos to ensure delivery of Conservative policy on the ground. By the mid-1990s the Welsh quangos accounted for £1.5 billion per annum. Over time the anger at this transfer of power was further exacerbated by the cavalier approach of successive Secretaries of State to the appointment of members to quango boards. Many Conservatives rejected at the ballot box were found positions, and a number of controversial multiple appointments were made (see Jones, 1997). Furthermore, it should be noted that Griffiths (1996) has argued convincingly that Welsh Office policy even in the Walker-Hunt era had much more in common with British-level policies than was often thought, that the quangos generally operated according to a Thatcherite agenda and that the economic results which were achieved were not as spectacular as often claimed. As a result, even the Walker-Hunt era which in its style attempted to be more sympathetic to Welsh concerns, did not fully placate concerns about the centralizing and anti-democratic tendencies of Conservative governments.

All of these developments suggested a highly assimilationist drift in the approach of Conservative governments to Wales during the 1980s and early 1990s and produced dissent, focused around the revival of calls for an assembly. However, in contrast to the Conservative approach adopted in Scotland after the 1992 Election which sought to re-emphasize distinctive treatment, the Conservative response in Wales showed little such contrition. Indeed after the Walker-Hunt era John Redwood was appointed as Secretary of State. He was widely perceived as using Wales as a laboratory for a post-Thatcherite political economy. He placed emphasis on the need for an enterprise culture, championed NHS and local government reform and supported the WDA in the face of charges of impropriety, while criticizing environmentalists for standing in the way of developments and attacking the culture of state dependency. The sanctioning of his approach by the Major government appeared to be confirmation that the Conservative party had moved towards a view of ruling Wales which was quasi-colonial.

Not surprisingly, the Redwood era 1993–95 saw a significant hardening of anti-Conservative opinion. The appalling Conservative losses in the 1995 Welsh local government elections, in particular, suggested the need to take ameliorative action. Even then, it was only Redwood's fortuitous resignation from the Cabinet to contest the Conservative Party leadership which allowed a change of approach in Wales, and the change itself was modest. The appointment of another Englishman and one not previously in the Cabinet, William Hague, as Secretary of State, with a continued emphasis on enterprise policies, suggested further contempt for providing for administrative devolution in sympathy with the distinctive needs of Wales. There was a move from 1995 to head off possible dissent by actively celebrating Wales' special governing arrangements and to remind the Welsh of the economic benefits of the link with England. This new approach was given some substance by the announcement in November 1995 of a reform of the Welsh Grand Committee: providing for more meetings, some outside Cardiff, with senior Cabinet ministers possibly attending. However, there were obvious limitations to this reform. The Welsh Grand Committee remained in 1996 a glorified talking shop that still rarely met. Hague also tried to conjure up the idea of a new relationship with local government, in which the latter would enjoy more powers. However, this tactic fell flat in the context of the manifest development of the quangos since 1979. There was little that could hide the fact that the Conservatives had moved from a model of distinctive treatment of Wales and local government regionalism in the 1970s to one of increasing assimilationism and executive regionalization in the 1990s. A policy agenda continued to be pursued which was of central design and any mix of assimilationism with concessions to Welsh sensitivities was clearly asymmetrical (Bradbury, 1997).

There were clear potential problems in this approach in that it alienated the Welsh non-Conservative elites as well as the general public. However, in Conservative circles, the tilt towards reminding the Welsh of the advantages of the Union combined with new concessions, was generally thought sufficient to reassure the general public if not the elites. At the same time, Hague went confidently on the offensive in attacking Labour's renewed advocacy of devolution, arguing that it would create a costly extra tier of government; that it would reduce the influence of the Secretary of State within the British Cabinet leading to the abandonment of the position; that it would lead to a reduction in the number of MPs; and that it might well be the precursor of independence. The party had no expectations that this approach would lead to a good General Election result in Wales but there was a view that it would help to sustain compliance with Conservative policies if in power and bolster anti-devolution sentiment in the event of a Labour government and a referendum. Such was the Conservatives' confidence that there remained little explicit party debate. In the Welsh Conservative Party Sir Wyn Roberts (1995) reflected the simple adherence to government by Westminster so long as there remained the capacity for some Welsh influence. Meanwhile, at Westminster there were many English MPs, particularly those still committed to the uniform implementation of the Thatcher project, who contemplated further erosions of the special treatment of Wales in the event of the Conservative Party getting re-elected. All of this pointed to a long-term collapse in Conservative sympathy for distinctive treatment of Wales, a powerful reminder of the vulnerability of any notion that Wales' role in the British state should be governed by respect for a union state tradition.

LABOUR, NEW LABOUR AND PROPOSALS FOR WELSH
DEVOLUTION

Dissent at Conservative government was channelled from the late 1980s into a new movement for political devolution. Advocates in this movement sought to stress the greater pressures for the assertion of Welsh rights to representative self-government which were now in place and the historic opportunity for New Labour to deliver devolution within a more far-reaching reconstruction of the British state which implicitly conceived of Britain as a union state. In so doing there was an awareness of the weakness of pressures and of Labour's case in the devolution debate in the 1970s. An evaluation of the significance of the movement of the early-mid 1990s warrants a brief review of the problems encountered in this earlier debate.

When looking back at the 1970s it should be noted that the basis of support for devolution even within the Labour Party was highly problematic. Both in the party in Wales and at Westminster there were clear divisions, with opponents arguing that devolution contradicted the desirability of being able to implement uniform democratic socialist policies from a Westminster power base. The push for devolution within the party also came predominantly as a result of the fear of the growth in support of the separatist Plaid Cymru by the early 1970s and out of a need to have devolution in Wales as a logical corollary to Scottish devolution. The Labour Party leadership's commitment was, therefore, based primarily on cynical party political considerations. Further, the basis of support for devolution in the 1979 Referendum was very weak. During the campaign the Labour Party was itself split between the *Yes* and *No* campaigns; even from sympathizers there were criticisms of the limited nature of the proposals. Local government was hostile because of the threats an assembly posed to its powers; business was hostile because of the perceived threats to the link with the British economy; and trade unions remained broadly in sympathy with the democratic socialist critique. The public also had many doubts. These were raised especially with respect to the implications for the economy, taxation, and the stability of Wales' place within the Union. There were also fears that an assembly would be captured by a Welsh language mafia, which would then discriminate against non-Welsh speakers. Arguably there were greater suspicions in North and West Wales of being governed by a Cardiff-based Welsh elite than by a London-based elite. As a result of all these factors only 20.3 per cent voted Yes on a 58.3 per cent turn-out in the referendum (Foulkes *et al.*, 1983).

Labour's proposals were in any case highly problematic. The 1979 Wales Act provided for an assembly based on a first-past-the-post voting system and proposed that the assembly have executive and not legislative powers, and these only in a limited number of policy areas. The right of Parliamentary override was maintained and the position of Secretary of State was to remain to advise Parliament on responses to Welsh decisions. The Welsh Office was to remain as the administrative arm of executive power and the judicial committee of the Privy Council was to adjudicate over the interpretation of powers between the assembly and Parliament.

There was to be no reform of Wales' representation at Westminster. According to Bogdanor (1979) such proposals failed because they did not provide for clear decentralization or democratization because the powers to be transferred were limited and only executive and there would be no transfer of fiscal responsibility. They suggested a lack of clarity concerning assembly–Parliament relations because Westminster would retain powers to override assembly decisions. Finally, they did not provide for the successful legitimation of the assembly throughout Wales, because a first-past-the-post system would turn the assembly into a South Wales Labour Party preserve. In addition, the distinctively weak nature of the Welsh proposals contributed to the asymmetry of Labour's devolution proposals as a whole, which Labour did not try to defend. This was a cogent critique in itself but it was also clear that Labour's thinking about how the assembly would fit into the British system of government in practice was muddled. While the assembly was discussed in terms of the rhetoric of decentralization it remained obvious that Labour was still a party committed to Westminster power as a basis for engineering policies across the whole state.

Against this background it is clearly the case that the movement for Welsh devolution in the 1990s needed to make significant developments. To support the view of advocates of change there were a number of differences concerning the movement. The pressures promoting consideration of devolution in Wales were clearly different. Separatist nationalism was not really a concern as Plaid Cymru effectively had not made an electoral breakthrough. Between 1970 and 1987 its vote fell from 11.5 per cent to 7.3 per cent and in 1992 a vote of 9 per cent still left it as a marginal party. Its vote, moreover, was regionally concentrated within Wales. It was still perceived as the Welsh language party and Welsh language-speaking, as shown by the 1991 census, was still a minority attribute (see Jones, 1997). Moreover, it would be wrong to suggest that Welsh devolution was just being advocated as a logical corollary to Scottish devolution. Instead one can point to three novel sets of pressures which promoted consideration of Welsh devolution in its own right.

First, there were a number of issues which affected Labour Party thinking about how power should be distributed within the state. The party became increasingly aware of the electoral realities of where it won power most often and where it had strong majority support. Support within the party was also bolstered by the experience of regionalism in Europe, which was seen not only as good in terms of certain previously marginalized territorial interests but also in terms of pursuing the goals of democratic socialism in new ways. From a party leadership perspective devolution was also attractive for reasons of party statecraft. The New Labour Project in shifting the party from an automatic identification with state intervention had found a new concept around which to organize the rhetorical presentation of the Labour Party – a much more moderate collectivist notion but one which still contrasted co-operation within communities with the Conservatives' market individualism. Devolution offered itself as a prime policy for putting flesh on to the bones of New Labour's big new idea. At the same time New Labour's leaders were aware of the unpopularity of the move away from 'traditional values' in Labour's heartlands, of which Wales was certainly one: the promise of devolution offered a way of sustaining support while in opposition while the reality of devolution offered a way of off-loading some of the responsibility for meeting public expectations once in office. All of these points may suggest that Labour became more positively interested in devolution than in the 1970s.

Second, sentiments in the Welsh Labour Party merged with others in wishing to arrest what was perceived more idealistically as the democratic deficit in Wales. Many among the Welsh elites reacted angrily to quangoization, the control wielded by Secretaries of State with an English background and the overriding of special conventions of territorial representation at Westminster. As a result they set about finding alternative means of speaking for the nation, leading to a much higher and broader level of commitment to devolution among peripheral elites than had been the case in the 1970s. A more concerted campaign emerged with Labour at the heart of it. There was some internal Labour Party opposition but the number of public dissenters were fewer and it was hoped that in a referendum there would be few Labour Party MPs dissenting following the passage of the new code of conduct on party discipline. National Labour Party leadership support for devolution hardened rather than weakened after 1992 and the Welsh Assembly proposal was placed on Labour's 1997 General Election pledge card in Wales. More of the non-Conservative elite also became pro-devolution including, as might be expected, the Liberal Democrats, but also the trade unions, Welsh local government and some in the business world. In contrast to the narrow party-political origins of the push for devolution in the 1970s the case for devolution in the early and mid 1990s was put more positively as a good thing in its own right: to provide for a more democratic representation of Wales in the British political system and better government. To place a broad understanding on this subtly different expression of the politics of national identity, this phenomenon can be seen as an example of what Gladstone in debates over Irish Home Rule in the nineteenth century referred to as local patriotism (Bogdanor, 1979: 13). This is a form of politics which expresses itself as a desire to take more control of ones affairs as a nation while retaining loyalty to the overarching framework of the British state. This form of nationalism threatens no separatism. Previously it may be argued that this local patriotism had vested much faith in administrative devolution. The experience of Conservative governments after 1979 suggested that this had been misplaced and as a result the Welsh elite had moved on to considering political devolution more seriously.

The third novel impulse was the emergence of a new Welsh economic nationalism in the context of the Single European Market (SEM). In the 1970s the argument that Wales should take greater charge of its economic fortunes was problematic because the link with the wider British economy was seen as crucial. In that devolution might adversely affect economic fortunes by discouraging market activity or reducing central government financial subsidy from London, then it was to be opposed. After 1979, however, the economic context of the devolution debate substantially changed. Conservative reforms in Wales created an economy which was much less reliant upon nationalized industries or other heavy industries dependent upon government contracts and assistance. Instead the economic development focus became more orientated towards attracting inward investment and selling the advantages of a well-trained and disciplined industrial workforce and a deregulated economy with an export focus. This occurred at the same time as the development of a more global marketplace and European integration resulted in the pursuit of a SEM. As a consequence Welsh economic interests became less exclusively dependent upon the British economy than they had been in the 1970s. In many ways the domestic market became the SEM, necessitating the development of effective economic promotion in a European context. Given that after the late 1980s the pursuit of the SEM was accompanied by fiscal subsidies through the EU structural funds on a bigger scale than was the case in the past, it became necessary also to develop new regional capacities for effective lobbying. This functional necessity for regional capacity was exacerbated by the fierce competition over place marketing and accessing of EU funds which emerged across the EU from the late 1980s. A new Welsh economic nationalism was reflected in the greater operation of Welsh local authorities on the EU stage, experience of the networking activities with Baden Wurttemberg, Catalonia, Lombardy and Rhone-Alpes and the opening of the Welsh European Centre, at the instigation of Welsh local government rather than the Welsh office. It is not surprising, however, that the example of regional-level territories with their own elected political structures geared to the promotion of economic development within the SEM in other EU states should also prompt greater debate about whether an assembly would even better serve the Welsh economy. Extra support for the need for this debate was added by the Welsh Affairs select committee's criticisms of Welsh Office organization in relation to European work in late

1995. This policy rationale for regional governance and the support it gave to constitutional reform was particularly important in Wales, where politically based movements were much less dramatic than in Scotland (Jones, 1997; Bradbury and Mawson, 1997).

As well as there being new pressures for the consideration of Welsh devolution, there were some advances in terms of the composition of Labour's proposals, which is shown by comparison against Bogdanor's critique. It may be fortuitous but the growth of Welsh Office powers since the 1970s and the decision to vest all Welsh Office executive powers in the assembly did make for a more generous decentralization of executive powers. This would enable the assembly to deliver policies on economic regeneration, the health service as well as education and training which were more tailored to Welsh needs. The 1996 revision of the proposals developed plans to reform the quangos, notably to recreate the WDA as a super economic regeneration quango (Labour Party, 1995, 1996). The Welsh Labour Party's Policy Commission also moved to heed Tony Blair's call for the assembly to be elected on a basis similar to that proposed for the Scottish parliament. It was envisaged that the 60-member assembly would be elected on the basis of 40 members being elected on the first-past-the-post system and 20 according to the additional member system (Settle, 1997). It was hoped that this would provide for the legitimation which Bogdanor suggested the 1979 proposals lacked. Finally, some effort was made by the Labour Party centrally to defend the difference of the Welsh proposals from those in Scotland and England by reference to the Spanish case, where during the 1980s an approach of variable devolution was accommodated and no need was seen for the reform of representation in the national parliament. If it could be done there, why not in Britain.

There were also grounds for believing that the party leadership had developed a strategy which would give the assembly the best chance of being passed into law. That is to say, Blair made the decision not to sit and wait for a referendum to be forced into the legislation, a most likely eventuality which would put a Labour government on the back foot and mean probably that a referendum would be held mid-term when the party in government could be unpopular and party discipline fraying. Instead, Blair pre-empted such outcomes by positively proposing a referendum, thus ensuring that a referendum would be held early in a Labour term of office when it was possible the party would still be riding on the tide of election winning popularity. In addition, in terms of how the assembly might in practice fit into the British system of government, the advent of New Labour offered new promise. Its commitment to community and decentralization theoretically at least ended the clash with the centralism which characterized Old Labour. Irrespective of the actual degree of decentralization, such a change in the orientation of the Labour Party offered the potential for the relations between Westminster and the assembly, under a Labour government at least, to develop on the basis of co-operation and partnership, implicitly the philosophy of a union state concept of Britain.

Against this, however, there remained serious problems. These relate, first, to the bases of potential support. In the period prior to the 1997 General Election splits in the Welsh Labour Party were becoming increasingly evident, especially following the move to change the voting basis of the assembly. While Welsh Labour Action were strongly supportive, there was opposition from serious sceptics, including MPs Allan Rogers, Llew Smith, Sir Ray Powell, Denzil Davies and Ted Rowlands. Kim Howells was on Labour's front bench and was quiet on the issue but he was a well-known critic. There were also concerns that the wider elite unity in Wales could fray, especially as there had been no constitutional convention as occurred in Scotland, to provide a solid basis for co-operation between Labour and other interests. Such concerns were only partially ameliorated by Labour–Liberal Democrat talks at the Westminster level which concluded in 1997 with a shared position on promoting devolution in Wales. This occurred against a background of much resentment among the Welsh Liberal Democrats.

Business remained generally unsupportive. Similarly, it was recognized that the deterministic argument that functional demands would sustain support for an assembly was also questionable. For example, the announcement in July 1996 of the commitment by the Korean firm, LG, to develop semi-conductor and monitor assembly plants near Newport in South Wales, with its enormous economic development implications, cast in a positive light the promotional capacity of existing regional development structures when allied with the financial resources of the Treasury. Labour arguments that LG had gone to Wales because of its expectations of the supportive framework of a Welsh Assembly appeared rather hollow. This example highlights the fact that the impetus to devolution on economic grounds may have hinged too much on central government neglect and weaknesses in the use of the existing administrative machinery. It could be argued that such neglect could be reversed, thereby possibly converting cautious devolutionists back to support for the status quo and leaving others a much stiffer task in making the case for reform. Work by Harding *et al.* (1995) has shown that there is in any case some doubt as to whether there are clearly greater economic gains to be made by regions operating with formal elected structures or informal governance networks.

Even leaving aside these sceptical observations upon the nature of elite views on devolution, it was also clear that many believed the decision to hold a referendum effectively buried devolution in Wales because there was not the popular support to sustain a successful Yes vote. There was probably greater capacity for popular support than was the case in the 1970s. Opinion polls showed increasing support from the mid 1980s, with 1995 and 1996 polls revealing at least a 2:1 majority, but often the number of Don't Knows in such polls was competing for top spot. Moreover, it was likely that if public opinion were more rigorously analysed then the research findings in Scotland would be found to be true only more so. That is to say that there was a reasonable level of support for home rule but that it was rarely a first priority with voters and that while Welsh cultural identity was strong, political identity was not. Such findings suggested that the public would be open to persuasion away from supporting home rule and needed to be very strongly politicized to vote for it. In this regard it should be noted that fears that a Welsh Assembly would become a vehicle for promoting the Welsh language against an English-speaking majority and distrust by the public of Cardiff-based pro-devolution elites were still strong. It was clear that garnering public support in Wales would be a substantial challenge.

Second, there remained huge problems relating to the contents of the proposals. Essentially they provided for a model of devolution very much like that in 1979 – that is, executive devolution with no primary legislative or financial powers. Significantly, the more limited conception of the autonomy to be granted to a Welsh Assembly than to a Scottish Parliament was well reflected in the fact that in the Welsh policy documents the Labour Party talked far more in terms of unitary state concepts (such as decentralization) or vogue concepts (such as subsidiarity) than the granting of political autonomy to a historic national community. In terms of the detail, it was apparent that decentralization of power in practice would be entirely dependent upon legislative and financial settlements made by Westminster. In addition, the thrust of the competencies and purpose given to the assembly rested heavily on the business of reforming and controlling the quangos. This was not a role which provided much potential for achieving obvious success or becoming popular. Quangos by their very definition are arm's length agencies, of which operational autonomy is desired, and there are limits to how much control or new accountability an assembly can impose. The precise form of relations with Westminster and the future role of the Secretary of State were also not clearly defined, leaving potential for conflict. The decision that the assembly would conduct its business on the basis of the local government committee system rather than the cabinet-style system appeared to confirm that the assembly would struggle to define itself as a high-profile political body (see Deacon, 1996).

Ron Davies, Shadow Welsh Secretary, attempted to answer such concerns by stating that he saw Welsh devolution as a process, not an event, but in the short term this raised further potential problems. Generally, it raised the spectre of Labour having a hidden agenda. More specifically, it focused attention on the proposal that the assembly should not have primary legislative powers. This formal policy, although weakening the scheme of devolution, at least provided the advantage of meaning that there would be no Welsh version of the West Lothian question to be answered. The suggestion that legislative powers might emerge in due course meant that the question could justifiably be asked. Indeed, the 1996 revised proposals hinted at primary legislative powers in certain areas, notably over the quangos, affirming that this could indeed be the case. This inevitably opened up the issue of whether devolution should be accompanied by reform of Welsh representation in the Westminster Parliament, one that Labour preferred to keep closed. Overall, the feeling remained that the proposals for Wales were an illogical half-way house between the constitutional status quo and the proposals for Scotland. Comparisons with the Spanish case designed to bolster variable devolution seemed rarefied and unconvincing. On this basis many in Wales remained unconvinced, and long-standing critics such as Tam Dalyell in Parliament were unlikely to accept these proposals for a Welsh Assembly as a good contribution not only to the government of Wales but also to the government of Britain as a whole.

In looking forward to the working of the assembly in practice, there also remained uncertainties. The holes in the proposals left potentially huge discretion to any future government at Westminster. There would clearly be problems in the case of a Conservative government and a Labour assembly, exacerbated by the lack of a clear constitutional framework. Even in the context of a Labour government, though, there would be some uncertainties over the assembly's future. At the Welsh level there would clearly be some dispute between those who saw the assembly primarily in terms of its economic utility and those who prioritized issues relating to the democratic deficit. At the Westminster level there would also be dispute between the viewpoint that the assembly should think of itself in limited state terms, facilitating local provision and economic development, and that which suggested that the assembly should see itself much more as an interventionist body, superintending direct public intervention in economic development through equity shares and planning. In opposition the former regional political economy role was strongly identified with Gordon Brown and the latter view with John Prescott. There was the related issue of how centralist a Labour government would indeed be in relation to the working of the assembly. As Thomas (1996) has pointed out, the potential for central control in the proposals remained as high as in those of the 1970s. There continued to be expectations that much of that potential centralism would be turned into reality.

From this discussion emerges many points which support the view that by the early 1990s Welsh politics had begun to assert an autonomy consistent with the view that British state legitimacy in Wales can only be sustained if the state is conceived in union state terms: at least to reassert existing distinctive treatment and possibly to move on towards political devolution. However, there is also much evidence to support the view that the Welsh were still a divided people over the issue of asserting rights to self-government within the context of the British state and there are considerable grounds for scepticism that in its thinking New Labour had moved very far from Old Labour. In contrast to Mitchell's analysis of Labour in Scotland, there appeared still to be much thinking about Welsh devolution which was consistent with a view of Britain as a unitary state rather than a union state. This suggests that those seeking to assert Welsh rights still had a long way to go in achieving devolution and that even if devolution were achieved the constitutional framework for Welsh government had much potential for developing on a conflictual basis.

WALES AND BRITAIN: THE UNGROUNDED UNION STATE?

This discussion overall promotes an analytical case that the argument over what changes have occurred in the debate about the constitutional framework governing Wales is usefully conducted using the criteria of a developing union state. Advocates of a coherent historic Welsh political identity and analysts who suggest that Conservative governments after 1979 both confirmed respect for that identity during the Walker-Hunt era and then provoked the basis for a compelling move towards political devolution may be characterized as seeing the politics of Wales' role in the British state as informed by the development of a union state tradition, with the 1990s as a major phase in its evolution. This contribution provides some grist to that mill but generally promotes an opposing sceptical perspective both on the historical background and the interpretation of constitutional debate in the early–mid 1990s. In summary, it argues that historically there were developments in governmental arrangements which developed territorial distinctiveness in the configuration of the state, but that such developments often derived from contingent factors and expedient decisions of territorial management. Conservative governments after 1979 sustained much distinctiveness but they essentially worked on the assumption that a special approach to governing Wales had definite limits, meaning that arrangements built up over time were open to testing as to their utility and level of importance both to local elites and the public. It is clear that such testing resulted in rather more consistent reversal of distinctiveness in relation to the government of Wales than was the case in Scotland.

Similarly, while it clearly provoked anti-Conservative dissent and led along with other factors to a new movement for devolution, pressures for devolution were not conclusive and Labour policy prescriptions made the prospect of devolution both uncertain and potentially constitutionally difficult. This is not to argue normatively against the rightness of the development of Wales as an 'imagined community' or to argue against the merits of distinctive treatment, including devolution, for Wales within the British state. Indeed the possibility of Britain developing as a union state is explicitly accepted, and the novel pressures promoting Welsh devolution in the 1990s are highlighted. Rather it is to provide a sober argument that there are grounds for believing that politics in Wales and at Westminster still had much to embrace if that goal was to be realized.

Such an analysis has much in common with that provided by Marquand (1988) and Dunleavy (1989) of the relationship between political philosophy and state development in Britain. Chastened by the experience of Thatcherism, Marquand came to argue that the role of the state had grown earlier in the twentieth century because of particular contingent factors and the utilizing of the economic and social prescriptions made by such figures as Keynes and Beveridge, not because of any underlying philosophical commitment to state intervention and collectivism. The big state and more idealistic goals of a developmental state were vulnerable to the underlying assumptions in the electorate and in the political class of a limited state orthodoxy. In similar vein Dunleavy suggested that statism in significant ways had been ungrounded, leaving existing prescriptions for state activity vulnerable to attack and prescriptions for an extension of the state's role weak. The analysis of the devolution debate in Wales during the Major governments offered here may make a specific analogy by suggesting that rather than representing the politics of a developing union state, it reflected the complexities and problems of an ungrounded union statism.

REFERENCES

Birch, A. (1989) *Nationalism and National Integration* (Unwin Hyman).
Bogdanor, V. (1979) *Devolution* (Oxford University Press).
Bradbury, J. (1997) 'Conservative Governments, Scotland and Wales: A Perspective on Territorial Management' in J. Bradbury and J. Mawson (eds) *British Regionalism and Devolution* (Jessica Kingsley, 1997) pp.74–98.
Bradbury, J. and J. Mawson (1997) 'The Changing Politics and Governance of British Regionalism' in J. Bradbury and J. Mawson (eds) *British Regionalism and Devolution* (Jessica Kingsley, 1997) pp.273–309.
Constitution Unit (1996) *Scotland's Parliament, Fundamentals for a New Scotland Act* (Constitution Unit, University College London).
Deacon, R. (1996) 'New Labour and the Welsh Assembly: Preparing for a New Wales or Updating the Wales Act 1978?', *Regional Studies*, Vol.30, No.7, pp.689–93.

Dunleavy, P. (1989) 'Paradoxes of an Ungrounded Statism' in F. Castles (ed.) *The Comparative History of Public Policy* (Polity Press, pp.242–91).

Foulkes, D., J.B. Jones and R. Wilford (1983) (eds*) The Welsh Veto, The Wales Act 1978 and the Referendum* (University of Wales Press).

Gamble, A. (1994) 'Territorial Politics' in P. Dunleavy, A. Gamble, I. Holliday and G. Peele (eds) *Developments in British Politics 4* (Macmillan) pp.69–91.

Griffiths, D. (1996) *Thatcherism and Territorial Politics, A Welsh Case Study* (Avebury)

Harding, A. *et al.* (1995*) Regional Government in Britain – An Economic Solution?* (Joseph Rowntree Trust).

Jones, J.B. (1997) 'Welsh Politics and Changing British and European Contexts' in J.Bradbury and J.Mawson (eds) *British Regionalism and Devolution* (Jessica Kingsley, 1997) pp.55–73.

Marquand, D. (1988) *The Unprincipled Society* (Jonathan Cape).

Mclean, I. (1995) 'Are Scotland and Wales Over-represented in the House of Commons?', *Political Quarterly*, Vol.60, 250–68.

Mitchell, J. (1995) 'Unionism, Assimilation and the Conservatives', *Contemporary Political Studies* Vol.3, pp.1376-83.

Mitchell, J. (1996) 'From Unitary State to Union State: Labour's Changing View of the United Kingdom and its Implications', *Regional Studies*, Vol.30, No.6, pp.607-11.

Osmond, J. (1995) *Welsh Europeans* (Seren).

Roberts, W. (1995) 'Evolution the Key to Birth of an Assembly' *Western Mail*, 7 Dec. 1995 (1992).

Rokkan, S. and D. Urwin (1982), 'Introduction' in S. Rokkan and D. Urwin (eds) *The Politics of Territorial Identity* (Sage).

Settle, M. (1997) 'Second Rebel Splits Labour on Assembly', *Western Mail*, 13 Jan. 1997.

Sharpe, L.J. (1993) 'The United Kingdom: The Disjointed Meso' in L.J. Sharpe (ed.) *The Rise of Meso Government in Europe* (Sage), pp.247–95.

Thomas, A. (1996) 'The Moment of Truth: Labour's Welsh Assembly Proposals in Practice', *Regional Studies*, Vol.30, No.7, pp.694–703.

Urwin, D. (1982) 'Territorial Structures and Political Developments in the United Kingdom' in S. Rokkan and D. Urwin (eds) *The Politics of Territorial Identity* (Sage, pp.19–73).

Wales Labour Party (1995) *Shaping the Vision, A Report on the Powers and Structure of the Welsh Assembly.*

Wales Labour Party (1996) *Preparing for a New Wales, A Report on the Structure and Workings of the Welsh Assembly.*

Walker, P. (1991) *Staying Power* (Bloomsbury).

Strategies of Autonomist Agents in Wales

JONATHAN SNICKER

The idea of Wales and the Welsh has been transformed during the 1980s and 1990s, a process with significant implications for the British constitutional settlement. Such transformations depend upon on the ability of social and political actors to define, redefine, produce and reproduce identity in the course of interaction. Nationalism is not an adequate descriptor for this process. Since centrifugal and centripetal forces and anti-separation intentionalities are at work here the term 'autonomism' is employed.

This contribution proposes that under the Conservative administrations in the period 1979–97 Welsh identity was reinforced and transformed by institutionalization and key agents of autonomism. This process, termed 'Cymricization', implies that the Three-Wales model is being superseded by a far more complex political dynamic.

Balsom's Three Wales Model posits Welsh-speaking, Anglo-Welsh and British regions as primary structures of identity (Balsom, 1985). In addition to questioning the ongoing primacy of those structures, this study challenges traditional ideas concerning Welsh identity and its relationship with autonomism. Namely, that the various territorial identities within Wales are fixed and Welsh language culture is enshrined, or has undergone social closure. Second, recent history also challenges certain historically determined interpretations of the role of the state in explaining the persistence of Welsh identity. Third, that Welsh identity survival depends exclusively on core values centred around the Nonconformist tradition, the language and the Welsh literary heritage.

We assume, nevertheless, that language and education are key determinants in identity formation. In the context of Wales, where autonomist sentiment bears a close relationship with an ability to speak Welsh\Cymraeg, language itself becomes 'a form of political action' (Edelman, 1995: 125). The traditional state-oriented arguments posit an elite minority of Welsh 'who have survived by anchoring themselves within successive forms of Britishness' (Williams, 1981: 14). There is still some credence attached to this process, and the argument correctly reveals the contingency of Welsh identity, as well as implying strategic behaviour on the part of carriers of Welsh identity.[1] The strategy itself however is perhaps no longer so effective in the face of a weakening of British identity.

Welsh identity itself is complex and multi-faceted. The Welsh language, Cymraeg, employs more than one term to express the concept. This plurality of terms stems, it is argued, from a constant and pressing need for the Welsh to affirm their identity in response to a 'perceived...threat of cultural genocide' (Bowie, 1993: 169). The consequent plurality of possible identities results in a variety of labels that are derived from relationships with the Welsh language: these include Cymraeg (Welsh language), Cymreig (Welsh identity), Cymru-Cymraeg (Welsh-speaking), Cymru di-Gymraeg (Non-Welsh speaking).[2]

It follows that multiple loci of Welsh identity can be posited, and have existed over time. In addition to linguistic identity, one scholar makes the case for the salience of Welsh territorial identity as a 'process of the negotiation of a particular version of Welsh national identity through land and landscape'. Welsh identity has also been posited as residing in ideology or, at an earlier stage, morality. Socio-territorial differences have also informed debates over the validity of identity sources in the Welsh context, particularly over the contribution of the gwerin (rural folk) compared to that of the industrial working classes (Gruffudd, 1995: 220–21).[3]

One set of arguments suggests that recent Welsh identity formation has been reactive and exogenously determined. This may be generally ascribed to a 'paternalistic liberalism of multiculturalism' (Williams, 1994: 88).[4] Perhaps this is what Berlin had in mind when he said that

> to be the object of contempt or patronizing tolerance on the part of proud neighbours is one of the most traumatic experiences that individuals or societies can suffer (Berlin, 1990: 246).

'Intolerence' is perhaps not too outlandish an expression in the context of Mrs Thatcher's declaration: 'I'm an English nationalist and never you forget it' (Osmond, 1988: 43 ff.17).

Alongside this are more endogenous factors, such as the several politically salient categories of Welsh identity posited by the Three Wales Model (Balsom, 1985). These different versions of identity are not fixed, but in constant dialogue. Since the mid-1980s, moreover, new identities and accompanying dialogues have emerged, and herein lies the internal motor of change in Wales. The reassertion of identity since this time has been primarily focused on two areas: political and protest activities – engaged in by, for example Plaid Cymru (The Party of Wales) and Cymdeithas yr Iaith Gymraeg (The Welsh Language Society); and cultural activities – Urdd Gobaith Cymru (The Welsh League of Youth) and Merched Y Wawr (Women's League) – which are exercised across existing social, linguistic and cultural cleavages (Adamson, 1991: 126).

Exogenous and endogenous factors are often atomized by scholars. For instance local culture and issue politics which influence identity transformation are often placed by scholars on a tangent with external factors, such as the decline of partisanship, rise of protest voting and post-material values (Levy, 1995: 300). Too great a price has been paid for the analytical utility of this approach, especially when the transcending role of individual agency is considered.

AGENTS OF TERRITORIAL ADMINISTRATION IN THE WELSH OFFICE

The growth of state institutions in Wales has been well documented (Civil Service, 1995; Dynes, 1995; Griffiths, 1996). The Welsh Office possesses attributes akin to the state of which it is a constituent part, but paradoxically these qualities make it also separate and prone to further separation. Here we consider the effect of agents within the Welsh Office on Welsh identity mobilization and autonomist impulses. Within the Welsh Office, personnel can be broadly categorized into two types, political personnel and administrative personnel.[5]

Political Personnel

Between 1979 and May 1,1997 Wales had five Conservative Secretaries of State, namely Sir Nicholas Edwards, Peter Walker, David Hunt, John Redwood and William Hague. Over this period the ruling Conservative Party gradually felt more 'able to dispense with the tradition that the Welsh Secretary needed to be Welsh' (Randall, 1972: 368; Dynes and Walker, 1995: 296), the last two Conservative Secretaries of State having no discernible connection with Wales, although non-Welsh Secretaries of State had been the subject of controversy during previous administrations (Jones, 1984: 188).

The political culture changes at the Welsh Office are also important. Before the advent of John Redwood, Wales was regarded as a 'playground for the "wets"' (Williams and Lawrence, 1992). Both Peter Walker and David Hunt advocated a 'Toryism of partnership, political consensus and public spending', and tended to cultivate Welsh opinion (Williams and Lawrence, 1992; Thomas, 1994: 47). Some have suggested that Walker and Hunt encouraged the by-passing of Westminster by Wales-based institutions and agencies (Osmond, 1992: 37). John Redwood represented a significant break with these traditions. Already having articulated a position broadly defined as Eurosceptic, he entered the Welsh Office in May 1993 known as a champion of free-market liberalism and individualism. Furthermore, he did little to endear himself to the Welsh-speaking community – he refused, for instance, to sign letters written in Welsh (*Financial Times*, 1994). In addition to the decline in support for Redwood, Conservative Party support in Wales fell markedly. The 1995 New Unitary Authority elections provide a case in point – the number of Conservative seats fell to 42 out of a total of 1,273, with a ten per cent share of the vote (Gow, 1995). His successor, William Hague, though more popular, did little to ameliorate this trend – in the 1997 General Election the Conservatives lost all their Parliamentary seats (Jones, 1997).

The political culture in Wales has been transformed in a deeper sense. Curiously, the seeds of such were planted in 1979, in the immediate aftermath of the referendum. During the referendum campaign, however, the Welsh Conservative Party and an anti-devolution cadre (often known as the Gang of Six, but in fact much larger) within the Welsh Labour Party had committed themselves to change. The Conservatives promised to address the issue of public accountability in Wales, and the anti-devolutionists in the Labour Party were, in a sense, obliged to prove their ability to lobby for Wales in the Parliamentary arena. The vehicle for this, the Select Committee on Welsh Affairs, commenced business in January 1980. Leo Abse, a Labour member and one of the most vociferous anti-devolution campaigners,[6] was its first chairman.

The Committee, however, failed to live up to the expectations it generated. The source of failure lay in part with its dual role, lobbying for Wales and overseeing the Welsh Office, which was at times contradictory. It began by emphasizing the former role. Setting out to address the larger 'nationalist issues' such as unemployment, broadcasting, and water, the Committee produced its first report in August 1980. The unanimous report was critical of government policy, and linked unemployment with the prospect of unrest, particularly among the young. Despite the Committee's six Conservative MPs supporting the findings, the government rejected all but two proposals. For a considerable period thereafter the Committee avoided substantive policy issues (Balsom and Jones, 1984: 100).

The actions of the six Conservative MPs provide evidence for a territory/party loyalty cleavage in British politics. The most interesting individual in this respect is Sir Wyn Roberts, former Minister of State at the Welsh Office. Sir Wyn, who began as a junior minister in 1979 and lost his position during the July 1995 reshuffle, is the longest serving minister in a single government department this century (Wastell, 1994). His argument that 'Wales was never a kingdom and has never been united except under the Welsh Office' (Williams and Lawrence, 1992) may be disingenuous, hardly unusual among Conservative ministers in recent years, and especially given that certain individuals within Plaid Cymru regard Sir Wyn as, at the very least, a cultural autonomist (Davies, 1994).

Some evidence suggests that the Welsh Office became an institutional servant of Welsh autonomism, with Sir Wyn as its principal agent. This may be an overstatement, but a state of affairs not far from this was acknowledged in the Welsh language press (Iowerth, 1994). There is evidence supporting the 'principal agent' argument in the field of education, a policy area crucial to Welsh identity.[7] During the process of nationwide education reform Sir Wyn Roberts, with the acquiescence of David Hunt, ensured that a 'distinctive Welsh dimension' was promulgated (Hunt, 1992: 11). Former Plaid Cymru president Dafydd Ellis Thomas acknowledged Sir Wyn's role in an address to the Welsh Grand Committee (Thomas, 1991: 59; Ellis Thomas, 1992: 34). Later, after the decision by the Curriculum Council for Wales to temporarily drop Welsh as a compulsory school subject for children age 14–16 in English medium schools, Plaid Cymru sought to confer with Wyn Roberts (Stover, Bowen et al., 1994).

John Redwood, who was, of all the Secretaries of State since 1979, most resistant to Welsh autonomy on any level, paradoxically may have offered Sir Wyn greater latitude by refusing to deal with education correspondence. A leaked memorandum provided rich insights into his intentions. Redwood broke with the precedent set by previous incumbents in the Welsh Office by stating through his documents clerk that he would 'no longer automatically reply to letters addressed to him from other MPs, MEPs, councillors and prominent organisations' (Blackhurst, 1993). Critically Redwood narrowed his policy remit, specifically excluding education.

Sir Wyn contributed to the reinforcement of a separate identity for Wales in other ways. The Welsh language has received institutional and policy reinforcement under Sir Wyn's tenure, particularly the establishment of a 15-member Welsh Language Board to secure the use of Cymraeg in the public sector, announced as a package of measures in the Welsh Language Bill in December 1992. Sir Wyn pronounced it 'an historic day' (Jones, 1992) and left the impression that he regarded Welsh language revival as his primary achievement (Wastell, 1994). The Welsh Language Act came into force in 1993; public bodies in Wales are now obliged to use Welsh and English co-equally.

Other Welsh institutions were created. For example, Sir Wyn oversaw the establishment of the Countryside Council for Wales in April 1991, amalgamating functions of the Countryside Commission in Wales and the Nature Conservancy Council in Wales. These developments were a central pillar in the Welsh Office's Rural Initiative announced by Sir Wyn in February 1991 during a Welsh Grand Committee debate on rural Wales, and represented a significant change from the original idea of an 'England and Wales' institution. In the same year it was announced that the Wales Tourist Board (WTB) would be allowed to adopt its own marketing strategy independent of the British Tourist Authority (Thomas, 1994: 169).[8]

Sir Wyn is an autonomist whose support for Welsh identity is tempered by a unionist financial outlook. In 1992, for instance, he argued for a pragmatic view of Wales' relationship with England. He pointed out that public spending for 1990–91 ran at £2,964 per capita in Wales compared with £2,586 for the UK as a whole, and that the average poll tax bill for 1991–92 was £121, less than half of the English average bill of £252 (Williams and Lawrence, 1992). This is similar to arguments made elsewhere, especially from sources associated with neo-conservatism (Malcolm, 1989).

The dilemma for Welsh (especially Welsh-speaking) Tories is reconciling their Toryism with the neo-conservatism that now dominates their party. For this elite, and their fellow travellers in Scotland, the strain is telling.

Administrative Personnel

Welsh Office personnel with sympathies towards various types of Welsh autonomism are likely to colonize those policy areas most amenable to their inclinations. This process is, however, subject to interference from central state agencies, and there is little likelihood of a perfect correlation between a 'Welsh' policy area and its dominance by a 'closet autonomist'. The analysis is complicated further by the presence of administrative gatekeepers – individuals in strategic positions who have had the capacity to affect profoundly the development and direction of the Welsh Office.

In the early years, recruitment to the lower echelons of the Welsh Office was conducted primarily in the 'regional offices of Wales', such that in the initial period of operation 70 per cent of the administrative class was from a Welsh background (Rolands, 1972: 338). Current 'British' administrators persist in this expectation of Welsh 'colonization' (or 'infiltration' depending on one's perspective), and have reacted to it (Beckett, 1994). Thus even if intuition was proved to be incorrect in reality, shared expectations may produce real results.

Interviews conducted with WO personnel provided further support for our intuitive expectation of asymmetric levels of Cymricization across departments. On the basis, therefore, of historical, social, cultural and structural factors we expect agriculture and education to be highly Cymricized policy areas. One broad empirical indicator supports this hypothesis. According to sources within the Welsh Office, around 15 per cent of the Welsh Office administrative staff is Welsh speaking and the bulk of these individuals are concentrated in the departments of education and agriculture (Confidential Source #1247, 1995). These findings were confirmed by follow up questions (Confidential Source #1634, 1996).

The only verifiable linguistic data available uses the loosely defined criterion 'percentage who have notified they have some ability in the use of Welsh' and was submitted by the Welsh Office as a result of a parliamentary question. The submission to some extent corroborated our intuitive expectations, but the looser criteria for ability in Welsh given in the official figures would appear to indicate that not all the people classified as having an ability in Welsh are necessarily fluent Welsh speakers. This assumption receives, moreover, substantive vindication by the confusion arising over the Welsh-speaking ability of a Grade 1 civil servant which required a parliamentary answer to be corrected (House of Commons, 1995).

It appears that an internal survey covering Welsh speakers in the WO was conducted recently but is not available in the public domain. A copy for the purposes of this research was requested but it was not forthcoming. The Welsh Office Personnel Management Division asserted that the ability to speak Welsh was not 'a key determination (sic) in most postings'. This information directly contradicted data received from confidential sources within the Welsh Office during interviews. Several inferences can be drawn from this. In the first instance, vagaries of data may confirm the lack of overall coherence and autonomy within the WO (Jones, 1988: 53). Second, notwithstanding the lack of coherence within the institution, we find it more persuasive to surmise that the asymmetries in data are indicators of the politicization of the issues.

NDPBS AND QUANGOS

The development of the so-called quango state in Wales has engendered much discussion, particularly the issue of 'packing' with Conservative party supporters (Osmond, 1992: 16–20). Both the Countryside Council and the WTB would provide fruitful avenues for research into these matters, and the institutionalization of Welsh identity in general, not least because they have shared a Chief Executive. More importantly perhaps they symbolize the process of institutionalization of Welsh identity in the 1980s, and give precise indicators as to the process of that institutionalization. This process appears to occur in one of two ways – the more 'traditional' method is for an analogue body to be created in Wales which then goes on to evolve differently from its counterpart in England. A core feature in this evolution has been the development of co-operative networks between statutory agencies, local authorities and the private sector. This form of Welsh corporatism was directly referred to by one MP when he was asked to account for the success of Wales in gaining the investment from Lucky Goldstar of Korea in July 1996 (Evans, 1996). With regard to institutionalization the second, more recent, strand of the process concerns the creation of certain structures in Wales which are from the outset unique.

The development of this latter, more potent, process has been attributed to Sir Wyn Roberts (Confidential Source #1968, 1996). Though the link between the process of 'quangoization' and the widening 'democratic deficit' are constantly subsumed into discussions about the need for Welsh autonomy, less is said about the related processes of Cymricization and decentralization. Pluralist decentralization at a local level, for instance in education, has invariably diminished the functional power of local authorities, often Labour Party satrapies opposing Welsh autonomism.[9] The quangos and other constituency bodies in civil society that were created to interact over these removed functions have moreover proven themselves more amenable to Cymricization.

AGENTS OF COMMUNICATION

It must be understood that modern Welsh autonomism has less to do with control over the means of production than control over the means of cultural production and reproduction. In this sense the media, particularly the broadcast media, have been characterized as 'playing a central role, both positive and negative, in the development of the concept of a national community' (Davies, 1994: ix).

Education is another means of cultural production and reproduction. The general role of education in cultural reproduction has been documented elsewhere (Brock and Tulasiewicz, 1985; Khleif, 1980); here we focus on the role of human agency in the Welsh education system.

Education Personnel

Concerns about the role of teachers in social and cultural maintenance are not new. Socrates advises Adeimantus that children must be protected from 'views of life for the most part at variance with those which we think they ought to hold when they come to man's estate' (Plato, 1935: 58). One Welsh scholar has claimed that 'the state, at least since the time of Elizabeth I, has attempted to control teachers and teaching matter' (Elwyn Jones, 1990: 199). Control over the latter, and then in only legalistic terms, has always been the easier task.

Members of the teaching professions in Wales have had over time a close involvement with Welsh autonomism. A disproportionate number of Plaid Cymru general election candidates have come from the teaching profession (Morgan, 1982: 381). Welsh-medium education has exhibited marked growth in the period under examination, and in all sectors. The expansion is also taking place outside the core language areas, Y Fro Cymraeg, and there has been a consequent growth in demand for Welsh-speaking teachers. In addition, the Welsh immersion teacher has been found to be more committed than the average teacher (Baker, 1988: 109), though the physical teaching environment is often worse. The quality of the teaching within Welsh-medium education has two structural implications. First Welsh-medium schools are likely to be on average better educational institutions than their English-medium counterparts (Confidential Source #2068, 1996). Second, given the politicization of the Welsh language and given the empirical research revealing that 'attitudes are favourable when there is immersion in the indigenous culture' (Baker, 1988: 133–4), the teachers are likely to be more politicized and more efficient transmitters of distinctly Welsh-identity bundles than their colleagues in English-medium schools. Examination results bear the former claim out. The proof of the latter is more difficult, and is only likely to be verifiable some time after the 1997 Referendum.

We can however provide preliminary indicators of identity transformation that are likely to have future political effect. The percentage of Welsh speakers, for instance, has risen among all groups below 25 since 1981 (Jones, 1995: 1). At present around 37 per cent of the population of Wales under 18 receive education at least partly through the medium of Welsh – giving a non-normal distribution curve (Williams, 1996). We can attribute the increase to factors such as the provision of Mudiad Ysgolion Meithrin (MYM – Primary School Movement) playgroups, which have expanded greatly since the 1970s (Jones, 1995: 1). The major impetus behind the increase, however, has come from the state. The most significant legal instrument in this respect, the 1988 Education Reform Act, acquired a Welsh dimension for five main reasons. The first is the historical and political fact that 'in the 20th century, the state's position on the Welsh language has been generally indulgent' (Elwyn Jones, 1988: 93). Second, 'the concept of a National Curriculum raised the issue of which nation was to be served', and 'revolutionized the role of the state in education, thereby inadvertently raising questions about the relationship between the Welsh nation and the British state in a new context', creating 'almost by accident' a new dimension within which cultural and political autonomism could coalesce (Elwyn Jones, 1994: 8, 13, 14). Third, an institutional structure arose that was generally favourable to the development of separate policies. Fourth, political, administrative and education personnel were in place to translate the Act into the Welsh dimension. Finally, 'from the outset of discussions on the curriculum, Sir Wyn Roberts, the minister for Wales responsible for education, insisted on a Welsh dimension' (Smith, 1991).

It has been in the latter half of the twentieth century that state 'indulgence' emerged as a significant factor; particularly as a result of the growing role of the Welsh Department of the Ministry of Education. The creation of a new dimension in which Welsh identity could undergo a transformation is more recent and was in large part due to the Education Reform Act of 1988, though its authors did not realize this at the time (Elwyn Jones, 1994: 13). The Curriculum Council for Wales (CCW), formed in August 1988, and its more powerful successor, which replaced it in 1994, Awdurdod Cwricwlwm ac Asesu Cymru (ACAC – the Curriculum and Assessment Authority for Wales), have provided an institutional framework for the input of specifically Welsh concerns. The National Curriculum in Wales began to develop a separate identity, which was deliberate and purposive; so much so that the process is actually outlined and justified in official documentation.

It is the role of agents within these institutions that interests us here – those, for instance, who composed the CCW's second report which declared, uncontroversially, that the Council's immediate task was to 'respond to statutory consultations, and to establish appropriate machinery to enable it to do so'. The Council however posited the need to differentiate itself from the 'the larger National Curriculum Council in England' and 'to establish a clear identity of its own' (Curriculum Council for Wales, 1992: 1).

As a consequence since 1988 the National Curriculum in Wales has progressively acquired a Welsh dimension. The table below depicts the National Curriculum in Wales as it stood in 1990.

TABLE 1
NATIONAL CURRICULUM IN WALES IN 1990

Core Subjects	Other Foundation Subjects
Mathematics	Welsh**
Welsh*	Design and Technology
Science	Music
History	Art
English	PE
Geography	
Modern Foreign Language***	

*   For schools designated as Welsh speaking under Section 3(7) of ERA 1988
** In schools where Welsh is not taught as a core subject
***At KS3 and KS4 only (KS1 5–7YRS, KS2 7–11, KS3 11–14)

Source: Curriculum Council for Wales, 1990, p.1.

The curricular structure of education in Wales has changed little since then. The 1992 Education Act and the subsequent review of the National Curriculum and its assessment framework in Wales, however, afforded an opportunity for continued development and Cymricization of the content of the Curriculum (Curriculum Council for Wales, 1993: Appendix B).

The role of teachers in the execution of the Curriculum Cymreig and the responses of their pupils also supports the fourth component of the argument. From attitudinal changes among teachers in areas previously apathetic or even antipathetic to the Welsh language we can infer changes among the attitude of administrative and political agents. The inference must be qualified however by the likelihood of interference by structural factors, particularly institutional and power rivalry between 'British Wales' LEAs and the more Cymricized CCW/ACAC. Given that qualification the findings are nevertheless revealing. Several schools in the former Gwent area were surveyed, a process which included interviews and analysis of inspectors' reports.

Most inspectors' reports included positive statements on the development of the Welsh language in this 'British Wales' region. The 1995 report on Cwm Primary school, for instance, found that 'the enthusiasm for Welsh... is well-supported throughout the school by the incidental use of Welsh in all classes', and it is 'used incidentally by all teachers throughout the school'. Furthermore a 'Welsh Dimension in the Curriculum' is being 'established through studies of local, national and geographical topics and through activities such as the popular lunch time folk dancing club'. Other aspects of a burgeoning Welsh Curriculum include a school eisteddfod which is held on Dydd Gwyl Dewi (St. David's Day) (HMI Inspectorate, 1995: 5, 13). It is clear that in many of the region's infants, primary and junior schools the pupils have come to 'regard Welsh as a natural part of school life' (Palmer, 1995b: 14). The consequences of these developments extend beyond the boundaries of the schools. One inspector cited as evidence of the growth of a Welsh ethos the 'attempts to enlist the interest of parents' in what was clearly a profound change taking place in the identity of one particular school and its occupants (Adams, 1995: 16).

Among older age groups Welsh and the 'Welsh ethos' has become increasingly integrated into the school curriculum. At Betws Comprehensive School in Newport, for instance, Welsh was being 'taught for the first time to year 7' with the implementation of the National Curriculum Welsh Order of September 1993. The inspector found that 'most pupils enjoy the lessons and have positive attitudes to the language' (James, 1995: 23, 24).

The establishment in 1988 of the first designated Welsh-medium comprehensive school in the region is also significant. The school was intended to be 'an island of Welshness in a sea of Englishness' (Raybould, 1995: 6, 7). With an inaugural intake of 52 pupils Ysgol Gwynllyw was opened 'in consequence of strenuous efforts made by the parents'. A Sixth Form was established in September 1993 'again as a result of similar parental pressure' (Raybould, 1995: 2). It is clear from the report that the entire ethos of the school is centred around a Welshness with the Welsh language at its core:

> furthered by the respect and unfailing care offered to all pupils by the teachers, Welsh is to be heard on the lips of all in school, unprompted and unhindered (Raybould, 1995: 15).

Autonomist agency is also demonstrated by the example above. The school inspector for Gwynllyw, Bill Raybould, is the former director of Pwyllgor Datblygu Addysg Gymraeg (Welsh Language Education Development Committee) which was established by the government to promote Welsh in schools.[10] Interviewed in this capacity he expressed concern at the consequences of the demise of his committee (Smith, 1992). Earlier, and more controversially, he argued that Welsh should be given foundation status in England:

> It is an insult to Welsh people that their language is not accorded the same status as foreign, or Commonwealth, languages...particularly when urban areas such as London, Liverpool, and Shrewsbury have concentrations of Welsh speakers (Smith, 1991).

His concerns proved, on one level at least, unfounded; though they may, in the long run, have had unintended career repercussions for the individual expressing them. Career repercussions were manifest for different reasons when ACAC took over the school-related duties of Pwyllgor Datblygu Addysg Gymraeg and the functions of CCW in April 1994. The new institution advertised for a bilingual chief executive thereby excluding, not without controversy, the previous chief executive at CCW, Bernard Jones (Heath, 1993).

To strengthen our arguments, the rate and spread of identity transformation must be addressed. Attitudinal change is not only visible among bureaucrats, within the teaching profession and, as a consequence, among students; the 1988 Education Reform Act may have induced also a change in parental attitudes to Welsh. The 1991 census figures reveal that 26.9 per cent of the 10–14 age group were designated by their parents as Welsh speaking, whereas in 1981, 13.3 per cent of 3–4 year olds (that is, part of the same cohort) were described as Welsh speaking (Jones, 1995: 1). Though we can doubt, as in all language surveys, the veracity of the figures, the statistics do unambiguously reveal the changing symbolic value of the Welsh language (Millar, 1995: 174, 178–9). Changing parental attitudes seem to be both a cause and a consequence of the rise in the status of the Welsh language.

Another significant factor in secondary schools has been the rise in the percentage of pupils taking Welsh as a second language, from around 40 per cent in 1988 (a proportion that had remained more or less steady since 1979) to over 65 per cent in 1994. Over the same period the proportion not taught Welsh declined from around 45 per cent to around 20 per cent (Jones, 1995: 4). It is estimated that by 1999 Welsh-language schools will constitute around 25 per cent of all secondary schools in Wales (Confidential Source #1247, 1995). Such schooling has proved popular with parents – the average academic performance of these schools is demonstrably better on the whole than the English-medium schools (Jones, 1995: 5). As a result of this popularity several Welsh feeder primaries have opened in British Wales, including such schools at Newport and Abergavenny. This evidence also undermines claims over the inhibiting educational effect of bilingualism (Jones, 1988: 108).

Moreover the new WelshBac proposals constitute an attempt to further entrench the Welshness of the education system (Elwyn Jones, 1997; Macleod 1997). Such reforms can only increase the rate of identity transformation in 'British Wales', where Welsh identity was previously deemed to be weakest. Across a range of measures there has been a significant increase in the number of parents in these areas wishing to send their children to Welsh-medium schools, and this trend is likely to persist (Confidential Source #1247, 1995).

CONCLUSION

Welsh identity is situationally and temporally contingent, and varies in response to a myriad of factors (Bhabha, 1990; Jenkins, 1995: 1). It has undergone resurgence when suppression has declined or after crises of various kinds. The identity transformation in Wales since 1979 however has been determined by key elite groups making proactive choices. They have discovered the power of self-categorization (Hechter, 1975: 40), and this has been mediated by Cymraeg. This power has also arisen from an education system which is now structurally capable of producing Welsh identity. Its personnel likewise have the capacity and in certain areas the willingness to reproduce Welsh identity. Moreover the alternative, 'British' identity, has been weakened by, inter alia, the successful challenge in Wales to the Conservative government's attempt to nationalize the curriculum and homogenize and create new patterns of uniformity.

The 'choices' made by the autonomists are perhaps better termed 'strategies', and have involved the colonization of 'identive' policy areas, the manipulation of the intent of statutory instruments, the by-passing of existing structures, particularly the old Councils in the case of the Education Reform Act, and on a ground level the attempt to diffuse identive behaviour and goals into the wider populace. There can be no doubt that key individuals within a Conservative and Unionist administration have presided over, and in some cases colluded in, the widening and deepening of Welsh identity particularly among younger people. Devolution under the Labour government, and the passing of political responsibility from one generation to the next can only serve to further this process.

New forms of autonomist behaviour are manifest in Wales, which weaken existing concepts, categories and theories of 'nationalism'. The evidence suggests that the 'Three Wales Model' may not have a long-term future, because the future political dynamic of Wales lies less in regional differences than in generational ones.

NOTES

1. For a general discussion on the renewed scholarly interest in the role of agency in 'the construction work of nations', see Hannerz and Löfgren (1993).
2. For perspectives on this diversity see Bell 1995, particularly Bell 1995a; Bell 1995b; Bianchi 1995, and the review article in the Welsh-language periodical *Barn* (Davies 1996).
3. The notion of a classless gwerin (folk) has been a consistent theme in autonomist discourse (see Adamson 1988: 7).
4. The quote also indicates that liberalism can be considered as a non-neutral ideology (Miller 1995: 439).
5. Categorizing the personnel within NDPB's and QUANGOS subject to the remit of the Welsh Office under the Conservatives is somewhat more complex and politically contentious.
6. For an insight into the strategies employed by Abse and Kinnock at the time see *The Economist* 1978.
7. For latest insight into the implications of the separate development of the Welsh education system since 1988 see Elwyn Jones, 1997; MacLeod, 1997.
8. See Tourism (Overseas Promotion) Wales Act 1992.
9. Structural 'presence' has also been altered by the creation of new unitary authorities.
10. The committee's functions have been taken over by ACAC.

REFERENCES

Adams, S.J. (1995) Inspection of Park Terrace Primary School, Pontypool Gwent, OHMCI.

Adamson, D. (1988) 'The New Working Class and Political Change in Wales.' *Contemporary Wales* Vol.2, p.7–28.

Adamson, D.L. (1991) *Class, Ideology and the Nation: A Theory of Welsh Nationalism* (Cardiff: University of Wales Press).

Aitken, I. (1995) 'Talkin' 'bout a Devolution: Regional Politics in the UK', *New Statesman & Society*, Vol.8 ,p.14.

Baker, C. (1988) *Key Issues in Bilingualism and Bilingual Education.* (Clevedon) Multilingual Matters.

Balsom, D. (1985) 'The Three-Wales Model: The Political Sociology of Welsh Identity. Recent Electoral Trends, Pressures for Change', in J. Osmond, *The National Question Again: Welsh Political Identity in the 1980s* (Llandysul: Gomer).

Balsom, D. and J.B. Jones (1984) 'Faces of Wales: The Nationwide Competition for Votes', in I. MacAllister and R. Rose, *The 1983 British Election* (London: Frances Pinter) p.98–121.

Beckett, A. (1994) 'How Clean Was My Valley?' *The Independent* (London) p.4.

Bell, I.A. (1995a) 'Introduction: The Politics and Place of Writing', in I.A. Bell, *Peripheral Visions*, p.1–5.

Bell, I.A., (ed.) (1995b) *Peripheral Visions: Images of Nationhood in Contemporary British Fiction* (Cardiff: University of Wales Press).

Bell, I.A. (1995c) 'To See Ourselves: Travel Narratives and National Identity in Contemporary Britain', in I.A. Bell, *Peripheral Visions*, p.6–26.

Berlin, I. (1990) 'The Bent Twig: on the Rise of Nationalisn' in I. Berlin, *The Crooked Timber of Humanity* (London: John Murray), pp.238–61.

Bevan, D. (1984) 'The Mobilization of Cultural Minorities – The Case of Sianel-Pedwar-Cymru,' *Media Culture & Society*, Vol.6, No.2, pp.103–17.

Bhabha, H.K., (ed.) (1990) *Nation and Narration* (London: Routledge).

Bianchi, T. (1995) 'Aztecs in Troedrhiwgwair: Recent Fictions in Wales'. in I.A. Bell, *Peripheral Visions*, pp.44–76.

Blackhurst, C. (1993) Minister outlines list of 'prominent' MPs. *The Independent* (London) p.5.

Bowie, F. (1993) 'Wales from Within: Conflicting Interpretations of Welsh Identity', in S. Macdonald, *Inside European Identities: Ethnography in Western Europe* (Oxford: Berg), pp.167–93.

Brock, C. and W. Tulasiewicz (eds) (1985) *Cultural Identity and Educational Policy* (London: Croom Helm).

Butt Phillip, A. (1975) *The Welsh Question: Nationalism in Welsh Politics 1945–70* (Cardiff: University of Wales Press).

Civil Service (1995) Wales: Departments and Other Organisations. *Civil Service Yearbook* (London: HMSO), pp.894–930.

Cohen, N. (1995) 'The Principality of Redwood,' *The Independent* (London) p.21.

Confidential Source #2068, 1996. J. Snicker. Cardiff.

Confidential Source #1983, 1996. J. Snicker. Cardiff.

Confidential Source #1634, 1996. J. Snicker. Cardiff.

Confidential Source #1247, 1995. J. Snicker. Cardiff.

Cormack, M. (1993) 'Problems of Minority Language Broadcasting: Gaelic in Scotland,' *European Journal of Communication*, Vol.8, No.1, pp.101–17.

Curriculum Council for Wales (1990) *Annual Report August 1988–March 1990*, CCW.

Curriculum Council for Wales (1992) *Annual Report 1990–1991*, CCW.

Curriculum Council for Wales (1993) *The National Curriculum and Assessment Framework in Wales*, CCW.

Davies, D.H. (1983) *The Welsh Nationalist Party 1925–1945: A Call to Nationhood* (Cardiff, Cardiff University Press.

Davies, D.W. (1996) 'Pe baech chwi'n genedl', *Barn*, pp.24–5.

Davies, J. (1994) *Broadcasting and the BBC in Wales* (Cardiff, University of Wales Press).

Davies, K. (1994) Interview, Plaid Cymru Chief Executive. J. Snicker. Cardiff.

Davies, R. (1996) 'The Tools for the Job,' *Agenda: The Journal of the Institute of Welsh Affairs* (Winter), pp.18–20.

Donald, C. (1992) 'Reading between the Lines,' *The Independent* (London) p.19.

Dynes, M. and D. Walker (1995) *Wales. The Times Guide to the New British State: The Government Machine in the 1990s* (London, Times Books,) pp.296–306.

The Economist (1978) 'Devolution: Wales's Turn', 25 February, p.18.

The Economist (1992) 'Britain Stands Alone', 8 August, p.51.

The Economist (1994) 'The Best and the Brightest', pp.29–30.

Edelman, M. (1995) *From Art to Politics* (London: University of Chicago Press).

Ellis Thomas, D. (1992) Address to the Welsh Grand Committee, HMSO.

Elwyn Jones, G. (1988) 'What Are Schools in Wales For? Wales and the Education Reform Act', *Contemporary Wales*, Vol.2, No.1, 83–97.

Elwyn Jones, G. (ed.) (1990) *Direction and Devolution in Welsh Education in the Twentieth Century* (Cardiff, University of Wales Press).

Elwyn Jones, G. (1994) 'Which Nation's Curriculum? – The Case Of Wales', *Curriculum Journal*, Vol.5, No.1, pp.5–16.

Elwyn Jones, G. (1997) 'The WelshBac – A Defining Moment in Education'. *Agenda* (Summer), pp.41–2.

Evans, G. (1991) *Fighting for Wales* (Talybont: Y Lolfa).

Evans, H.I. (1990) Foreward. *Annual Report August 1988–March 1990*. Curriculum Council for Wales, CCW.

Evans, J. (1996) Lucky Goldstar Investment. V. Roderick. (Cardiff: BBC Radio Wales).

Evans, S. (1996) 'Exiles in Whose Country?' *Times Literary Supplement*, p.30.

Financial Times (1994) 'On Redwood Not Signing Letters in Welsh', (London) p.23g.

Financial Times (1994) On Unpopularity of the Secretary of State for Wales' (London) p.11a.

Gow, D. (1995) 'Domination Of Principality Encourages Resistance To Devolution, *The Guardian* (London) p.11.

Grant, W.P. and R.J.C. Preece (1968) 'Welsh and Scottish Nationalism,' *Parliamentary Affairs*, Vol.21, No.3, pp.255–63.

Graubard, S.R. (1993) Preface, *Dædalus*, Vol.122, No.3, pp.v–viii.

Green, L. (1982) 'Rational Nationalists,' *Political Studies*, Vol.30, No.2, pp.236–46.

Griffiths, D. (1996) *Thatcherism and Territorial Politics : A Welsh Case Study* (Aldershot: Avebury).

Gruffudd, P. (1994) 'Tradition, Modernity and the Countryside: The Imaginary Geography of Rural Wales,' *Contemporary Wales*, Vol.6, pp.33–47.

Gruffudd, P. (1995) 'Remaking Wales: Nation-building and the Geographical Imagination, 1925–50,' *Political Geography*, Vol.14, No.3, pp.219–239.

Hannerz, U. and O. Löfgren (1993) 'Defining the National: An Introduction,' *Ethnos*, Vol.58, No.3–4, pp.157–60.

Harris, C. and R. Startup (1995) 'The Church in Wales: A Neglected Welsh Institution,' *Contemporary Wales*, Vol.7, No.1, pp.97–116.

Heath, T. (1993) New Rule Drives Top Man from Post, *Times Educational Supplement* (London) p.3.

Hechter, M. (1975) *Internal Colonialism: The Celtic Fringe in British National Development, 1536–1966.*(London, Routledge & Kegan Paul).

Heylings, M.R. (1995) *Inspection of Lliswerry High School*, Newport Gwent, OHMCI.

HMI Inspectorate (1995) *Report on Cwm Primary School*, Gwent, HMI.

House of Commons (1995) Parliamentary Question for Answer on Monday 4 December 1995: Staffing. *Hansard* (London).

House of Commons (1995) Parliamentary Question for Answer on Monday 4 December 1995: Staffing II. Corrected version (London).

Hunt, D. (1992) Address to the Welsh Grand Committee. Minutes of Evidence, HC 410. Welsh Grand Committee (London: HMSO).

Iowerth, D. (1994) 'Ble mae'r bwrdd?' *Golwg.*, Vol.6, pp.10–11.

James, R.G. (1995) *Inspection of Betws Comprehensive School*, Newport, Gwent.

Jenkins, R. (1995) 'Nations and Nationalism: Towards More Open Models'. Mimeograph provided by the author, pp.1–42.

Jones, H. (1995) *The Welsh Language: Children and Education*, Swyddfa Gymreig.

Jones, J.B. (1984) 'Labour Party Doctrine and Devolution: The Welsh Experience,' *Ethnic and Racial Studies*, Vol.7, No.1, pp.182–93.

Jones, J.B. (1988) 'The Development of Welsh Territorial Institutions: Modernization Theory Revisited,' *Contemporary Wales*, Vol.2, No.1, pp.47–61.

Jones, J.B. (1997) 'The Landslide Inheritance', *Agenda* (Summer), Vol.8–9.

Jones, P.E. (1988) 'Some Trends in Welsh Secondary Education, 1967–1987', *Contemporary Wales*, Vol.2, No.1, pp.99–108.

Jones, R.M. (1992) 'Beyond Identity? The Reconstruction of the Welsh' *Journal of British Studies*, Vol.31, No.4, pp.330–57.

Jones, T. (1992) 'Devolution Arguments Fail to Sway Unconverted', General Election 1992, *The Times* (London) p.11.

Jones, T. (1992) 'Welsh Tongue Fails to Placate: Official Language'. *The Times* (London) p.7.

Khleif, B.B. (1979) 'Language as Identity: Towards an Ethnography of Welsh Nationalism,' *Ethnicity*, Vol.6, No.4, pp.346–57.

Khleif, B.B. (1980) *Language, Ethnicity, and Education in Wales* (The Hague: Mouton).

King, P. (1980) *Federalism and Federation* (London: Croom Helm).

Landy, R. (1995) Inspection Report under Section 9 of Education (Schools) Act on Ebbw Vale Comprehensive School, Waun-y-pound Road, Ebbw Vale Gwent NP3 6LE.

Levy, R. (1995) 'Finding a Place in the World Economy. Party Strategy and Party Vote: The Regionalization of SNP and Plaid Cymru Support, 1979–92', *Political Geography*, Vol.14, No.3, pp.295–308.

Lord Annan (1977) Broadcasting Commission.

MacLeod, D. (1997, Thursday, June 24) 'It's Bac to the Valleys', *The Guardian*, p.2 (Schools).

Malcolm, N. (1989) 'Just Another Typically Unusual Welsh Election', *The Spectator*, p.6.

May, J. (1994) *Reference Wales* (Cardiff: University of Wales Press).

Millar, S. (1995) 'The Meaning of Language: Ethnolinguistic Identity in the United Kingdom', in N.A. Sorenson, *European Identities: Cultural Diversity and Integration in Europe since 1700* (Odense: Odense University Press), pp.173–88.

Miller, D. (1995) 'Citizenship and Pluralism,' *Political Studies*, Vol.43, No.3, pp.432–50.

Morgan, K.O. (1982) *Rebirth of a Nation: Wales 1880–1980* (Oxford: Clarendon Press).

Nairn, T. (1993) 'Internationalism and the Second Coming,' *Dædalus*, Vol.122, No.3, pp.154–70.

Osmond, J. (1988) *The Divided Kingdom* (London: Constable).

Osmond, J. (1989) 'Walker's Welsh Tales', *New Statesman and Society*, p.13.

Osmond, J. (1992) *The Democratic Challenge: Changing Wales* (Llandysul: Gwasg Gomer).

Osmond, J. (1995) *Welsh Europeans* (Bridgend: Seren).

Palmer, H.R.D. (1995a) Inspection of Fleur-de-lis Primary School, Blackwood Gwent, OHMCI.

Palmer, H.R.D. (1995b) Inspection of Trenant Infant School, Crumlim Gwent, OHMCI.

Parry, B. (1995) 'Some Good Vibrations from the Beach Boyo', *The Daily Telegraph* (London), p.38.

Phillips, A. (1988) 'Welsh Nationalists', *Maclean's.*, Vol.101, pp.50–52.

Pirsig, R.M. (1992) *Lila: An Inquiry into Morals* (London: Black Swan).

Plato (1935) *The Republic* (London: J.M. Dent & Sons).

Prime Minister (1993) Permanent Under Secretary of State, Welsh Office, 10 Downing Street.

Randall, P.J. (1972) 'Wales in the Structure of Central Government', *Public Administration*, Vol.50 (Autumn), pp.353–72.

Raybould, W.H. (1995) Inspection Report under Section 9 of Education (Schools) Act 1992 on Ysgol Gyfun Gwynllyw.

Richardson, J. (1994) 'Doing Less by Doing More: British Government 1979–1993,' *West European Politics*, Vol.17, No.3, pp.178–97.

Rolands, E. (1972) 'The Politics of Regional Administration: The Establishment of the Welsh Office,' *Public Administration*, Vol.50 (Autumn), pp.333–51.

Sharpe, L.J. (1993) 'The European Meso: An Appraisal', in L.J. Sharpe, *The Rise of Meso Government in Europe* (London: Sage), pp.1–39.

Smith, I. (1991) 'Wisdom of the Welsh Rubs Off', *The Times* (London).

Smith, I. (1992) 'Welsh Pupils Find Their Longue', *The Times* (London).

Spivey, N. (1993) 'A Totem of the Celtic Fringe', *Financial Times* (London: Books) p.xv.

Stover, G., E. Bowen, *et al.* (1994) 'Rhif 1,' *Y Monitor Cymraeg.*, Vol.7, pp.1–2.

Thomas, A. (1994) 'The Myth of Consensus: The Local Government Review in Wales,' *Contemporary Wales*, Vol.7, pp.47–60.

Thomas, D. (1991) 'The Constitution of Wales', in B. Crick, *National Identities: The Constitution of the United Kingdom* (Oxford: Blackwell).

Thomas, D. (1994) 'Wales in 1991: An Economic Survey', *Contemporary Wales*, Vol.6, pp.137–207.

Urwin, D. (1982) 'Territorial Structures and Political Developments in the United Kingdom', in S. Rokkan and D. Urwin, *The Politics of Territorial Identity: Studies in European Regionalism* (London: Sage), pp.19–73.

Wastell, D. (1994) 'Long-playing Welsh Record', *Sunday Telegraph*. London, p.12.

Welsh Affairs Committee (1981) Broadcasting in the Welsh language and the Implications for Welsh and Non-Welsh Speaking Viewers and Listeners: Report, Session 1979–80, House of Commons.

Williams, C.H. (1996) Designer Ethnicity: A View from Wales, ASEN.

Williams, G. (1994) 'Discourses on "Nation" and "Race": A Response to Denney *et al.*,' *Contemporary Wales*, Vol.6, pp.87–103.

Williams, G.A. (1981) 'Mother Wales, Get Off Me Back', *Marxism Today*, Vol.25, pp.14–20.

Williams, R. and T. Lawrence (1992) 'Nationalist Pulse Beats Stronger in Welsh Hearts', *The Independent* (London), p.7.
Wilson, B.J.M. (1996) Letter from Head of Personnel Management Division, Welsh Office.
Wood, J. (1981) 'Secession: A Comparative Analytical Framework', *Canadian Journal of Political Science* (March), pp.107–34.
Woodward, T.J. (1994) Inspection of Trevethin Comprehensive School, Ponypool, Gwent.

English Regionalism and New Labour

JOHN MAWSON

English regionalism has been described as the 'dog that never barked' (Harvie, 1991). This contribution considers recent developments in the politics and administration of the English regions and the wider implications for the debate surrounding devolution in the UK. It explores the nature of contemporary regionalism in England, identifying the manner in which certain underlying economic, political and administrative developments are leading to new forms of regional governnance. Having charted the emergence of regionalism in the first half of the century, the study focuses in detail on the events surrounding the Labour government's devolution proposals of the 1970s. It highlights how the failure to satisfactorily resolve the English regional question played a significant part in the ultimate failure of the devolution project. It then goes on to explore why the regional issue took on increasing significance in the latter part of the 1980s and how the Conservative government and the opposition parties responded with new policy agendas. The challenges of a new form of regional governance are examined, focusing on the increasingly important role played by local government and the business community. Having explored the features of an emerging regional consensus prior to the 1997 general election, the contribution concludes with an assessment of New Labour's initial response to the English dimension.

While media attention and political argument has focused on Scotland and Wales, this has occurred within fairly familiar well-rehearsed sets of arguments. The position in England, however, remains much less clear or predictable (Bradbury and Mawson, 1997). Failure to correctly address the English regional dimension proved to be the 'Achilles heel' of Labour's previous devolution initiative in 1979. It could again prove problematic in Labour's attempts to reshape UK territorial politics.

THE ORIGINS OF THE ENGLISH REGIONAL DEBATE

It is instructive to reflect that many aspects of the contemporary debate concerning devolution and regionalism in England were present in the latter decades of the nineteenth century and in the years up to the First World War. During this period there were bitter political disputes surrounding the form and structure of the British state related in particular to the issue of Irish

Home Rule and the reform of the House of Lords. The decentralization of government administration was a key issue underlying the establishment of elected County Councils in 1888. The English dimension was taken a stage further when the Labour Party conference of 1918 declared the aim of 'separate statutory legislative assemblies for Scotland, Wales and even England with autonomous administration in matters of local concern' (Labour Party, 1918: 70). However when a Speaker's Conference on devolution (1919–20) addressed parliamentary concerns about 'Home Rule All Round' England was treated as a single unit for devolved government rather than proposing regions within England.

It was during this period that the emerging academic disciplines of sociology and geography began to study the region as a physical, social, cultural and political entity. Moreover some of the founding fathers of the town planning profession, such as Sir Patrick Abercrombie and Raymond Unwin, saw the value of regions as an important focus of planning practice and were to go on to heavily influence the Royal Commission on the Distribution of the Industrial Population and Industry (Royal Commission, 1940) which established the legislative framework for the postwar system of land use planning and regional policy (Hall, 1978).

An important influential figure in the early academic and professional discourse surrounding regionalism was the Scottish intellectual and polymath, Sir Patrick Geddes, who advocated the adoption of regional surveys. One of the driving forces behind his regional interest was hostility to the domination of London in British society. In commenting on contemporary politics Geddes was to observe: 'The movement of politics is no longer a question between Empire and nationalist Home Rule, between Ulster and Irish Free State; it is really between centralized government – and civic regionalism' (quoted in Defries, 1927: 238). Geddes in his postwar series, *The Making of the Future*, commissioned the geographer C.B. Fawcett to write *The Provinces of England: A Study in Some Geographical Aspects of Devolution*; a book-length adaptation of an earlier paper 'The Natural Divisions of England' (Fawcett, 1917). In this study Fawcett made the key connection between the achievement of successful devolution to Scotland and Wales and the need to resolve the issue of regionalism in England. He argued:

> The obvious remedy is the division of England into several provinces each of which should have local self government on a par with Wales or Scotland. Such a division is rendered desirable by the great variety of the problems of government in the different parts of England, and the magnitude of the task of providing for the local government of its thirty-four millions of inhabitants. It is probable that in an English

parliament the congestion of business would soon resemble that which has been for many years the normal state of the British Parliament. Hence when the question of the devolution of parliamentary powers again becomes urgent, that of the subdivision of England will naturally arise (Fawcett, 1917: 124–5).

Fawcett did not see the English regions as the building blocks for a federal system but rather as playing an administrative role in receipt of functions devolved by Parliament. After the end of the First World War debates surrounding territorial politics died down and the next half century was marked by a broad constitutional consensus extending across the political spectrum surrounding these matters. Regionalism was kept alive by a small band of political advocates, academics and professionals particularly those engaged in the emergent town planning profession.

ENGLISH REGIONALISM 1945–79

Regionalism was to resurface as the political and institutional certainties of the postwar welfare state began to break down in the 1960s and 1970s. As part of the Wilson government's experiment with French style national indicative planning, Regional Economic Planning Councils were established in 1964 to prepare regional strategies linking economic and physical planning. The centralization of power started to become an issue again in the late 1960s following the growth of nationalism in Scotland and Wales. In 1968 Edward Heath committed a future Conservative government to an elected Scottish Assembly. The Labour government responded by establishing a Royal Commission on the Constitution 'to examine the present functions of the central legislature and government in relation to the several countries, nations and regions of the United Kingdom' (Royal Commission, 1940). It reported in October 1973 and became known as the Kilbrandon Report.

The Commission attributed the resurgence of interest in decentralization to dissatisfaction with the remoteness and unresponsiveness of 'London based' government to the needs of the more distant parts of the UK as well as a growing sense of national identify in Scotland and Wales. The commission noted that there was a general demand from people in England 'to win back power from London' (paras 1–7). In its conclusion the Kilbrandon Commission rejected a federal solution or separatism for Scotland and Wales. It recommended devolution – 'a delegation of central government powers which would leave overriding control in the hands of Parliament' Kilbrandon 1973: para.543) – and included four alternate schemes each supported by different groupings of Members of the

Commission. The minority submission by Lord Crowther-Hunt and Professor Peacock focused particularly on regional government. The Kilbrandon Report was not debated in Parliament but in September 1974 (shortly before the second general election of that year) the government announced its intention to set up elected Assemblies for Scotland and Wales.

Labour's election manifesto of that year committed the party to the establishment of elected regional authorities in England as a counter to the devolution proposals for Scotland and Wales. But once in office while pressing ahead with its home rule proposals for Scotland and Wales in the form of a draft bill it chose to issue a consultation Green Paper for England Devolution: 'The English Dimension', since 'consultation undertaken in the Summer of 1974 showed not only much greater desire for change in Scotland and Wales than England but also a clearer view as to what form it should take' (HMG, 1976: para.3).

The Green Paper emphasized a key problem which had been regularly raised by the Labour MP for West Lothian, Tam Dalyell, in parliamentary debates, namely the question as to whether Scottish MPs should have the right to vote on English legislation in subject areas which were devolved to Scotland, especially if Scotland were to continue to have the same number of MPs at Westminster. The consultation paper concluded with various ways in which the double representation problem could be addressed. It rejected the notion of an English assembly or assemblies with legislative powers since it would amount to a form of federalism and an unbalanced one in which one partner would have 85 per cent of the regulation and resources. Instead it plumped for a series of regional assemblies with legislative powers overseeing a range of strategic functions. Failure, however, to satisfactorily resolve the matter and in particular provide an economic and political counterweight to the perceived advantageous position of Scotland (at a minimum, a development agency for the North) was to lead to problems in the passage of the devolution legislation. English MPs, particularly from northern constituencies, were in due course to show their dissatisfaction by supporting legislative amendments which they felt would reduce the prospects for a home rule vote.

After an abortive attempt to secure the passage of a single Scotland and Wales Bill, the legislation was withdrawn in June 1977 and Labour then turned for support to the Liberals. Under the so-called Lib–Lab pact, a second attempt was made to legislate for devolution in two separate bills in the 1977–78 Parliamentary session. However, the bills were subject to amendments which required referenda before the legislation could be brought into effect. A further amendment introduced by Labour backbencher George Cunningham, and supported by a substantial group of backbenchers against government wishes, made the referenda in Scotland and Wales subject to a 40 per cent rule. Unless 40 per cent of the electorate voted in favour, the acts could be repealed. In the event, in Scotland a majority were in favour but this only amounted to 32.9 per cent of the electorate while in Wales a mere 20.2 per cent of votes cast favoured devolution – some 11.9 per cent of the electorate. A matter of weeks later, on 28 March 1979, a motion of 'no confidence' in the Labour government was carried with the support of the SNP who had been backing the government prior to the referendum. Certainly failure to satisfactorily address the English regional question had been one significant element in the failure of the devolution measures and in turn the collapse of the government.

At this juncture it is evident that there was little political or policy rationale within England to support the case for some form of regional government that would have been sufficiently strong to over-ride the objections of prominent national Labour Party figures, opponents of regionalism in local government or the apathy of the general public.

FORCES FOR CHANGE IN THE ENGLISH REGIONS AND THE CONSERVATIVE RESPONSE

During the course of the 1980s Conservative governments dismantled the remaining elements of Labour's regional machinery and adopted a strong 'pro Union' 'status quo' position in regard to the constitution. It was nevertheless in this period that new pressures emerged which were to lead to the re-emergence of the regional agenda in England (Mawson, 1996). The fragmentation of the public realm arising from privatization, the establishment of arm's-length agencies and the marketization of public services, when taken together with a limited and poorly coordinated presence of government departments, highlighted the need to improve management at the regional level. The business support structure and institutional capacity for handling regional development and inward investment was widely seen as inadequate in comparison with that of other EU countries and Scotland, Wales and Northern Ireland. Moreover the need for civil servants to manage the implementation of European Structural Fund programmes at regional level and prepare regional strategies to access European funding resulted in pressures from the Treasury. Added to these administrative and policy considerations there were those outside government circles who expressed political concerns about the accountability and openness of government agencies and quangos at the regional level.

There were, moreover, fundamental changes in the policy context within which regional activities were taking place. The dismantling of traditional regional economic policy reflected the evening out of inter-regional unemployment disparities (albeit at a higher absolute level than prevailing in the previous three decades) and the increasingly diverse, complex and unpredictable nature of spatial economic change often with greater variations within than between regions. Given the powerful forces of economic restructuring unleashed by the single European market and the increasingly interdependent nature of the international economy commentators argued, there was a need for policy interaction at several scales from international down to local (Albrechts *et al.*, 1989). Within this new context the region was seen by many influential policy makers as playing a critical pivotal coordinating role as expressed in the many debates surrounding the 'Europe of the Regions'. To facilitate this new role the view was that there was a need to devolve powers downwards from national government in order that policies could be shaped to local circumstances. The task of the region was to provide direction and coordination to the wide range of institutions and agencies established to facilitate economic, social and physical development. The marshalling of resources both human, financial and institutional was to be accomplished by facilitating networks and partnerships within and between public and private sectors. In this process the aim was to devolve responsibility downwards in applying principles of subsidiarity and negotiating an efficient division of labour in terms of the roles and responsibilities of different organizations. Regions which succeeded in developing their institutional capacity were seen as the ones best capable of responding to the opportunities and threats of the modern economy.

It was against the background of these pressures that in April 1994 the Conservative government launched its new network of ten integrated regional offices in the English regions. Regional civil servants in the Training, Enterprise and Employment Division (TEED) of the Department of Employment (DE) and the Departments of Environment (DoE), Transport (DT) and Industry (DTI) were made accountable to one Regional Director (RD). Subsequently in 1995 the DE was merged with the Department of Education, adding a further significant dimension to the work of Government Offices. Reporting to the relevant Secretaries of State, the RDs were made responsible for all staff and expenditure routed through their offices and for ensuring that the necessary coordination and links were established between main programmes and other public monies.

Early successes of the GORs included the introduction of the Single Regeneration Budget and Challenge Fund, securing greater integration of the management of European funding and TECs, Business Links and Careers Service contracting; and the establishment of the network of Business Links, introducing a regional dimension to the competitiveness

White Paper, and facilitating local and regional partnerships to secure policy development and implementation (Mawson and Spencer, 1997). However, there was a reluctance by Ministers to allow the GORs to engage in any form of open forum debate with the key regional players on the development of various regional strategic priorities. The Regional Directors became subject to criticism that they were powerful unaccountable bureaucrats who were in a position to pick and choose regional opinions and play off one group of regional actors against another in the exercise of their policy discretion. However, in his speech on regionalism in 1995, David Curry, the then Conservative Minister of Local Government, argued that the GORs' encouragement of regional joint working on issues such as Europe and Regional Planning Guidance had fostered the development of successful regional partnerships. This form of regional governance between central and local government and other partners worked well, he argued, and therefore he saw no need to establish formal political structures to replace them (Curry, 1995).

Meanwhile the Labour Party's agenda for the English regions had gone full circle, and it is important to understand the reasons for this return to regionalism.

LABOUR'S LONG MARCH TO REGIONALISM

Following the unsuccessful outcome of the devolution referenda, the Labour Party's commitments were watered down in the 1979 Election Manifesto with withdrawal of support for a Welsh Assembly and no mention of regional devolution in England. The election of the Conservative government in 1979 effectively killed off devolution as an immediate political issue. The lack of interest shown by the general public and the absence of any great enthusiasm for English regionalism among key constituents within the Labour Party, *viz* local government, the trades unions and regional representatives, added to the devolution débâcle and put the issue on the back burner for a decade. Despite the campaigning efforts of the shadow Regional Affairs Spokesperson John Prescott who issued in 1983 a detailed economic and political case for elected regional authorities and development agencies in the Alternative Regional Strategy (Miller and Mawson, 1986; Labour, 1982), the English dimension did not figure in the 1983 Manifesto and only received a commitment to consultation on regional structures in 1987. Even the federalist Liberal Party which had strongly advocated elected English regional government in the 1970s recognized political realities and retreated in the 1983 and 1987 elections to taking action in England 'as the need and demand is established' (1987). In the case of the Conservative Party the 1970s flirtation with devolution and regionalism under Edward Heath was firmly squashed by the strongly unionist Mrs Thatcher.

However Scottish antipathy to the Thatcherite policy agenda was expressed in the outcome of the 1987 General Election and undoubtedly reflected a widespread resentment that for over a decade policies had been imposed on Scotland which had been rejected by a large majority of the electorate. Labour Party activists in Scotland felt more frustrated than ever that overwhelming support in Scotland had no impact in Westminster and many who had been hostile or lukewarm now became active supporters. There were of course dangers in this situation for an emasculated Labour majority in Scotland, and the facts of life were brought home in the Govan by-election of November 1988 when Jim Sillars won a former Labour stronghold for the SNP. These political events together with various other underlying pressures highlighted above brought devolution and regionalism back to the fore. Brian Gould, shadow Environment Spokesman, signalled this new phase in a speech in Manchester in May 1990 when he claimed 'this new commitment by Labour to regional devolution is an important moment in British politics' (Gould, 1990). In 1991 the Labour Party published a consultation paper 'Devolution and Democracy' (Labour Party, 1991) which highlighted the issues in more detail, particularly the democratic deficit at the regional level, the need for a more effective and accountable regional structure to access European funding and to facilitate economic development. Based on earlier party documents it suggested a phased approach to elected regional government in which the move from unelected regional structures would be based on the widest consensus possible. The 1992 Manifesto drew on the Prescott report emphasizing the key role of regional development agencies and resurrected elected assemblies for the English regions but without a firm commitment in the first term of a Labour government.

The other two major parties also responded to the revival of the regional agenda in their Manifestos but with the Conservatives launching an attack on the destabilizing effect of the devolution proposals on the Union. However the party recognized the validity of a number of the emerging arguments concerning the weakness of the regional administrative structure in the English regions and so their Manifesto also stated:

> We will strengthen the machinery for coordination in the regions. New, integrated regional offices of the appropriate Whitehall departments will be established so that business and local government will have only one port of call (Conservative Party, 1992: 39).

Thus the Conservative solution was to be one of administrative decentralization as expressed in the launching of the ten Government Offices for the Regions (GORs) in April 1994.

Meanwhile the Labour opposition had embarked upon a wide-ranging consultation exercise in the run-up to the production of the party's local government policy document, 'Rebuilding Democracy, Rebuilding Communities' (Labour Party, 1995) under shadow Environment Spokesman Jack Straw. Initially the proposals for regional devolution were to be prepared alongside the party's local government policies. However the tensions present in resolving the relationship between the regional and local tiers was such, particularly against the background of the complex and varied outcome of Local Government reorganization, that the brief was split when Jack Straw became shadow Home Secretary in the Spring of 1994. The apparent uncertainties in Labour policy were seized upon by the Conservatives when John Major launched his attack on the devolution proposals as 'teenage madness' and 'one of the most dangerous propositions ever put before the British nation' (Major, 5.1.95). The ferocity of the attack drew media attention, and for the first time in many years the English regional dimension began to be considered as a significant political issue.

THE PHOENIX RISES? THE EMERGING VIEWS WITHIN NEW LABOUR

Labour responded swiftly to the Conservative attack: an immediate media rejoinder which was followed by the launching of a consultation process. A Labour spokesman commented to the press that John Major's pitch for the English nationalist vote had helped the opposition by highlighting the issue at an early stage, thus giving time to formulate policy (Castle, 1995). The skeletal framework of a new strategy which Straw and his team had been working on was presented to a meeting of the Parliamentary Party early in February and was revealed in an interview on BBC 1's *On the Record* programme. Labour's sensitivity to the accusation that regional government would create more bureaucracy was highlighted in Straw's statement: 'One thing we are clear about in England – you cannot establish regional assemblies as well as having shire counties and districts underneath them' (Straw, 12.2.95). This position was reiterated in a speech by the leader of the opposition in St Helens when he argued that the Local Government Commission had reduced only eight of the 39 shire county areas to anything like single district authorities, it meant that the task for elected assemblies was now 'longer than had been anticipated' (Blair, 10.2.95). In a clearly orchestrated campaign 'party sources' were quoted as saying that the need to subject local government to a further reorganization and consult widely before elected assemblies were created, made the establishment of elected regional bodies ahead of a second election highly unlikely because shire counties could not generally co-exist with a system of elected regional assemblies since it was argued that in the field of land use planning, transport, economic development and European aid (all of which would be key functions of the regions), there would be considerable overlap with the activities of the County Councils. Nevertheless, the requirement for a two-tier system: 'was not set in stone. We accept that in some very sparsely populated counties there may be exceptions to the general rules of unitary local government (Straw, 1995)'.

The Labour Party consultation document, 'A Choice for England' published in June 1995 argued the case for making the GORs, quangos and other agencies more open and accountable to the regions and their local authorities. The emergence and development of local authority joint working at the regional level was seen as the basis for a more accountable and democratic regional structure. In September 1995, Jack Straw set out the thinking which underlay the proposals in a speech to the Regional Studies Association (Straw, 1995). Straw suggested that two apparently conflicting trends had to be taken account of:

> On the one hand there is a patent need all over England to make the existing system of regional government more responsive and accountable to people in each region and to do so swiftly. On the other hand, it is a simple fact of life, that the support for directly elected assemblies varies across the country... So the question is how to secure change which allows those regions with strong support for elected assemblies to move ahead at their pace and not at the pace of the slowest.

The solution proposed was a two-staged process with the creation of indirectly elected regional chambers made up of a relatively small number of nominated councillors (40 was suggested) in the first phase. Nominations would come from an electoral college based on formula reflecting a geographical and political balance. The chambers would co-opt other regional partners (CBI, Chambers of Commerce, TUC, voluntary organizations) to key policy committees and regional development organizations. 'A Choice for England' stated that the assemblies would not have tax raising or legislative powers but consideration would be given to transferring certain functions held by the GORs and quangos, or at least sharing responsibility with the GORs. They would have the responsibility for establishing the elected regional authorities.

As to the timescale, Straw stated that it would vary from region and would be dependent on three safeguards:

- the plan for the chamber should be drawn up by democratic representatives in the region;

• Parliamentary approval; and

• popular consent tested through a referendum.

In June 1996 the Labour Party launched the second key component of its proposals for the English regions in the form of the Report of the Regional Policy Commission (Regional Policy Commission, 1996). The Commission had been established some 12 months earlier under the Chairmanship of the former EU Regional Policy Commissioner, Bruce Millan, at the instigation of Labour's Deputy Leader John Prescott. Working under the framework of the proposals contained in 'The Choice for England' the report was designed to develop regional economic policies which would complement the emerging proposals for regional political structures. Central to the Commission's thinking was the establishment of a regional development agency for each region under the remit of the relevant Chamber or Assembly. This mirrored earlier Labour Party thinking in the Alternative Regional Strategy (Labour Party, 1982) and Labour's 1994 policy statement 'Winning for Britain' (Labour Party, 1994) which acknowledged the valuable practical experience of local authority controlled enterprise boards or companies as one model for the proposed regional development agencies (RDAs). The support of senior Labour Party figures meant that it was likely to be taken seriously in providing the framework for future policy development. Indeed, the wider significance of these developments was highlighted in a press leak in May 1996 which suggested that the Labour leader was seeking to avoid a rebellion of English MPs against the Scottish devolution proposals by supporting the immediate implementation of the proposals for the RDAs (Condon, 1996). Labour Party sources were quoted as saying that the promise of the speedy introduction of RDAs would be sufficient to persuade the 40-strong northern group of MPs, second only to the Scottish MPs within the Parliamentary party, to drop its plan to disrupt the devolution legislation in protest at the lack of the immediate establishment of elected assemblies in England.

To some observers the package offering the establishment of chambers throughout England and the prospect of moving to elected assemblies in a second term was a pragmatic response to the political reality of varying enthusiasm for regionalism and the need to avoid more costly local government reorganization. It further had the advantage of 'going with the grain' of developments in regional governance and was a comparatively low-cost solution.

The promise of early legislation to establish the RDAs was seen as securing the passage of devolution legislation by securing the support of the powerful North East block of Labour MPs as well as others from the North of England. Moreover it could be argued that those regions which took early steps to establish elected assemblies would set in train a 'domino effect' with other regions following quickly behind, not wishing to lose comparative advantage. The Straw staged approach was therefore interpreted as a robust strategy fitting in with the short-term 'low cost' priorities of New Labour, addressing immediate political pressures arising from devolution, while at the same time providing the scope for a more ambitious form of English regionalism in the longer term.

However for those wishing to see more fundamental constitutional change, the Straw approach was viewed with suspicion. The so-called 'triple safeguards' in this interpretation were there simply to ensure that major reform remained a distant and unlikely prospect. As the Constitution Unit (1996) argued, the chambers in anything other than a short time-frame might well find difficulties in exercising influence within Whitehall and could quickly lose authority within their regions if it were seen that the chambers commanded few real powers, resources and political clout. They could well serve a useful purpose as a transitionary vehicle but probably would have much less utility as a permanent feature. In relation to this latter scenario it is interesting to note that John Rentoul's recently published biography of Tony Blair commented: 'Blair does not expect (English) devolution to go beyond regional development agencies and joint boards of local councillors to oversee them' (Rentoul, 1996).

THE REGIONAL STAKEHOLDERS

As the views of the political parties on the need for a new regional agenda became increasingly focused, so other key actors with a stake in the regional scene also began to recognize the force of the arguments for change. During the course of 1994 and 1995 a number of these issues were aired during the House of Commons Trade and Industry Committee review of regional policy under the chairmanship of the Labour regional spokesman, Dick Caborne. The Association of British Chambers of Commerce argued in evidence to the Select Committee 1995, that a stronger regional voice was needed if Britain's views on regions were to be properly represented in Europe and that this could be best accomplished by a regional forum which also provided an advisory and co-ordinating remit in economic development (Trade and Industry Select Committee, 1995: para.138). Concerns about regional coordination and the transparency and accountability of government were also raised by the CBI. Reflecting these feelings the CBI decided to launch a regional Business Agenda initiative involving a survey of members in England and Wales covering their attitude to the Government Offices and regional issues. In announcing the initiative, Howard Davies said that 'there was a growing consensus that a regional focus for decision making across the public sector needed to be created which allowed input from the business community' (Davies, 1995).

The CBI's report 'Regions for Business' published in the run-up to the 1997 election confirmed the growing consensus surrounding a new form of regional governance involving the establishment of formal regional partnerships based on all the main public and private sector organizations (CBI, 1997). It argued that there was a need for better resourcing of these nascent partnerships which had sprung up in most regions and had the potential to guide policy making by establishing regional priorities for action as well as advising the GORs on land use and transport issues, EU and SRB funding. It was felt that they could also achieve greater coordination of the work of agencies such as English Partnerships and the Highways Agency as well as inward investment and business support services. Similar proposals were set out by the British Chambers of Commerce in its Regional Policy Brief which advocated the establishment of regional strategic form based on 'regional partnerships' comprising the key stakeholders: trade unions, Chambers of Commerce, CBI, TECs, local authorities and educational bodies (BCC, 1997). The TEC National Council also supported this approach in its Regional Development Principles Paper which advocated the establishment of nominated Regional Chambers comprising a similar group of stakeholders who would develop regional priorities with the GOR and set the framework for a Regional Development Agency (TEC National Council, 1997).

It was not just the business community however, which was to recognize and respond to the new regional agenda. Regional issues have always been a key matter of concern for local government in relation to issues such as transport, planning, environmental issues, regeneration, economic development and European funding. Over the years the need to engage in policy development, advocacy and implement various strategic initiatives at this geographical scale has necessitated the creation of regional joint machinery though much of this type of work has been undertaken through the County Councils. Perhaps the best known examples of local authority joint working are the so-called 'standing conferences' of regional local authority associations which have their origins in the early post-war attempts to disperse population and industry from the congested cities. The activity survived in some regions and this continuity of experience in the South East, West Midlands and North East. was matched elsewhere by a revival of joint working during the latter part of the 1980s in response to the need to provide Regional Planning Guidance for central government. Their work was extended into other activities such as economic development and the preparation of European strategies.

With the restoration of a comprehensive geographical coverage of regional working by the early 1990s, and an increasing recognition of the need to articulate local authority interests at the regional level, a decision was taken to establish an English Regional Association (ERA) in 1993. A survey of these regional local authority associations showed that the composition of the nine associations encompassed all the local authorities in England (bar three councils) including Counties Districts, Metropolitan Districts and London Boroughs (English Regional Associations, 1995). The prospect of an election within a comparatively short time-frame which held up the possibility of a change in government, and in turn the emergence of a new regional structure based on the building blocks of local authority regional organization, was undoubtedly a major factor behind the various reviews of ERA roles and constitutions which began to take place. Further pressures leading in the same direction were the strengthened presence of central government in the regions as represented in the work of the GORs and the establishment of a single Local Government Association in April 1997 with an electoral college organized on a regional basis. Irrespective of the outcome of the general election it was recognized that for all the reasons listed above and others, local government would need to speak with a more powerful single voice at the regional level.

THE MISSED OPPORTUNITY?

It is clear from the developments described above that at the time Labour took office there had emerged a degree of consensus as to the way forward in the regions. Labour moved swiftly to establish a new Department of the Environment, Transport and the Regions under the Deputy Prime Minister. A bill to establish Regional Development Agencies was announced in the Queen's speech. However there were no direct references to taking forward the 'Straw component' of the package. This came as a surprise to many in the regions, given the level of consensus which had been building up in the run-up to the election across sectors and among the various regional stakeholders as to the need for regional governance if not government.

In a number of regions steps had been taken to establish regional chambers and/or regional partnerships, and in others plans were well advanced in anticipation of the staged approach. It is not entirely clear why this decision was taken. Perhaps it reflected the sheer volume of legislation for the first session and/or continuing uncertainties as to the extent which was necessary to set in train a process towards more formal regional government. Whatever the reason it was to become a significant issue in the consultation exercise on the RDA proposals which was launched by the Minister of the Regions in June 1997 (DOE, 1997a).

The issues paper indicated that for each region there would be single RDA based on existing GOR boundaries and that

> the functions to be given to the agencies would include promoting inward investment, helping small businesses and coordinating regional economic development (DOE, 1997b).

Those responding to the paper were invited to consider some 20 economic development functions or remits in which it was suggested that the RDAs might legitimately become involved. The RDAs were to rationalize and reduce the duplication of effort among the various agencies and institutions engaged in economic development.

The government indicated that it did not wish to impose a blueprint from Whitehall. The bill would not specify a single prescriptive model but rather allow each region to have arrangements which fitted its own circumstances building on the work of existing organizations. As to their accountability, in the short term it was intended that the boards of the RDAs would be formally appointed and be accountable through ministers to Parliament. In making appointments, the Secretary of State ' will wish to be guided by the wishes of the regions'. The consultation paper talked of small boards of eight to ten directors, private-sector led, but with a reasonable balance of regional stakeholder interests. To the extent that they were financed through government spending from existing public expenditure programmes the normal arrangements for accountability to Parliament would apply and there would be no new public monies forthcoming.

The consultation paper indicated that the bill would specify the mechanisms by which the relationship between the RDAs and government (including the Government Offices for the Regions) would be overseen in regard to public accountability. Ministers wanted the RDAs to be fully responsive to the needs of their region and the paper suggested that the government would 'support the establishment of non-statutory regional chambers possibly formed by local authorities acting in partnership with regional business interests as a step towards these objectives'.

The regions were given a matter of weeks from June to early September to respond to the consultation paper. A focus of much concern was the extent to which the RDAs would be accountable to the full range of regional interests given the government's stated preference for a small board which would be private sector led. This concern was compounded by the lukewarm attitude displayed by central government towards a formal statutory regional partnership or chamber which many wished to see establish regional priorities both for the GORs and the RDAs. Not surprisingly therefore in the consultation response there was a generally expressed desire, particularly from the local authority side, for large boards alongside requests for the establishment of formal regional chambers to which the RDAs would be made accountable.

In terms of the range of RDA functions: inward investment, regional selective assistance, coordination of business support services including Business Links, European and UK technology programmes and the powers and functions of English Partnerships were widely seen as obvious activities for the RDAs albeit that implementation might be undertaken through subcontracting. Influence over the strategic priorities of the Single Regeneration Budget, European funding and other relevant public programmes such as transport and planning were regarded as important roles for the RDAs but with the caveat that such priorities should be determined ultimately through democratically accountable structures. As far as the modus operandi of the RDAs was concerned most saw them as fulfilling a limited number of functions directly, such as inward investment, but that much of their work would be concerned with that of strategic coordination and subcontracting. Another dimension of the enabling/facilitating role of the RDAs was seen as that of the encouragement and allocation of funding to subregional and local partnerships.

It could be argued that Labour's wish to establish RDAs (particularly in order to ensure support in the House of Commons to carry its devolution measures) seriously underestimated the momentum behind a more open and accountable approach to the management of the English regions. In terms of regional democracy the RDA initiative could be interpreted as putting the 'cart before the horse'. Moreover the proposal to transfer a significant range of government functions and programmes to the RDAs, particularly without the necessary organizational capacity, always seemed likely to incur the wrath of other Whitehall departments and their Ministers (Hetherington, 1997). Reports in the press that DTI and DFEE ministers were resisting the RDA proposals during the Summer of 1997 support such a contention (Wighton and Kamptner, 1997).

Surprisingly the consultation paper only briefly referred to the role of the GORs and then only as a mechanism to ensure scrutiny and accountability for the public funds transferred to the RDAs. It failed to acknowledge the progress made by the GORs in their first three years in developing more coherent and integrated policies and establishing close links with the other regional stakeholders. Indeed for those concerned with pursuing a radical social agenda at the regional level the scope for mobilizing the full potential of public policy programmes and expenditure through the GORs is considerable. One is tempted to consider whether it would have been more productive for the consultation paper to have devoted greater attention to the activities of the GORs and how their work could have been made more open

and accountable at the regional level. In this respect Labour's first foray into
the English regions may turn out to have been a missed opportunity.

REFERENCES

Albrechts, L., *et al.* (eds) (1989) *Regional Policy at the Crossroads: European Perspectives* (London: Jessica Kingsley).
Blair, A. (1995) quoted in *The Independent*, 14 February.
Bradbury, J. and J. Mawson (eds) (1997) *British Regionalism and Devolution. The Challenges of State Reform and European Integration* (London: Jessica Kingsley).
British Chambers of Commerce (1997) *Regional Policy – BCC Policy Brief.* (London).
Castle, S. (1995) 'Labour Treads Softly on Devolution' in *The Independent on Sunday* 12 February.
Condon, T. (1996) 'Blair Buys Off Home Rule Rebels', *Scotland on Sunday.*
Confederation of British Industry (1997) *Regions for Business: Improving Policy Design and Delivery.*
Conservative Party (1992) *Manifesto 1992: The Best Future for Britain* (London: Conservative Council Central Office) p39.
Constitution Unit (1996) *Regional Government in England: Regional Chambers and Regional Development Agencies* (London).
Curry, D. (1995) 'Regionalism: The Government's Perspective'. Paper delivered at the Association of Metropolitan Authorities/Birmingham University Conference, Westminster Hall. Regionalism: The Local Government Dimension, London, 20 March.
Davies, H. (1995) 'Regional Government', Paper delivered at regional newspaper editor's annual lunch. Newcastle, 6 January.
Defries, A. (1927) *The Interpreter Geddes: The Man and His Gospel.* (London: Routledge).
Department of Environment (1997) 'Regions Invited to Have Their Say?' *DOE News Release* 214, 11 June 1997.
Department of Environment (1997(6)) *Regional Development Agencies. Issues for Discussion* (London).
English Regional Associations (1995) *A Survey of the English Regional Associations.* (London).
Fawcett, C.B. (1917) 'Natural Divisions of England', *The Geographical Journal*, February, pp.124–5.
Gould, B. (1990) 'Power to the Regions Will Be the Lasting Legacy of the Next Labour Government', Centre for Local Economic Strategies, Spring lecture. John Rylands Library, Manchester 24 May.
Hall, P., *et al.* (1978) *The Containment of Urban England*, 2 vols. (London: PEP/Allen and Unwin).
Harvie, C. (1991) 'English Regionalism: The Dog That Never Barked' in B. Crick (ed.) 'National Identities. The Constitution of the United Kingdom', *The Political Quarterly* (Blackwell).
Hetherington, P. (1997) 'Whitehall Rearguard Action to Keep England a United Kingdom', *The Observer.* 7 September 1997.
HMG (1976) *Devolution: The English Dimension* (HMSO).
House of Commons, Trade and Industry Select Committee (1995) Fourth Report. Regional Policy. Session 1994–95 (London: HMSO).
Labour Party (1918) Report of the Labour Party Conference (London).
Labour Party (Parliamentary Spokesman's Working Group) (1982) Alternative Regional Strategy: A Framework for Discussion (London).
Labour Party (1991) 'Devolution and Democracy' (London).
Labour Party (1994) 'Winning for Britain' (London).
Labour Party (1995) 'Rebuilding Democracy, Rebuilding Communities' (London).
Labour Party (1995) 'A Choice for England: A Consultation Paper on Labour's Plans for English Regional Government' (London).

Major, J. (1995) quoted in *The Times*, 6 January.

Mawson, J. (1996) 'The Re-emergence of the 'Regional Agenda in the English Regions: New Patterns of Urban and Regional Governance?', *Local Economy*, Vol.10, No.4, 300–326.

Mawson, J. and K. Spencer (1997) 'The Government Offices for the English Regions: Towards Regional Governance?' *Policy and Politics*, Vol.25, No.1, pp.71–84.

Miller, D. and J. Mawson (1986) 'The Alternative Regional Strategy: A New Regional Policy for Labour', Chapter 5.3 in Nolan and Paine.

Regional Policy Commission (1996) *Renewing the Regions. Strategies for Regional Economic Development* (Sheffield: Sheffield Hallam University).

Report of the Royal Commission on the Constitution (1973) (London: HMSO).

Rentoul, J. (1996) *Tony Blair* (London: Warner).

Royal Commission on the Distribution of the Industrial Population (1940) (London: HMSO).

Straw, J. (1995) Labour and the Regions of England. The Regional Studies Association Guest Lecture. Labour Party Press Release. (London: Labour Party. 28 September.

Straw, J. (1995) quoted in the *Daily Telegraph*, 13 February.

TEC National Council (1997) 'Regional Development Principles Paper', Produced by the Economic Development Strategy Group (London).

Trade and Industry Select Committee, 1995.

Wighton, D. and J. Kamptner (1997) 'Beckett Beats Off Prescott over Regions', *Financial Times*. 16 July 1997.

Territorial Debates about Local Government: Or Don't Reorganize – Don't, Don't, Don't!

HOWARD ELCOCK

A SURFEIT OF REORGANIZATION

Issues and debates concerning regional and local government areas have a particular resonance in Britain, because British local government has been wholly or partially reorganized at least six times since 1958, after an abortive attempt to do so was made by the Attlee government in 1948. In this regard, Britain's local government history can be contrasted starkly with those of other West European states, even those which have suffered war and invasion in modern times, or which have been relatively recently united as nation states. Thus, the basic units of French or German local government have their roots in the histories and traditions of the communities of those countries despite wars, revolutions and invasions. By contrast, the history of British local government is one of repeated revisions of boundaries and structures, carried out for reasons which have often paid scant regard to historical community identities or communities of sentiment and interest (Ball and Stobart, 1996).

The Labour Party's plans for the introduction of regional government in England propose that further local government reorganization to create unitary authorities should be carried out before elected regional assemblies are introduced (Labour Party, 1995). However, more recent Labour pronouncements have indicated that the introduction of regional government will not depend on the creation of unitary local authorities throughout the region concerned, as had originally been proposed, but it is expected that such regions would have predominantly unitary local government systems, so the pressure for further reorganization might still be present.

The only European parallels with this orgy of reorganization are to be found in the new democracies in Eastern Europe, where the structures of local and regional government have been repeatedly changed to meet the demands of dominant ideologies and occupying powers. Thus Slovakia's regional and local government structures have been radically reorganized four times since 1923 and further reorganization is in prospect (Malikova and Bucek, 1996). Likewise in Poland, regional and local government structures have been changed several times since the Second World War but rather less drastically than those in Slovakia.

We may first consider the unstable history of British local government over the last 40 years, before looking at the reasons why this spate of reorganizations has been undertaken. In this initial account we shall confine our remarks mainly to England because the saga becomes impossibly complicated if all the events relating to Scotland and Wales are also taken fully into account. For the same reason, Northern Ireland is left entirely out of the reckoning, except to note that its local government was radically altered as part of the introduction of direct rule from London in 1972 (see Elcock, 1994, Ch.2 for more detail.) The principal English reorganizations were as follows:

The Boundary Commission of 1958

The 1958 Boundary Commission was appointed by the Macmillan government. Its members were charged with reorganizing the county boundaries of England in order to create larger counties and remove anomalies such as the county of Rutland – which had a population of 23,000 but enjoyed the same status, functions and powers as Lancashire with a population of over a million. Subsequently, the county councils were charged with carrying out a similar reorganization of the borough and district authorities within their counties. This was an incremental approach which ran into the sands of political opposition. The Commission's proposals for particular counties and county boroughs were repeatedly resisted by local authorities and their communities, with the result that a series of lengthy public enquiries had to be held and in some cases disputes over procedures and boundaries ended up before the Courts (Wednesbury Borough Council v. Minister of Housing and Local Government (1965) 1 Weekly Law Reports 261). In Shropshire, opposition to the abolition of Bishop's Castle Borough Council led the Minister to create a new category of local authority, the rural borough, which 'has no other raison d'etre but tradition' (Richards, 1966: 89). In the end, resistance by MPs and local authorities to the Commission's proposals led an exasperated Richard Crossman to wind up the Commission, of which he said, 'The more I looked at the work the Commission has been doing, the more futile I found their work' (Crossman, 1975: 65). He substituted a Royal Commission on Local Government in England, of which more later.

The Government of Greater London

Crossman's decision to seek comprehensive reorganization through a Royal Commission was encouraged by the success of the Herbert Commission's report on the government of London, whose work in the early 1960s resulted in the London Government Act of 1965, which created the Greater London Council and 32 new London Borough Councils, which took over the government of London from the London County Council and the old metropolitan borough councils in 1968. This was a radical reorganization which was implemented despite vocal opposition, including that of the London Labour Party, which believed that it would not be able to control the new GLC as it had its predecessor, the London County Council for many years – an ironic reason in view of subsequent events.

The Redcliffe-Maud Commission

The achievement of reorganization in London encouraged Crossman to establish a Royal Commission on Local Government in England chaired by Sir John Maud (who became Lord Redcliffe-Maud during the Commission's work), which reported in 1969. It recommended a unitary local government structure for most of England, with two tiers in three large urban conurbations. One member, Derek Senior, wrote a lengthy minority report advocating a two-tier structure throughout the country but both sets of proposals were based on city regions. Also, both the majority of the Commission and Mr Senior recommended the adoption of a regional tier of government in England.

Although its recommendations were substantially changed after the Conservative Party won the 1970 General Election, the Redcliffe–Maud Commission's work did result in a comprehensive reorganization of local government in England and Wales, under the Local Government Act of 1972. This Act established six metropolitan county councils and 47 non-metropolitan or 'shire' counties in England and Wales. Both types of county had district councils within them but the metropolitan districts had much more extensive powers than their non-metropolitan equivalents. This was an asymmetrical structure which was to prove a source of grievance which soon produced pressure for further reorganization because the larger non-metropolitan districts, especially the former county boroughs, persistently pressed for the restoration of their former powers and status. This almost came about through Peter Shore's proposals for 'organic change' in the late 1970s but the proposals were swiftly aborted by Margaret Thatcher when she came to power in May 1979 (Elcock, 1991: Ch.3; 1994: Ch.2).

A similar comprehensive reorganization occurred in Scotland a year later, where a new structure of Regional and District Councils plus three unitary Islands authorities, making a total of 65 new local authorities, was created following the report of the Wheatley Commission in 1972. Among them was Strathclyde Regional Council, the largest local authority in Europe.

Abolishing the GLC

Although pressures for further reorganization surfaced before the 1972 Act had been fully implemented, the structure remained stable until Mrs. Thatcher's Cabinet proposed the abolition of the GLC and the six metropolitan county councils in 1983. Although all but two of these authorities, including the GLC, had been controlled by the Conservatives between 1977 and 1981, after the elections held in the latter year they became major centres of opposition to the government's policies. In consequence, the government proposed their abolition in a 1983 White Paper (DoE, 1983) which provided a thin veil for the removal of political opponents from positions of office. Despite vigorous and widespread opposition, the necessary legislation was ruthlessly driven through Parliament, and the local authorities which governed the seven largest conurbations in England disappeared on 1 April 1986. London then became the only capital city in Europe without a city-wide governing authority (Norton, 1986).

The Banham Commission

Then, in the early 1990s the government appointed a Local Government Commission for England under the chairmanship of Sir John Banham to reorganize English local government yet again. This was a partial reversion to the incremental approach, with members of the Commission reviewing each county in four 'tranches'. The Commission's members were required to take account of local community sentiment but the government and in particular John Selwyn Gummer as Secretary of State for the Environment from July 1993 until May 1997 expressed a strong preference for unitary local authorities on grounds of efficiency. This resulted in a series of increasingly bitter disputes between Mr Gummer and Sir John Banham which culminated in the latter's resignation in March 1994. To cut the Commission's long, still unfinished and rather muddled story short, some of the most unloved counties have been abolished, including the estuarine counties of Cleveland and Humberside which were replaced with unitary authorities. Rutland County Council was restored as a unitary authority. Thus the local government map of England is now becoming more asymmetrical than ever; an untidy map of unitary authorities and two-tier systems as a result of the mixture of the Commission's work and the Secretary of State's modifications thereof (Pycroft, 1995; Leach, 1996a). At the same time, unitary systems were created in Scotland and Wales by the fiat of the relevant Secretaries of State, after processes of public 'consultation' carried out on their behalf. Hence, this time the government pushed through much of what it wanted, in contrast to the fate of many of the 1958 Commission's recommendations.

Contrast all this frenetic activity with France or even Germany, where parts or all of the local government structure date back for centuries and they have adjusted their structures incrementally, for example by merging small communes (Gunlicks, 1986). Furthermore, France, Italy and Spain have all added regional tiers of government to their structures relatively recently, without disturbing the established local authorities at the equivalent of the county and district levels (see Keating, 1988; Keating and Loughlin, 1997).

THE RATIONALES FOR REORGANIZATION

These successive reorganizations have been justified in terms of a number of reasons, many of which might very loosely be described as attempts to establish local government on a more rational footing (see Stacey, 1975). This notion of rationality can be summed up as a belief that reorganizing the structure of local government will produce specific benefits, for instance greater efficiency, economies of scale or closeness to local communities (Leach, 1996a). More specifically, motivations for reorganization have included the following:

1. The need to recognize changing patterns of settlement and the changing relationship between town and country. The problem of urban expansion must be mentioned here too, which is somewhat akin to the 'consolidation' issue in the US(Rusk, 1993). The issue was and is how suburbs and rural areas can be brought to take their share of the costs of dealing with the problems of the inner or downtown cities and supporting the urban services which their residents use but do not support through local taxation because they live close to but outside the city boundary. The increasingly fashionable solution proposed in the 1960s and 1970s was the establishment of 'city-regions' consisting of major towns and cities together with their surrounding hinterlands – the suburban and rural areas whose inhabitants work in the city as well as shopping and spending their leisure time there (Senior, 1966; Redcliffe-Maud, 1969). Despite the urgings of the proponents of city-regions, this issue has been repeatedly ducked by British governments since the early 1960s, when a number of county boroughs' proposals to extend their boundaries were rejected because of suburban opposition (Jones, 1964). Similarly, the boundaries of the metropolitan counties were drawn very tightly around their built-up areas and the same applies to many of the new unitary authorities established in large towns and cities in the mid-1990s. The abolition of many county councils has now considerably reduced the capacity of any local authority to think strategically about such spatial issues because neither the metropolitan

boroughs nor the new unitary authorities are large enough for this purpose.

2. The notion has often been urged that there is an 'ideal' size for a local authority responsible for a given range of services but there is no agreement on what this ideal size should be. The poles of this argument can be summarized as 'Big is Efficient' versus 'Small is Beautiful'. On the one hand it is argued that large authorities can achieve economies of large scale and can employ a wider range of specialist staff. On the other hand, small authorities should be able to maintain close contacts with their citizens. Since most citizens identify with small areas, such as a village, a town, an estate or a street, small local authorities may more nearly reflect community sentiment, although it is widely argued that the areas with which people identify are too small for efficient administration (see Leach, 1996a: 54f)

Although the debate over economies of large scale versus the accessibility of small authorities has raged for many years, the validity of neither proposition has been proven! (see Newton, various). This issue does not seem to arise in the same way in the rest of Europe but it is a factor in US consolidation reforms. Larger size would permit more efficient government but consolidation proposals are usually rejected in the necessary referenda of local citizens, who will not usually accept the absorption of their local government by a larger unit, especially where this larger unit is a downtown city with poverty-stricken populations, high local taxes and Democratic political control (Rusk, 1993; Peters, 1997).

3. British local authorities are very large by general international standards and have got larger as a result of the successive reorganizations described earlier. Thus before 1973 the UK had some 1,400 local authorities, but even then this was only the same number that New York City alone had (Newton, 1969). Under the 1972 Local Government Act the number of local authorities was set at 404 in England, 65 in Scotland and 45 in Wales. This may mean that councils are more remote from their communities, or it may mean that they are more efficient. Increasingly, these large local authorities are being urged to establish sub-units which will allow local people immediate access to services and control over them. Such proposals include:

- Extending parish councils to urban areas – at present they exist in rural counties but not towns and cities, apart from small ones in rural areas.
- Developing forms of political decentralization – creating neighbourhood fora, committees or councils (Burns, Hoggett and Hambleton, 1993; Elcock, 1983).
- Developing departmental or corporate decentralization through the

creation of neighbourhood offices or teams which allow access at the neighbourhood level to the staff of one or more of the council's departments (Hambleton, 1979; Elcock, 1986). This idea has also been proposed by the Local Government Commission for England, which has urged local authorities to establish 'One stop shops' (LGCE, 1993, para.43)

Lastly, many councils have sought to reduce their remoteness from their citizens by developing various forms of consumerism, from cosmetic improvements to consumer surveys (Fenwick, 1995).

THE DANGERS OF REORGANIZATION FROM ABOVE

However, many of these arguments assume that it is possible to impose community government from the top down. This has been the cause of a great deal of controversy. The issue must be raised of whether local government structures should be imposed by Commissions or Ministers, or whether they should only be created or changed as a response to community opinion. Thus, there was a provision under the 1972 Local Government Act for holding local referenda on proposals to create town or parish councils – one such was held in Withernsea, East Yorkshire in the early 1970s and as a result, a town council was established there. The research undertaken for the Local Government Commission has indicated that the concept of community is highly ambiguous and within a single local government area there may be a series of geographical, economic and functional communities, all of which citizens feel a degree of identity with (Ball and Stobart, 1996).

The difficulties involved in imposing local government structures from above can be well illustrated by the sorry tale of the estuarine counties which were created under the 1972 Act but which have now all been abolished – the major achievement, if it is to be regarded as such, of the Banham Commission. The basis for their creation was the argument that estuaries should be regarded as unifying features rather than as dividing lines. Traditionally, estuaries such as the Humber, the Tees or the Severn have been regarded as dividing lines because before the advent of modern transport, the communities on each side of the estuary had few dealings with one another and were often hostile rivals. However, when these estuaries were crossed by bridges or tunnels, the relationships between the communities on the banks of the estuary changed and there was therefore a case for securing the development of the estuary as a coherent unit, rather than treating it as a dividing line.

Humberside County Council: A Case Study

A good example is the estuary of the Humber, which traditionally divided the East Riding of Yorkshire from the Parts of Lindsey in Lincolnshire. However, as part of the creation of a nationwide regional planning structure by the Department of Economic Affairs, in 1965 a Yorkshire and Humberside Regional Economic Planning Council was established by the Department of Economic Affairs, whose area included the whole of the Parts of Lindsey as well as all three Ridings of Yorkshire, in order to secure the coherent development of the Humber Estuary (see Hogwood and Keating, 1982). In early 1966, the then Minister of Transport, Barbara Castle, promised that the long awaited Humber Bridge would at last be built. Although many have alleged that this was a political bribe offered during the vital Hull North by-election campaign, it is now clear that the decision to build the Humber Bridge was related to two national strategic decisions. The first was the decision, taken in the light of the then population projections, to build a New Town of half a million people on North Humberside (see Crossman, 1975). However, shortly afterwards the population projections declined rapidly and the New Town was never built. The second was the perceived need for a third North–South motorway link, from Teesside through North Yorkshire, over the Humber Bridge and then via Lincoln to join the M11 at Cambridge.

A consequence of the decision to build the Humber Bridge was that despite long-standing animosities between the communities on the two banks, interest in the need for coherent physical and economic development of the estuary increased. A Humberside Feasibility Study was carried out by a team of Department of the Environment civil servants which was published in 1969. It recommended the coherent economic development of the estuary, arguing that 'the building of the Humber Bridge would alter radically the whole pattern of economic and social interchange in the sub-region' (p.31, para.4–105). This study also indicated that major urban development would be required in the Humberside area after 1980 as the population continued to grow – however, falling population projections removed the need for this development by the early 1970s. Also in 1969, Derek Senior's lengthy minority Royal Commission report (Redcliffe-Maud, 1969, Vol.2) recommended the establishment of an estuarine county of Humberside. The eventual outcome, after much hesitation, was the creation of Humberside County Council under the 1972 Local Government Act, although the decision to create Humberside was taken late in the process of preparing the bill – it was not included in the first set of proposals for new county councils in England published in 1971; it was introduced in the final bill the following year. In any case, two parishes in the South of the new county were so insistent that they wanted to remain in

Lincolnshire that after an investigation by a junior Environment Minister, one Michael Heseltine, they were excluded from Humberside – a decision which probably enabled the Labour Party to secure marginal control of the new county council at the first elections in April 1973 (Elcock, 1975).

Humberside County Council was thus created because it was believed that it would enable the estuary to be developed coherently, as well as to plan for the changes in movement and settlement patterns which would follow the opening of the Humber Bridge. The new county council attempted to assuage hostile community sentiments by establishing a divisional structure for its major services which respected the traditional local government areas in the county. However, a ham-fisted demand in Autumn 1973 by the Post Office requiring that letters be addressed to North or South Humberside (instead of East Yorkshire or North Lincolnshire) provoked hostile popular reactions which were to lead to Humberside's eventual destruction by the Banham Commission in 1996. A Yorkshire Ridings society, with its origins in Bridlington, led a persistent campaign which finally persuaded Ministers that the county was so unacceptable to community sentiment that it ought to be removed, although it was generally acknowledged that Humberside County Council was efficient and provided high quality services. In March 1989 the then Secretary of State, Nicholas Ridley, ordered the Local Government Boundary Commission to review Humberside with a view to 'dissolving' the county council (*The Times*, 18 March 1989). A year later the Commission recommended Humberside's retention because although the county was not popular, its opponents could not agree on what should replace it (*The Times*, 8 March 1990) but the Commission reversed this recommendation eight months later and recommended Humberside's abolition because it was 'unwanted and unwelcomed' by local people (*The Times*, 29 November 1990). However, Humberside was not without friends. In 1993 the regional council of the Confederation of British Industry recommended retention of the county council (LGCE, 1994, para.47). It had also proved its worth as a strategic planning authority by producing its Structure Plan by December 1976, three and a half years after its creation and more quickly than any other county council in the Yorkshire and Humberside region (Elcock, 1985). However, the Local Government Commission for England came to the same conclusion as the Boundary Commission; that '...the weight of evidence in relation to community identity and interests is against the continued existence of Humberside County and that the strength of feeling generated by people's loyalty to the historic counties of Yorkshire and Lincolnshire must be recognized' (LGCE, 1994, para.45). Ministers were also undoubtedly influenced by the secure control the Labour Party had established in Humberside by the early 1990s. A similar fate was visited upon Cleveland County Council for similar reasons. In the end, Humberside County Council ceased to exist in April 1996. It was replaced by four unitary authorities, and the Humberside concept survives only in the retention of the Humberside County Fire and Police Authority. Structure planning is now to be carried out separately by the unitary authorities on the North and South banks (LGCE, 1994, para.93), so that the concept of planning the estuary as a coherent whole has now been lost sight of. As Steve Leach has put it, 'Avon, Cleveland and Humberside – imaginative responses to the realities of economic and social activity patterns – have gone whilst historic counties with much less coherent identities in this sense are to remain' (1996b: 171). It is perhaps not overly cynical to suggest that reasons of political advantage have underlain this reversion to traditional structures with little regard for changing geographical economic and social realities.

In this context, we should note that the legislation which established the Local Government Commission for England required the Commissioners to draw up the new local authority boundaries to reflect community sentiment. There was undoubtedly an assumption from the start of the Commission's work that hostile community sentiment should lead to the abolition of the unpopular estuarine counties. The Commissioners commissioned extensive market research from MORI in an attempt to ascertain what that sentiment was. On the South Bank of the Humber 39 per cent of the people surveyed by MORI favoured retaining Humberside County Council but only 27 per cent favoured its retention on the North Bank (LGCE, 1994, para.47; Leach, 1996a: 48).

However, such popular sentiment may be invoked only when it is politically convenient to do so. When it ran counter to the Secretary of State's desire for unitary authorities on grounds of their greater efficiency, the Minister sought to override the Commission's attempts to reflect community sentiment by retaining two-tier structures. In many areas popular sentiment supported the existing local authorities and in some but by no means all cases, this has been accepted, albeit reluctantly, by the Secretary of State (Pycroft, 1995). However, in Humberside the unitary solution was adopted in 1996 but this is already giving rise to new problems and hence pressures for further reorganization. The boundaries of the largest city, Kingston upon Hull, were not extended into the surrounding suburbs, because of strong public opposition in the suburbs (LGCE, 1994, para.44) so that its council still faces problems concerning urban expansion, as well as those presented by the limited size and wealth of the community available financially to support its services and meet its needs. York's city boundaries were extended, by contrast, because public opposition to this extension was weaker (ibid). There are already increasing indications that the new unitary authorities in Humberside are too small to support the levels of services which had been provided by the former county council. Also, the strategic capacity of local government to plan the area's development has been significantly reduced.

REORGANIZATION: THE IMPLEMENTATION DEFICIT

We have seen that local government reorganizations have tended to be obstructed or to founder on a series of problems or issues, as well as violations of community sentiment. Among the unresolved issues are these:
    First, threats to the political balance of council areas which have wholly or partly thwarted reorganizations. Suburban and rural local authorities are usually controlled by the Conservative Party and the acceptance of the fringe areas of cities, which tend to contain large numbers of Labour voters especially if overspill estates have been built on the city's peripheries, may well endanger the security of the Conservatives' control of the suburban local authorities. It may also result in the levying of higher local taxes to pay for the services needed in the cities areas. Equally, Labour MPs have on several occasions resisted the absorption of Conservative suburbs into city boundaries because Parliamentary redistribution resulting from the new local authority boundaries might endanger their seats. The 1958 Boundary Commission ran into the sand of such political resistance, as Richard Crossman (1975) vividly documented. The Banham Commission's recommendations in 1994 and 1995 suffered a somewhat similar fate on several occasions.
    Another source of political pressure has resulted from the emergence of some local authorities as centres of resistance to government policies, for example the GLC and the metropolitan county councils after 1981. They were abolished to remove powerful focal points of opposition to the government's policies from a 'new urban Left' generation of councillors (Gyford, 1984; Lansley et al., 1989). A similar political spleen on the part of the then Secretary of State for Scotland against Strathclyde Regional Council may have been reflected in his determination to ensure that it was fragmented when he reorganized Scottish local government in 1995.
    Second, doubts about the efficiency of particular structures, especially that of two-tier systems because of inter-authority failures of communication, rivalry and conflict, yet in other countries, such as Germany and the United States, small local government units work together successfully to pursue common objectives or to provide services which are too expensive for each to provide alone.
    However, two-tier local government has other virtues, notably that it enhances democratic accountability and prevents local dictatorships

developing because it creates a system of checks and balances under which decisions may have to be considered from two different points of view. Large regional or sub-regional authorities such as county councils can take a relatively detached strategic view of issues like the location of industrial plants, gypsy sites, highways and other developments, while the district councils play their own legitimate role in pressing local residents' objections to unwelcome development proposals. Without the two-tier structure, the strategic issues might not reach local political agendas (see Elcock, 1979). There is a real debate about the relative merits of single or multi-tier local government, either in general or in the context of developing differing systems for different kinds of areas. Thus it seems to be generally accepted for the present that two-tier local government is appropriate for sparsely populated areas such as Northumberland, whereas densely populated cities benefit from being governed by a single, all-purpose council. Little evidence has been adduced in support of either view. The advent of regional government under the Blair government will add a new dimension to this debate because regional chambers or assemblies will be well placed to undertake the strategic reviews and plan preparation of which relatively small metropolitan borough or unitary councils are not capable because of their relatively small geographical size.

The third issue, which was been rendered acute by the former Conservative government, concerns the democratic accountability and control of single purpose local bodies. The Thatcher and Major administrations favoured the creation of single-purpose bodies ruled by appointed, not elected, members in the interest of speedy decision-making, leading to accusations that it has created a 'new Magistracy' (Stewart, 1993; Jenkins, 1995). This, it is argued, has weakened local accountability and therefore responsiveness to citizens' needs and desires, in the interest of securing greater managerial efficiency and quick decision-making (see Thornley, 1990). Hence the growing problem of the 'Quangocracy' – appointed governors who are now responsible for the spending of more public money than elected councillors but whose public accountability for that expenditure is at best obscure and tenuous (Robinson and Shaw, 1995). The issue has been made the more acute by unwise actions which have provoked allegations of corruption or at best malpractice. Many of these quangos could be absorbed into new regional administrations which will be accountable to indirectly elected regional chambers or directly elected assemblies (Elcock, 1996).

An example of the difficulties caused by the imposition of a quango on local communities was the conflict that developed between the London Docklands Development Corporation and the local authorities in the East End of London, whose representations on behalf of local citizens were almost completely rejected by the Development Board during its first years of existence (Batley, 1989). However, more recently established Urban Development Corporations, such as Tyne and Wear, have from the beginning stressed their desire to work in partnership with the local authorities within their areas.

A final impediment to effective reorganization, which has also been an important reason for the instability of reorganizations once they have been carried out, has been the desire of those local authorities which lose power and status as a result of a reorganization, to recover their lost powers and status the next time round. A graphic illustration of this was the response of the former County Borough Councils which were incorporated in 'shire' counties in 1973. They lost control over education, social services and libraries – three of their major service responsibilities – and almost at once, they began an agitation, led by the 'big nine' cities in 'shire' counties, to recover these functions, which was on the verge of success when Labour lost office in 1979 (DoE, 1979). There is also a noticeable pleasure at the recovery of these lost powers by the new unitary authorities which have been created where county councils have either been abolished, as in the case of Humberside where Hull City Council is now closer again to its former status as a county borough, although they have still lost the control over water, police and fire which they enjoyed before 1973 (Doyle, 1996). The latest reorganization has already given similar hostages to fortune:

> There is a strong case for relative stability in general but most particularly in relation to territorial reorganization. Sadly, the outcome of this review makes such stability less rather than more likely. The scars of the 1991–1994 battles are unlikely to be forgotten. The anomalies … – a unitary York but not a unitary Oxford – will continue to rankle' (Leach, 1996b: 171).

Hence we will all be driven to return to the opiate of reorganization sooner or later.

These issues have been further muddied in recent years by a serious debate about the relative merits of single and multi-purpose local bodies. Much has been asserted but few proofs have been offered in favour either of single purpose or multi-purpose bodies. Single purpose bodies could be used to levy additional taxes to support popular services such as health or social care. They also permit their governing members to become well informed about a specialist field of activity. On the other hand, multi-functional local authorities are able to transfer funds between services as patterns of demand or need change (Stewart and Clarke, 1996; Cole and Boyne, 1996; Davis and Hall, 1996).

REGIONALISM

Another factor which is of increasing importance in the territorial debates about British local government is the regional dimension, despite the absence of a regional tier of government, as opposed to regional and sub-regional administrative agencies, of which there are a lot in the UK (see Hogwood and Keating, 1982). Such agencies include Regional Tourist Boards, Regional Sports Councils, Regional Arts Associations, Training and Enterprise Councils. This substantial but fragmented regional tier of administration was strengthened by the establishment of the Integrated Government Offices in 1993. Major issues concerning the development of a regional tier of government include:

Regional accountability: Should the extensive regional administration, including the Government Offices for the Regions, be subject to democratic accountability and control? There is much regional administration in Britain but there are no democratic structures of accountability to match it. This issue has been rendered the more acute by growing concern about the lack of accountability of the 'Quangocracy' (see Robinson and Shaw, 1995)

Nationalist popular sentiment: Growing nationalist sentiment in Scotland and Wales which led to the acceptance of devolution by the opposition parties at Westminster, as well as stimulating debate about the treatment of the English regions. The Labour Party was committed to introduce limited devolution to Scotland and Wales, together with the establishment of indirectly elected 'regional chambers' in the English regions, which will be composed of local councillors and representatives of regional interests, which may in some cases serve as the basis for the establishment of elected assemblies at the regional level (Labour Party, 1995). However, it is commonly argued, for no very cogent reason, that the creation of elected regional assemblies requires a move towards single tier local government in the regions, such as the North of England, where demands for regional government are most vocal. However, the arguments adduced earlier against undertaking reorganization constitute a powerful argument for not undertaking more reorganization and there is no doubt that regional assemblies could quite properly be established without the need for abolishing what remains of the county tier of local government. However, the major doubt about regional assemblies concerns the extent of public support for elected regional assemblies, given the requirement that their establishment must be approved by referenda.

The 'Europe of the Regions: The growing importance of the 'Europe of the Regions' and the establishment of the Committee of the Regions puts the

United Kingdom at a disadvantage, because of the increasing importance of the EU Structural Funds and their allocation to disadvantaged regions since the reforms of 1989, which both increased the importance of the Structural Funds, required the preparation of regional strategies to support applications for funding (Elcock, 1997). Effective representation in Brussels at the regional level is therefore needed in order to lobby effectively for development funds. This was one reason for the establishment of the Integrated Government Offices for the regions. Furthermore, the basis of British representation on the Committee of the Regions is at present unsatisfactory – although the government's original intention to nominate the British members without reference to local authorities was successfully resisted. The longer term issue is whether the importance of regions is increasing and that of nation states declining within the European Union as the 'Europe of the Regions' develops (Loughlin and Keating, 1997). The creation of the Government Offices for the Regions was in part a response to this development but many argue that democratic regional structures are needed if the nations and regions which make up the United Kingdom are to play a full part in developments at the European level.

Sources of Opposition

However, many, especially in industry and on the right of the political spectrum, are hostile to proposals for regional assemblies because they believe that they will mean more bureaucracy and higher taxation. Such opposition is most clearly reflected in the campaign by the Conservative Party and business interests against the Labour Party's proposal to permit a Scottish Parliament to vary the rate of income tax, which they have denounced as the 'Tartan Tax' (Lynch, 1997). Similar opposition from the business community is apparent to proposals for regional government in the North of England (Lanigan, 1996; North-East Chamber, 1996)

Popular Sentiment

The other major doubt concerns whether there is a real and substantial public demand for devolution and regional government. In particular, whether any of the English regions are in any sense civil societies is open to doubt. Even in the case of the Northern region of England, with its political solidarity, its industrial inheritance, its distinctive local accent and social culture, many doubt whether this constitutes a sufficiently coherent regional identity to warrant the establishment of a regional assembly (Fenwick, Harrop and Elcock, 1989; Elcock, 1996, 1997).

CONCLUSIONS AND DILEMMAS

The most fundamental question arising from the history of local government reorganization is whether reorganization was ever either necessary or desirable. Arguably, a process of incremental adjustment would have been less expensive and less disruptive, although we have seen that incremental approaches tend to founder on the rock of local political opposition.

However, there is serious doubt as to whether reorganizations have been effective. The evidence is overwhelmingly that any efficiency gains that may have resulted from reorganization are not sufficient to offset the costs of the reorganization itself. Furthermore, every reorganization produces both winners and losers, so the success of a reorganization will be asserted only by the winners. The losers will retreat sulking to their tents and prepare to fight for the reversal of their losses. Hence success or failure must be evaluated in terms of who gains and who loses.

Third, it is clear that reorganization is addictive (Elcock, 1991). Each reorganization makes the next one inevitable as the losers fight back and as doubts grow about the efficacy of the new structure – or as it becomes apparent that the political goals of the reorganizers have not been achieved. Reorganization may also follow a change of government if the new government sees political advantage for itself in restructuring local government, either to improve its own members' chances or to weaken the power of the opposition in local authorities, especially as opposition control of local government strengthens because the government becomes unpopular and this is reflected in local election results.

Fourth, there is no easy way of resolving the question of how many tiers – one, two, or several – constitute an effective local government system (Leach, 1996a). The issue of single purpose and non-elected bodies is a further difficult issue which is not easily resolved (Cole and Boyne, 1996). It may be preferable to accept an asymmetrical form of local and regional government, with differing structures which reflect the varying economic, social and political structures of different regions and localities (Keating, this volume).

Fifth comes the issue of how to determine the ideal size of local government units. Should the structure vary in different parts of the country, for example between urban and rural areas? If so, on what basis should single or multi-tier structures be accepted?

In the event of devolution and regional government being introduced, its implications for local government will need careful consideration, although if considerations of local government structure have to be introduced before devolution and regional government have been established, the resulting delay while the rival merits of single and multi-tier solutions are debated, will probably prevent the implementation of either devolution or regional government within the reasonable life span of any government. The government should therefore uncouple regionalism and devolution from questions of further local government reorganization.

Lastly, the long-term implications of membership of the European Union need to be considered, in terms of the principle of subsidiarity and the developing 'Europe of the Regions'. The 'Europe of the Regions' probably renders the development of a regional level of government inevitable; it ought to be made accountable to elected regional assemblies. Such regional governments and assemblies would also be able to carry out the strategic planning functions which cannot be effectively carried out by the relative small metropolitan borough and unitary councils (Elcock, 1996, 1997).

In the end , the debate about the territorial structure of local government remains what it has always been: a debate between the demands of 'national efficiency', as perceived through either red or blue-tinted political spectacles, versus arguments relating to community sentiment which may or may not be well founded. Although it may perhaps be too cynical to dismiss reorganization as dramaturgy, as Aaron Wildavsky vividly argued when he compared reorganization to looking for a lost button not where it was dropped but in the kitchen because the light is better there (1980 79), it is nonetheless clear that the debate about the British local government structure has been based neither on a clear perception of what reorganization might be expected to achieve, nor on any sound evidential basis. Rather, it is based on the advocacy of a series of propositions about efficiency and community sentiment whose validity is not established: which of them gain acceptance at any given time depends on one's political persuasion. Devolution and regionalism add a further dimension to this policy conundrum of asymmetrical government.

REFERENCES

Ball, R. and J. Stobart (1996) 'Community Identity and the Local Government Review', *Local Government Studies*, pp.113–26

Batley, S. (1989) 'London Docklands: An Analysis of Power Relations between UDCs and Local Government,' *Public Administration*, Vol.7, pp.167–87.

Burns, Hoggett and Hambleton (1993*) The Politics of Decentralisation; Revitalizing Local Democracy* (London: Macmillan).

Cole, M. and G. Boyne (1996) 'Evaluating the Structure of Local Government: The Importance of Tiers,' *Public Policy and Administration*, Vol.11, pp.63–73.

Crossman, R.H.S. (1975) *The Diaries of a Cabinet Minister*, Vol.1, Minister of Housing and Local Government (Hamish Hamilton and Jonathan Cape).

Davis, H. and D. Hall (1996) *Matching Purpose and Task: The Advantages and Disadvantages of Single and Multi-purpose Bodies*, INLOGOV

Department of the Environment (1969) *Humberside: A Feasibility Study* (HMSO).

Department of the Environment (1979) 'Organic Change in Local Government', White Paper, Cmnd 7457 (HMSO).

Department of the Environment (1983) White Paper, 'Streamlining the Cities', Cmnd 9063 (HMSO).

Doyle, P. (1996) 'Mayors or Nightmares?' *Public Policy and Administration*, Vol.11.

Elcock, H. (1975) 'English Local Government Reformed: The Politics of Humberside', *Public Administration*, Vol.53, pp.159–66.

Elcock, H. (1979) 'Politicians, Organisations and the Public: The Provision of Gypsy Sites', *Local Government Studies*, Vol.5, pp.43–54.

Elcock, H. (1983) 'Disabling Professionalism: The Real Threat to Local Democracy', *Public Money*, Vol.3, No.1, pp.23–7.

Elcock, H. (1985) 'Theory and Practice of Structure Planning: Writing the Humberside Structure Plan', in H. Elcock and M. Stephenson (eds), *Public Policy and Management: Case Studies in Improvement, Polytechnic Products* (Newcastle upon Tyne, pp.64–78.

Elcock, H. (1986) 'Decentralisation as a Tool of Social Services Management', *Local Government Studies*, Vol.12, No.4, pp.35–49.

Elcock, H. (1991) *Change and Decay? Public Administration in the 1990s* (Longman).

Elcock, H. (1994) *Local Government: Policy and Management in Local Authorities*, third edition (Routledge).

Elcock, H. (1996) 'A Choice for the North', Public Policy Research Unit Research Papers No.1 (University of Northumbria at Newcastle).

Elcock, H. (1997) 'The North of England and the Europe of the Regions, or When Is A Region Not A Region?' in Loughlin and Keating, pp.422–36.

Fenwick, J. (1995) *Managing Local Government* (Chapman and Hall).

Fenwick, J., K. Harrop and H. Elcock (1989) *The Public Domain in an English Region: Aspects of Adaptation and Change in Public Authorities*. Studies in Public Policy No. 175 (Glasgow: University of Strathclyde).

Gunlicks, A. (1986) Local Government in the German Federal Republic (Durham: Duke University Press).

Gyford, J. (1984) *The Politics of Local Socialism* (Allen & Unwin).

Hambleton, R. (1979) *Policy Planning in Local Government* (Hutchinson).

Hogwood, B. and M. Keating (eds) (1982) *Regional Government in England* (Oxford University Press).

Jenkins, S. (1995) Accountable to None: The Centralisation of Modern Britain (London: Penguin Books).

Jones, G.W. (1964) 'County Borough Expansion: The Local Government Commission's Views', *Public Administration*, Vol.42, pp.277–90.

Keating, M. (1988) *The State and Regional Nationalism: Territorial Politics and the European State* (Harvester Wheatsheaf).

Keating, M. (1998) 'What's Wrong with Asymmetrical Government?' Chapter of present volume, pp.195–218.

Keating, M. and J. Loughlin (eds) (1997) *The Political Economy of Regionalism* (London and Portland OR: Frank Cass).

Labour Party (1995) 'A Choice for England: A Consultation Paper on Labour's Plans for English Regional Government'.

Lanigan, C. (1996) 'Supporters and Opponents of Regional Government in the North-East', *Public Policy and Administration*, Vol.11, pp.66–78.

Lansley, S., S. Goss and C. Wolmar (1989) Councils in Conflict: The Rise and Fall of the Municipal Left (Macmillan).

Leach, S. (1996a) 'Local Government Reorganisation: A Test Case,' in Steve Leach, Howard Davis and Associates, *Enabling or Disabling Local Government* (Open University Press) pp.41–58.

Leach, S. (1996b) 'Conclusion' in Leach and Davis, pp.158–72.

Local Government Commission for England (1993) *Renewing Local Government in the English Shires: A Progress Report* (HMSO) December.

Local Government Commission for England (1994) *Final Recommendations for North Yorkshire, Humberside and Lincolnshire* (HMSO) January.

Lynch, P. (1997) 'Reactive Capital: The Scottish Business Community and Devolution', chapter of present volume, pp.86–102.

Malikova, L. and J. Bucek (1996) 'Meso-level in Slovakia: The history and politics of territorial reorganisations', paper read to the International Political Science Association Research Committee on Local Politics and Government Conference, Wroclaw, Poland.

Newton, K. (1969) 'City politics in Britain and the United States', Political Studies, Vol.17, pp.208–18.

Newton, K. (1976) *Second City Politics: Democratic Processes and Decision-making in Birmingham* (Oxford University Press).

Newton, K. (1978) *Is Small Really So Beautiful? Is Big Really So Ugly?* Centre for the Study of Public Policy (University of Strathclyde).

North-East Regional Chamber of Commerce, Trade and Industry (1996) 'Everybody's Business', North-East Chamber Election Manifesto, Autumn.

Norton, Alan (1986) *The Government and Administration of Metropolitan Areas in Western Democracies* (INLOGOV).

Peters, B.G. (1997) 'Regional Economic Development and Political Mechanisms: Western Pennsylvania in Comparative Perspective', in Loughlin and Keating, p.262–74.

Pycroft, C. (1995) 'Restructuring Local Government: The Banham Commission's Failed Historic Enterprise', *Public Policy and Administration*, Vol.10, pp.49–62.

Redcliffe–Maud (Royal Commission) (1969) Local Government in England, Cmnd 4040, Volume 1 Report; Volume 2, D. Senior, Memorandum of Dissent, Cmnd 4040–1, HMSO.

Richards, P. (1966), 'Rural Buroughs', *Political Studies*, Vol.4, pp.87–9.

Robinson, F. and K. Shaw (1995) *Who Runs the North?* (Unison)

Rusk, D. (1993) *Cities without Suburbs* (Washington, DC: Woodrow Wilson Foundation).

Senior, Derek (1966) *The Regional City* (Longman).

Stacey, F. (1975) *British Government 1996–1975: Years of Reform* (Oxford University Press).

Stewart, J.D. (1993) *Accountability to the Public*, European Policy Forum.

Stewart, J.D. and M. Clarke (1988) *Managing Tomorrow* (Local Government Management Board).

Thornley, A. (1990) *Urban Planning under Thatcherism: The Challenge of the Market* (Routledge).

Wildavsky, A. (1980) *The Art and Craft of Policy Analysis* (Macmillan).

What's Wrong with Asymmetrical Government?

MICHAEL KEATING

THE DEMAND FOR ASYMMETRY

The renewed debates on constitutional reform in the United Kingdom have revived a question which has bedevilled discussions since the nineteenth century – whether it is possible, just or reasonable to concede self-government for one part of the state, without giving the same treatment to others. Where those other parts do not desire the same treatment, the problem becomes even more acute. This issue has arisen in the current debates on devolution, in which proposals are being made for constitutional change to apply to Scotland and, in a different form, Wales, while England is treated differently again. This will create an asymmetrical constitution.

Neither territorial assertion nor asymmetrical government are entirely new. The premodern European order was a patchwork of territorial, functional, ecclesiastical and civil authorities. One of the features of the modern state is its tendency to impose uniformity in law, administration and representation, in the name both of administrative rationality and of democratic equality. Yet even in the heyday of the interventionist nation-state, between the late nineteenth and late twentieth centuries, states were obliged to recognize territorial peculiarities and engaged in elaborate policies of territorial management (Keating, 1988) to preserve their territorial integrity. This has produced a wide range of asymmetrical features, some of which are little known, while others go unremarked because of their very familiarity. So the question is not whether asymmetry is possible, but rather just what degree and type of asymmetry is tolerable. This contribution first reviews the experience of asymmetry in a number of countries, before addressing the issues of principle raised and their application to the debate in the UK. Three examples are particularly relevant, since they illustrate the scope for asymmetry in liberal democratic systems, and they have provoked long-standing debates on its applicability. These are Canada, the UK and Spain.

ASYMMETRY IN PRACTICE

None of these states has ever had a uniform constitution. Rather, as diverse
and multinational compositions, they have tended to deal individually with
their component parts. All the provinces of Canada entered confederation
on specific terms, which were then incorporated into the constitution. The
nations of the UK similarly came into the union on different terms. The
most elaborate bargain was that with Scotland which, under the Treaty of
Union of 1707 was guaranteed its established church, its system of law, its
education system and local government system. Wales was largely
assimilated administratively to England after the union of 1536, but
differential provision has since been made in matters of religion and
language. Ireland was united with Britain in 1800 but kept its own laws,
which henceforth were, like those of Scotland, regulated by the Westminster
Parliament. Spain was also created by a process of union, in which the
component parts kept their own customs and institutions. While these were
gradually eroded in the course of the eighteenth and nineteenth centuries,
they never entirely disappeared. Under the Second Republic there was a
recuperation of powers in the historic nations, a process which
recommenced with the transition to democracy in 1978.

Canadian provinces all have the same legislative powers, as do Spanish
autonomous communities. The range of competences is the same for all
Canadian provinces, except that Quebec has powers in relation to the
province's system of civil law. Not all provinces use their powers fully; only
Ontario, Quebec and Newfoundland have their own provincial police
forces. In Spain, the powers devolved to the autonomous communities vary
though, in principle, all can accede to the same level. Catalonia, the Basque
Country, Galicia, Andalusia, Valencia and the Canary Islands have an
advanced degree of functional autonomy. Only the Basque Country and
Catalonia have control of their own police forces. In the UK, the exception
is Northern Ireland, which had a devolved legislature for 50 years; the 1998
peace accord provides for scheme without parallel in the UK, but this
asymetry has not, in general, been seen as a problem.

Administrative arrangements vary considerably in the UK. Most
Scottish domestic administration comes under the Scottish Office and its
executive agencies. There is some argument over the extent of discretion
available to the Scottish Office and its local policy networks (Kellas, 1988;
Midwinter, Keating and Mitchell, 1991; Paterson, 1994) but agreement that
it represents a concession to Scottish national distinctiveness. The Welsh
Office is more recent and has fewer responsibilities. The Northern Ireland
Office was established to supervise the work of the departments of the
Northern Ireland government after the suspension of the Stormont regime in

TABLE 1
FEATURES OF ASYMMETRY, CANADA, UNITED KINGDOM AND SPAIN

Feature	Canada	UK	Spain
Legislative powers	uniform	N.Ireland, 1922–72. Scotland proposals	
Functions	Quebec civil law		extended powers for some ACs
Distinct administrative status	uniform	Scotland, Wales	ACs with extended powers
Civil law	Quebec	Scotland	Catalonia
Fiscal powers	uniform	Scotland proposals. N Ireland, 1922–72	Basque Country, Navarre
Representation in national parliament	more for small provinces	separate determination for Scotland, Wales, N Ireland, England	no special status
Reservation of posts in national executive	informal accommodation of Quebec and other regions	Secretary of State for Scotland, Wales. Formerly reserved positions in UK departments	none
Language laws	Quebec	Wales, Gaelic areas of Scotland	Basque Country, Galicia, Catalonia, Valencia, Balearics
Distinct party system	Quebec	Scotland, Wales, N Ireland	Basque Country, Catalonia
Religion	provision for religious education varies	separate church establishments in Scotland and England. No established church in Wales or N Ireland	uniform
Symbolism	Quebec National Assembly, flag	term 'nation' in official usage for component parts. National cultural institutions, sports teams, flag.	use of terms 'nationalities' and 'nations', flags

1972. In Canada, the federal government has different arrangements for collaboration with the various provinces according to political convenience. In Spain, the responsibilities of the national administration vary according to what is devolved to the respective autonomous community. There are proposals that, in those autonomous communities with full powers, there should be a single administration on German lines, allowing the devolved administration to administer national policies which, if ever carried through, would create further differentiation.

The fiscal powers of the Canadian provinces are equal, though not all choose to exercise them in the same way. Quebec administers its own income tax, while the others share in the federal income tax system. Quebec, on the other hand, harmonizes its sales tax with the federal government, while Alberta does not have a sales tax at all. In Spain, the Basque Country and Navarre have a special fiscal status, which allows them to collect taxes locally and pass on a negotiated contribution to Madrid. Another peculiarity is that in the Basque County it is the constituent provinces which have the fiscal power, and not the autonomous regional government itself. Elsewhere, taxes are collected by the national government and then divided, except for those minor taxes which are exclusive to the autonomous communities. Further complications are raised by the current proposals to allow those autonomous communties that wish, to take control of 30 per cent of the personal income tax. In the UK, the Stormont regime collected its own taxes and then negotiated an 'imperial contribution', though the latter soon became a negative amount.[1] The opposition parties propose that the Scottish Parliament will have a limited power to alter income tax rates not available elsewhere in the UK.

A striking feature of all these states is that representation in the lower house of the national legislature is determined partly by population but also by territory; the two principles do not always coincide. A provision in the Canadian constitution stipulates that no province shall have fewer Members of Parliament than it has Senators and another ensures that no province will have fewer MPs than it had in 1976.[2] So Prince Edward Island has four MPs, giving it one per 31,441 inhabitants in 1996, while Alberta and Ontario have over 97,000 per MP. In the UK, the representation of Scotland after the Union was initially based on exchequer contributions, and was less generous than that of England. During the nineteenth century, the franchise rules were made uniform and Scottish representation was increased to reflect population relativities. As Scotland's relative population has declined in the twentieth century, however, there has been no corresponding reduction (McLean, 1995). Since 1945, there have been separate parliamentary boundary commissions for England, Scotland, Wales and Northern Ireland. The Scottish and Welsh commissions have to create at least 71 and 35 seats respectively, but there is no upper limit and the latest redistribution produced 72 and 40. During the life of the Stormont Parliament (1922–72) Northern Ireland was under-represented, with 12 MPs but in the 1970s this was increased to 17 (now 18). The English commission has no numerical instructions. The result is a disparity of representation in favour of Scotland and Wales. In Spain, representation in the national parliament is determined on a state-wide basis but there is a rule that each province must have a minimum of three members. This benefits small provinces whose population would not otherwise entitle them to this number. For elections to the Basque autonomous parliament, all three provinces are represented equally, despite huge disparities in population.

Surprisingly, these disparities in representation have rarely been a major political issue. Although the Scottish and Welsh over-representation is little more than a historical accident (McLean, 1995), it has subsequently been defended as a compensation for peripherality, and for the absence of self-government for the minority nations (Rossiter et al., 1997). Northern Ireland's treatment reinforces this interpretation. Its under-representation from 1922 to 1972 was justified by its having a devolved parliament; the abolition of Stormont was used to justify the increase. Thus the parties have recognized that territories and not just individuals are represented. In practice, political considerations were critical. Under-representation in the Stormont era served to insulate Parliament from Northern Ireland politics. It also helped ensure the two-party duopoly of Westminster politics, which had been seriously upset by the presence of independent Irish members between 1868 and the First World War. Scottish and Welsh over-representation did not upset this duopoly because before the 1970s there were no electorally competitive territorial parties there. Nor did over-representation upset the UK party balance unduly. No government has ever had a working parliamentary majority simply because of Scottish or Welsh seats, and the party advantage arising from the disparities in representation has been calculated as rather small (Rossiter et al., 1997).[3] The lesson is perhaps that territorial asymmetries in representation are tolerable as long as they translate into disparities in seats for the British parties, rather than introducing territorial parties into Westminster, and that these disparities do not upset the system of alternating party governments. In their effects on the British parties, territorial imbalances in representation contribute a great deal less to misrepresentation than does the single-member plurality electoral system; twice since the war, governments have been returned to office with less votes overall than the losing party (in 1951 and in February 1974).

Much the same can be said for Canada. Large distortions are introduced through the constituency-based plurality system of election, so that it is not uncommon for the winning party to gain fewer votes than the runners-up.

They are compounded by uneven territorial representation, but neither has been a major political issue as long as state-wide parties dominate politics and accept the rules of the game. Should the Bloc Québécois ever hold the balance of power in the federal parliament, they could play a similar role to the Irish Party in the late nineteenth and early twentieth centuries. In Spain, the Catalan and Basque nationalist parties have held the balance in the last two parliaments, but these territories do not have special arrangements for parliamentary representation.

There are also provisions in the UK and Canada for the representation of territories in the national executive. Canadian federal governments are constructed with an eye to territorial balance, and there is a system of 'regional ministers' for the distribution of patronage. In the UK, the Secretary of State for Scotland is by binding convention a Scottish MP, as are the junior ministers in the Scottish Office. The Secretary of State has a recognized role in lobbying for Scottish interests in Cabinet, as do the Scottish Office civil servants within the Whitehall network. The Secretary of State for Wales has a weaker and less clearly defined role. Indeed, from the late 1980s the Conservative government was able to dispense with the requirement that the Secretary of State for Wales be a Welsh MP. At one time, there was an even broader system of special representation for Scotland. From the early 1950s to the end of the 1970s, there was always a Scottish MP in the Ministry of Agriculture. Following an election pledge in 1974, a Scottish MP was appointed to the Ministry of Energy, a convention which lasted until the late 1980s. Past Labour governments always found a place for a Scottish miner.[4] So Scots have been able to penetrate the British administrative system, while keeping a fence around their own, a tendency noted by Lowell (1908)[5] early this century and Richard Crossman (1977) in the 1960s.[6] The Scottish MPs seek to insulate Scottish affairs from English influences by taking them into special Scottish committees. At the same time, they penetrate UK politics, especially where there is a Scottish material interest at stake (Keating, 1975). The system has allowed Scotland to mount a considerable territorial lobby, especially at times when Scotland has been crucial politically to the government of the day, or marginal between the parties (Midwinter *et al.*, 1991). In Spain, territorial representation was an issue in the Socialist governments of the 1980s and 1990s and, while no binding conventions have developed, governments need to have political managers for Catalonia and the Basque Country.

Guarantees of equal citizenship rights are often seen as one of the features of the nation state, yet here too we see asymmetries. Canada's Charter of Rights applies equally to all provinces and the federal government, but contains a 'notwithstanding' clause allowing governments to opt out of certain of its provisions. This clause, originally inserted at the insistence of some western provinces, was used extensively by the nationalist government of Quebec between 1982 and 1985. In 1989, Quebec's law mandating the exclusive use of French in commercial advertising was found contrary to the Charter and the then Liberal government invoked the notwithstanding clause to cover a new compromise. Since 1993, however, both Liberal and Parti Québécois governments have been careful not to provoke legal disputes over the charter since, apart from some language questions, there is little dispute over its content, as opposed to the legitimacy of it being imposed on Quebec. Differences in civil rights are, ironically, much greater in the non-federal UK. Exceptional legislation has been imposed in Ireland regularly since the nineteenth century, to the consternation of both nationalists and the more consistent unionists.[7] Some differences have also arisen from the difference between English and Scottish law – for example between 1966 and 1976 homosexual acts were legal in England but not in Scotland.

Foreign representation is one of the powers most jealously guarded by national governments, yet even in this sphere there are asymmetries. Quebec has an extensive programme of foreign activities, pursued in parallel with the Canadian government. By agreement, it is represented separately in the organization of French-speaking countries, the Francophonie.[8] In an effort to maintain its French culture, Quebec is allowed to select its own immigrants. Within Spain, Catalonia and the Basque Country also have extensive programmes of external promotion, which allow them to project themselves as something more than mere regions of Spain particularly in the European Union. In 1996 the Basque Country upgraded its mission in Brussels to an official government office; this followed a court ruling that autonomous communities could represent themselves abroad where matters affecting their own competences were at stake. Even in the UK, the territorial departments have acted to secure their position in Europe (Keating and Jones, 1995). Scotland and Wales have been increasingly active overseas in matters related to economic development, such as tourism, inward investment and export promotion, despite a series of highly publicized battles with the Foreign Office and other UK departments.

Underlying these constitutional asymmetries is an asymmetry in identity and self-representation. In the minority nations, there has long been a widely-shared dual identity so that citizens can be, for example, both Scottish and British. For some nationalists, these are competing and incompatible identities, but for most citizens being Scottish is rather a particular way of being British. The asymmetry arises in that there is no corresponding intermediary identity for the majority populations. Indeed, English people tend to conflate English and British identity. Spaniards outside the minority nations do not have a collective identity distinct from Spain. Similarly, there is no common identity for Canadians outside Quebec, as the inelegant terms coined to refer to their territory show (ROC, or 'rest of Canada'; Canada-hors-Quebec). These asymmetries in identity have led to asymmetries in symbolic recognitions. This is not possible in a state like France, where the principle of national unity is an absolute and the constitutional court in the 1980s ruled that the expression 'Corsican people' was impermissible. In Britain, on the other hand, symbolic recognition is given freely to the minority nations. Their cultural institutions are given the title 'national', official usage accords them the status of nations, and they even have their own teams in some international sports competitions. Their flags are flown on all manner of occasions, without any serious conflict. Northern Ireland is another matter, as symbols are highly conflictual there. In Canada, Quebec has assumed to itself much of the symbolism of nationhood, using the term 'national' for its institutions including its legislative assembly, though these symbolic differences are not generally recognized by the federal government and certainly not by the other provinces. The Spanish minority nations receive recognition in the constitution, with the help of a clause which talks of the Spanish nation and the nationalities and regions which compose it, so allowing territories to negotiate their own symbolic title.[9] Some use is made of the term 'national' in cultural and other social institutions, though not as extensively as in Scotland.

OTHER ASYMMETRICAL CONSTITUTIONS

Belgium has adopted an extremely complex federal arrangement to manage its linguistic and territorial diversity. There are three language communities: the Flemish, the French and the German; and three territorial regions: Flanders, Wallonia and Brussels Capital. The institutions of the Flemish community and Flanders region are effectively merged, although the former includes the Flemish-speaking inhabitants of Brussels. In Wallonia the institutions remain separate. European integration and regional devolution are between them emptying the Belgian state of much of its competence but it can be argued that, by removing issues over which national consensus is not possible, they are helping it maintain its existence. Devolution may also serve the interests of fiscal discipline if it ends the tradition whereby each spending initiative in one region needs, in the interests of symmetry and balance, to be duplicated in the other, whether or not local circumstances justify it.

On a smaller scale, asymmetrical arrangements abound in Europe. Italy has five special status regions in Sicily, Sardinia and on its northern borders, all with their own statutes. The Swedish-speaking Ålund islands have a special status within Finland. Even the French state conceded a special status for Corsica. On the Atlantic fringe of Europe is a whole swathe of islands with special constitutional status: the Faroes; Greenland; the Azores; the Canaries. All these special-status regions are islands or border territories, and are small enough for their special status not to affect state politics as a whole. Yet their existence breaches the principles of uniformity and symmetry on which their respective national constitutions are ostensibly based. There are also territories which were passed over by the expansion of the European state system. The Isle of Man and the Channel Islands do not belong to any state, but hardly qualify as states in their own right. San Marino, Andorra, the Vatican City and Liechtenstein are formally sovereign states but are for most purposes integrated into neighbouring or surrounding states.

Asymmetry and special status are thus an enduring feature of the European state system. They have not usually caused serious political problems. Yet at times of constitutional change, the issue of asymmetry comes to the forefront of political debate. It may be that it is easier to tolerate old and familiar anomalies than to introduce new ones, regardless of the magnitude of each; or it may be that there are specific types of asymmetry that are intolerable, and others with which we can live. To explore this, we need to examine the arguments for and against asymmetry in constitutional reform, and the issues raised.

THE CASE FOR ASYMMETRY

Whether asymmetry presents fundamental problems for the constitution depends on what model of the state is assumed. In a unitary-jacobin state on French lines, in which citizenship is by definition uniform and no intermediaries are tolerated between the sovereign people and its expression in the state, there is no room for differential status for territories. In a different way, classical federalism, while it allows for different public policies in different units, is based on a uniform division of powers.[10] A third constitutional formula is the 'union state' (Rokkan and Urwin, 1983; Mitchell, 1996), a state without a formal federal division of powers but in which parts of the territory have been incorporated by treaty and agreement; 'while administrative standardization prevails over most of the territory, the union structure entails the survival in some areas of variations based on pre-union rights and infrastructures' (Rokkan and Urwin, 1983: 181). In fact, these variations are not merely survivals from a pre-union era but many result from the need to adapt the union arrangements to modern needs. The union state is based upon a pact or contract, though this is usually unwritten and its terms vague. Since the parties have acceded to the union on different terms, it is often asymmetrical in origin, but needs to be adapted and renegotiated in each generation, in order to meet contemporary needs and continue to legitimize the state and its authority. The multinational states of Canada, the United Kingdom and Spain are all union states and their constitutional practice illustrates the extent to which asymmetry is already an accepted constitutional feature.[11]

Asymmetrical decentralization is based on the theory that the state is not a homogeneous whole, to be divided according to administrative convenience and undifferentiated principles of representation, but a union of territories brought together in a pact. This language of union and pactism was, ironically, used by the British Conservatives in a paper opposing constitutional change, when John Major (1992) wrote of Scotland that 'no nation can be kept in a union against its will'. The Campaign for a Scottish Assembly's Claim of Right (CSA, 1988) insisted that sovereignty belonged to the Scottish people, who had the right to negotiate their place in the union. In the case of Northern Ireland, British governments have positively insisted on the principle that local parties should agree on a constitutional settlement, which could then be accommodated to the UK constitution. The Basque Nationalist Party refused to recommend a vote for the constitution of 1978 because the provisions for home rule were presented as concessions from the Spanish state and not as a recognition of the inherent rights of the nationalities. All the political parties in Quebec agree that the unilateral patriation of the Canadian constitution in 1982 was illegitimate because it was done without the consent of the Quebec National Assembly.

Against this particularist argument, opponents present a universalist case, insisting that the minorities should be prepared to dissolve their special status into a homogeneous whole, which would not benefit any group in particular. There is something disingenuous in this argument when it comes from the majority community, since dissolving particular identities into a common whole will mean that the common whole is defined by the values of the majority. This majority can then use universalist and majoritarian arguments against the minorities.[12] Successful nation and state-builders, from the French Revolution on, have often asserted their own values as universal. Yet even the classic civic nationalisms and liberal state-building projects contain a value set, which is often blind to the values of minorities (Requejo, 1996). To say this is not to fall into the post-modernist trap of regarding all values as particularistic and relative; rather it is simply a warning on the need to recognize that there are different ways of realizing values such as liberalism and democracy.

One indication of the tendency to confound the majority with the whole is the confusion among unionist English writers about the use of the terms England and Britain. A.V. Dicey's celebrated tracts against Irish home rule use the terms interchangeably, and at one point he even writes that 'the interest of Great Britain, or, to use ordinary language, of England, is that the English government should be strong' (Dicey, 1912: 44). A.J. Balfour (1912), in another polemic against Irish home rule, argued that it was the superior English polity which had brought a 'higher grade of civilization' to Ireland, as it had to the Scottish Highlands. A.J.P. Taylor, arguably another English nationalist, took great care in his works on the Habsburg monarchy (Taylor, 1948) to distinguish the nationalities and territories of the Austro-Hungarian realm and their proper names, but failed completely with his own state, referring to it consistently as 'England'. A whole genre of scholarly works in the nineteenth century was devoted to what was called the 'English Constitution'. This could stem either from an ignorance unforgivable in reputable scholars, or from a recognition that the British constitution was indeed the English constitution extended to the other parts of the union. This being so, it is hardly surprising that these other parts should seek to safeguard their own particular interests where possible.

The union principle provides a different intellectual frame to approach the issue of asymmetry, at least in relation to Scotland and possibly to Wales and Northern Ireland. It does not, however, provide the solution, nor does it resolve the specific issues raised by critics. Arguments against asymmetry focus on issues of sovereignty; autonomy; equality of rights; issues of representation; issues of influence and access; and issues of fiscal equity and economic competition. There is also a more speculative argument to the effect that asymmetrical arrangements are inherently unstable and will therefore lead eventually to the secession of the special-status territory.

A common argument in the British debate is that it is impossible to divide sovereignty, which resides in Parliament. Yet the English principle of parliamentary sovereignty was never recognized in Scottish constitutional practice before the Union of 1707 and, while Dicey and Rait (1920) insisted that the new Parliament of Great Britain introduced the principle to Scotland, Lord Justice Cooper in McCormick vs. Lord Advocate (1953) ruled that it had not (Mitchell, 1996). The issue must be regarded as unresolved and somewhat academic. A clause in the Labour Government's Scotland Act (1978) declaring that nothing in it detracted from the sovereignty of the Westminster Parliament was defeated by an unholy alliance of unionists and Scottish nationalists, without any appreciable effect on the bill (Keating and Lindley, 1981). While the precise issue of sovereignty is not easily resolved, it may be possible to fudge it in practice, since Great Britain has done this for nearly 300 years, and European integration has emptied it of much of its old meaning. Yet underlying the debate is an important question about nationality and legitimacy. Dicey (1886) observed in the last century that a vital difference between home rule for Ireland and a system of mere local government, however generous, was that a home rule parliament would take on itself the right to speak for an Irish nation, so that claims to sovereignty would inevitably follow. Similarly, Charles Wilson (1970) in his note of dissent to the Conservatives' Scottish Constitutional Commission, insisted that a Scottish 'assembly with real powers would seek to make itself the effective forum of political interest' and that separation would be the inevitable consequence. Now in so far as these objections hold, it would seem that Scotland, precisely because it is a nation, cannot be conceded even the modest form of autonomy proposed by the Scottish Constitutional Convention and others, an ironical outcome. Since the Conservatives themselves have conceded that no nation can be kept in a union against its will, they have set up the argument as one of stark alternatives. This at least has the merit of intellectual consistency.

Labour, on the other hand, has been pursuing two contradictory tracks. After going along with the Scottish Constitutional Convention's assertions of Scottish sovereignty, it has now retreated to its 1970s position, insisting that nothing in the scheme will affect the sovereignty of the Westminster Parliament. As George Robertson put it in June 1996, 'The UK Parliament will of course remain sovereign, but the essence of devolution is that for the better government of our country, certain powers are passed on to an elected Scottish Parliament. That is what devolution means – that all Westminster MPs decide that they should exercise some of their powers relating to Scottish affairs by devolving them to a parliament set up by them for that purpose. And it follows from that that the devolution legislation will explicitly recognize the fact of parliamentary sovereignty.' This is an echo of Dicey's (1886) view a 110 years earlier that it is for the UK as a whole to decide on the appropriate institutions for each part of it. This argument is, strangely, used as a defence of asymmetry, on the grounds that Parliament still has ultimate control, yet it goes clean against the union state principle, according to which the constituent parts have not altogether given up their rights, and which implies that a settlement must be negotiated and not imposed. It is this, as noted above, that legitimizes an asymmetrical settlement.

The question of autonomy hinges on the argument that it is unfair for one part of the country to have more powers of self-government than another. This is a serious objection if any territory is being denied self-government while another is being given it. Here there is a simple solution, to concede the same to the others. In Canada, concessions to Quebec are followed by demands from other provinces for the same treatment. These have usually been conceded, though arguably this represents a power game for political elites rather than a desire for more autonomy on the part of provincial electorates. A similar process is at work in Belgium. More serious is the argument between those who favour autonomy and those, in other territories, who prefer a centralized regime. Here it might be argued that it is unfair to thrust home rule onto people who do not want it. Yet this depends on their motivation. If, say, the English, or anglophone Canadians, favour a centralized system because it gives them effective control of the whole, then they can be accused of a wish for domination (as in the case of Dicey) and reasonably told to look to their own affairs. Alternatively, they may have a principled preference for centralized government because of the opportunities it gives for redistribution or radical policy making. In that case, the argument flows into that about fiscal equalization and social solidarity.

The threat to equality of civil rights has often been used against asymmetrical arrangements. Experience in Northern Ireland between 1922 and 1972 and in the southern states of the United States until the 1960s certainly shows that this danger can be real. On the other hand, since the rights in question are universal ones it is not clear why they should in principle be better guaranteed at the level of the nation state than at that of the minority community or the suprastate level. Even the most moderate Quebec nationalists bridle at the suggestion that theirs is inherently a less liberal community, unfit to be entrusted with civil rights issues. In so far as there are rights to be secured across the territory of the state, then the solution might be a state-wide or supranational charter of rights legally enforceable on all governments. In practice, this solution has not found favour in Quebec, where the Canadian Charter of Rights is regarded by nationalists as an illegitimate imposition upon them (Laforest, 1992). In the UK, devolution is part of a programme of constitutional reforms which includes a more positive commitment to Europe and more guarantees of individual rights. With a commitment to the European Convention on Human Rights, there is less need to worry about what devolved governments might get up to. The Scotland Act stipulates that the Parliament will be subject to the European Convention, and the Irish Accord goes even further, allowing the courts to strike down legislation that violates it. This is thought more acceptable than a purely British charter, imposed by the majority nation. Here the problem lies on the other side, since those most opposed to Scottish devolution tend also to be opposed to a written charter of rights or to the intrusion of the European Courts (of Justice and of Human Rights) into domestic affairs, insisting on the untrammeled supremacy of the Westminster Parliament. Nor has the insistence on Westminster's role as the sole guardian of civil rights prevented UK governments from introducing special restrictions in Ireland for over a hundred years.

In the modern welfare state, equality of social rights poses further questions. British (and perhaps even UK) national unity has been buttressed in the twentieth century by the welfare state and a commitment to equity in the provision of basic social services, health and education. A similar process has been under way in federal countries like Germany and Canada and even, to some extent, the United States. There are also efficiency arguments for maintaining relatively uniform social provisions and costs, to ease labour mobility and provide a level playing field for investment attraction, as the European Union is showing. Radical differences in the way of providing services like health could be difficult to accommodate within a devolution settlement (Heald and Geaughan, 1996) but the scope for variation is debatable. Since a Scottish Parliament or Welsh Assembly would be unlikely to dismantle those parts of the welfare state under its control, the issue is perhaps academic, but in the event of an extension of devolution to English regions, it might be asked whether a minimum charter of social rights would be needed and, if so, how this would extend to Scotland with its extensive system of legislative devolution.

Perhaps the most difficult issue is that of representation at the centre, the celebrated 'West Lothian Question' posed in the 1970s by anti-home rule Scottish MP Tam Dalyell, who asked why he should be permitted, as a Westminster MP, to vote on matters in England while neither he nor English MPs would be allowed a vote on Scottish domestic matters (Dalyell, 1977). An identical question had arisen in the Irish home rule debates of the late nineteenth and early twentieth centuries. It has also featured in the Canadian debate and, to a lesser degree, in Spain. There is of course no answer to the West Lothian question, but the response depends on the terms in which the question is put and to whom it is put. If addressed to Scots, it is easy to turn it around and tell the English that, if they are worried about it, they should go for federalism, or home rule all round. If they choose not to go for this, then they must accept the consequences. This is merely to reverse the question which English centralists are prone to put to Scots, that they are free to secede but, if they choose to stay, must accept the unitary state. Neither argument helps solve the immediate practical problem. The political issue has both territorial and partisan/ideological dimensions. Where elections are contested among territorially-based parties, then the issue of territorial representation becomes critical. This is only partially the case in Spain, the UK and Canada. In practice, territorial cleavages overlap with ideological and class ones to produce complex party systems. So the English left has a stronger interest in keeping Scottish MPs at Westminster than do English Conservatives. Dicey was well aware of this, writing that 'The friends of Disestablishment, the Welsh, or the Scottish home rulers, the London Socialists, all the revolutionaries throughout the country, know that with the departure of the Irish representatives from Westminster their hopes of triumph must be indefinitely postponed. England is the stronghold of British conservatism' (Dicey, 1912: 65–6). Canadians attached to bilingualism, or collective values, have more interest in Quebec representation in Ottawa than do supporters of the right-wing Reform Party. Any political compromise is likely to reflect these interests – and once we depart from the strict model of the unitary, national and uniform state and accept the notion of the state as a pact or negotiated order, then the constitution is going to end up as a compromise among principles. The issue then becomes entangled with other forms of over- and under-representation and of power, including the electoral system and the House of Lords, not to mention the weight of the City of London in economic and monetary policy.

There have been many proposals for overcoming the West Lothian conundrum. Gladstone's first home rule bill of 1886 made no provision for Irish representation at Westminster. It is likely that such a parliament would have evolved into a self-governing dominion like Canada or Australia and gradually acceded to independence. Unionists objected to the exclusion of Irish MPs on precisely these grounds. The 1893 bill at first excluded the Irish MPs from Westminster but was then changed to provide for a reduced number, who would be prohibited from voting on matters which concerned only the other nations of the UK. This 'in and out' provision was unworkable in a parliamentary system of government since it would mean that the executive would be dependent on a parliamentary majority whose composition could change from issue to issue. The clause was deleted during the passage of the bill and Irish MPs were to be given full voting rights. Unionists, having criticized the exclusion of Irish MPs, now criticized their inclusion on 'West Lothian' grounds. Both sides had thus reversed themselves and their arguments.[13] In the 1912 home rule bill there was a compromise in which Irish MPs retained full voting rights at Westminster, but their numbers were reduced from 103 to 42.

Some Conservative MPs have been arguing recently for an 'in and out' system for Scottish MPs in the event of devolution and a 1995 poll showed a large majority of them against allowing Scottish MPs to vote on English and Welsh matters (McCormick and Alexander, 1996). More common has been the argument that Scottish representation should merely be reduced, as the government has now accepted. In so far as over-representation in both Parliament and in the executive has been accepted as a trade-off against home rule, this seems reasonable. Yet the trade-off between representation and home rule has been a political compromise rather than a constitutional principle, and reduced representation hardly addresses the constitutional issues. The issue of principle is not whether there should be 56 or 72 or any particular number of Scottish MPs at Westminster, but whether any Scottish

MPs should vote on matters pertaining to the non-Scottish parts of the UK. There is only one practical argument for linking the number of Scottish MPs to devolution. At present, Scottish MPs carry an extremely heavy load in legislative committees, since 72 of them have to deal with the whole body of Scottish legislation (Keating, 1975). In the event of devolution, this would no longer be the case.[14]

Under a home rule settlement, Scotland's and Wales's special representation in the central government would go. Even were the Secretaries of State to remain, they would be shorn of their administrative support and the access to the networks of central decision making which comes from their status as functional departments. The Constitution Unit (1996) has proposed intergovernmental institutions such as those found in Germany, while recognizing that these could not, in the British system, be as elaborate. The German constitution, however, is symmetrical and founded on the principle of a sharing of power over both national and regional affairs between the federation and the Länder. It is rooted in a system and culture in which power is highly institutionalized and bound by legal norms. There is a tradition of political consensus which facilitates intergovernmental co-operation even across party lines. These conditions do not apply in the UK. Since it is not at all likely that the British government would share power over all-British matters with the Scottish executive, in this case the negotiation would be exclusively over Scottish affairs. Nor would the power of the two levels be remotely equal. It is likely, then that the relations between the two governments would be determined by political considerations. In this respect, Spain offers a more likely precedent than Germany. After a period of legal wrangling and hundreds of references to the Constitutional Court in the 1980s, the relations of Catalonia and the Basque Country with the central government moved into the political realm. The need of successive socialist and conservative Spanish governments for support from the Catalan and Basque deputies in the Cortes forced them to recognize the distinctiveness of the two nations and negotiate with their leaders over policy issues.

Similar considerations apply to access to the decision-making apparatus of the European Union. There have been proposals to allow Scottish and Welsh ministers access to the British negotiating team in the Council of Ministers, or to use the Maastricht Treaty provisions allowing a regional minister to represent the state in the Council of Ministers. Again, it is difficult to see how this could apply in an asymmetrical constitution, except perhaps in relation to matters (if any such exist) that bear on Scotland alone. The Maastricht provisions are generally considered applicable only to federal states and have been used exclusively by the three federations in the EU – Germany, Belgium and, to a lesser extent, Austria. In the German case, where matters of Land competence are involved, there is an agreement through the Bundesrat and one of the Länder takes the lead in pursuing the agreed line in the Council. Belgium is more complicated since the regions and communities have full competence in devolved matters and the federal government is not allowed to represent them. Instead, the regions and communities take turns in representing the Belgian case. The German system rests on a tradition of compromise and intergovernmental negotiation, the Belgian on the exclusion of the federal level altogether from devolved matters. Neither provides a precedent for the UK. It is inconceivable that a British Conservative government would allow a Scottish Labour minister to represent the UK in Europe, on even the most technical matter. Nor is it likely that English MPs would tolerate a Scottish minister speaking for England. Precedents drawn from present experience, in which Scottish and ministers co-operate with their UK colleagues on European matters are also of limited relevance, since at present they form part of a single government. This is not to say that there could not be a great deal of co-operation between the two levels of government. Spanish experience shows that the interests of the centre and the regions coincide in Europe more often than they conflict. There is much scope for exchange of information and experience and Scotland's influence here would be enhanced where the Scottish administration possessed the relevant information and experience (Constitution Unit, 1996). Policy differences, however, will be resolved politically and not through institutional devices.

Direct representation of devolved governments in Europe is another issue which has caused conflict in many member states. In the UK, as in Spain, the issue is complicated by the national character of Scotland and Wales and the international legitimacy which this confers. It is likely that any Brussels office established by the Scottish Parliament will be more than a mere regional listening post and the head of the Scottish government may enjoy a high status in Europe because of Scotland's historic standing and name recognition. This could be a cause for conflict with central government, notably the Scottish Office, and only recognition of Scotland's distinct status can resolve the matter. Over time, Canadian governments have got used to the idea of Quebec promoting itself abroad and have come to live with the symbolism this produces, even if they do not much like it.

A common objection to asymmetrical devolution is that it gives some parts of the state a material advantage, especially in relation to public expenditure. The standard solution to problems of this sort is a system of fiscal equalization under which resources are passed to the various territories so as to allow each to maintain the same level of services for the same fiscal effort. The actual distribution of these resources would be at the discretion of the devolved governments according to their priorities, thus reconciling territorial justice with autonomy. Unfortunately, matters are in practice more complicated. There are immense conceptual difficulties in defining and operationalizing the idea of fiscal equalization. There are practical difficulties in measuring fiscal effort and devising indicators of need. There are immense political difficulties in changing existing patterns of spending to make them conform with whatever formula is chosen. Consequently, efforts to achieve fiscal equalization typically start with existing spending patterns and seek to change these at the margin. This is in effect what happens in Spain and is likely to be the pattern for devolved governments in the UK.

One problem that arises from differential taxation and spending powers is the possibility of market distortion and unfair competition, if some regions are able to give tax breaks and subsidies. This is a serious problem in Canada, where there is no federal regulation of location incentives, and only a weak inter-provincial anti-poaching agreement. In Spain, the Basque Country is accused by other governments of using its special fiscal status to give tax derogations to incoming investors. There are provisions for regulating this type of competition at the European level, though they are not always effective, and it is generally accepted that a regime in which no-one has the right to subsidize investment is better than a free-for-all, which allows firms to play off governments against each other to get the best deal. Where one government has a special fiscal regime and the others do not, however, it is going to be tempted to use its powers to gain advantage in the competition for investment.

A final argument against asymmetrical devolution is that of the 'slippery slope'. This is to the effect that a territory given a special status, particularly if this is accompanied by recognition of its national identity, will not be content with the status of devolution but will press for further concessions and ultimately for independence. There is not much historical support for this view, but on more general grounds it is argued that asymmetrical solutions are inherently unstable (Tarleton, 1965) and likely to generate tensions between the central government, with its comprehensive responsibilities, and the devolved administration. Where the status of a national minority is defined by a special statute, then concessions to other territories in the interests of symmetry will provoke further demands from the national minorities to retain their lead. Evidence for this might be provided from Quebec and Spain where concessions to minority nationalism have fed rather than demobilized the national minority movements. What is less commonly observed is the concessions made on the nationalist side, where the idea of national sovereignty has been watered down to the point that it is difficult to describe it as separatism (Keating, 1996).

CONSTITUTIONAL REFORM

Analysis of the experience in the UK and elsewhere suggests that asymmetry may be more of a problem in theory than in practice. The principles of recognition of the rights of territorial societies and of citizen equality within the state must be reconciled but, as long as neither is pushed to its absolute limit, compromises are possible. Absolute uniformity has never existed outside the imagination of jacobin centralists; British Conservatives are highly vocal in stressing how differently Scotland is managed, and, for internal Scottish consumption, how it receives more than its due share of resources. Perfectly symmetrical federalism is possible only under highly unlikely conditions. Independence for the distinct territories concerned provides no easy solution either since all but the most hard-line separatists accept that shared authority and joint policy making will remain a reality after independence. European integration brings in further elements of asymmetry, as a multi-speed or variable geometry Europe looks inevitable, and this will strain relations not only between states but within them, as some territories adopt a more enthusiastic attitude to Europe than others.

A federal solution to the UK's constitutional conundrum is not on the agenda, since there is virtually no demand for this in England, or in the individual English regions. A uniform system of devolution is impracticable, given the differing demands of the various parts of the UK, and the question of Scots law. Crowther-Hunt and Peacock's (1973) proposals to provide symmetrical devolution by denying both Scottish and English regional assemblies legislative powers would create even more anomalies. Separate legislation would still have to be passed for Scotland, unless the whole system of Scots law were abolished, but the Scottish Assembly would have no say on this. Presumably, it would be drafted by UK departments, representing a centralization rather than a devolution of power. Any system for the UK needs to take account of the system of Scots law and, thereby, accept an existing and important asymmetry.

What principles, then, can be used to frame an acceptable asymmetrical solution for the nations and regions of the UK? Firstly, the question of sovereignty needs to be addressed. If we stick to the doctrine of absolute parliamentary supremacy, then we cannot get far. If, on the other hand, there is a recognition of the UK as a union forged by negotiation and renegotiation, we have a different starting point. Ironically, the Conservative government recognized this in its *Scotland and the Union* statement, but completely failed to follow the logic of this recognition. They similarly refused to accept the constitutional consequences of membership of the European Union. The Scottish Constitutional Convention takes a more constructive route by insisting on the sovereignty of the Scottish people and the principle of negotiation, but without denying the need for a solution to be approved by the UK Parliament.

The second objection to asymmetry, that it is unfair to give different powers to different nations and regions, can be resolved by the principle of giving equal effect to the aspirations, rather than imposing a single solution. There are dangers in this procedure, as the Canadian experience shows. In an effort to defuse opposition to distinct society status for Quebec, the Charlottetown accord proposed a whole series of categorical rights for groups, together with a reformed Senate to accommodate the western provinces. The agenda became overloaded and the process failed (Lusztig, 1995). The Spanish system of rolling devolution provides another model. This too had wider consequences than were intended, as the imitation effect rapidly regionalized the entire state, while the Basque and Catalan nationalists continue to insist that, whatever the other regions have, they should have a bit more. Yet in so far as this model is likely to produce a snowball effect in the UK, as English regions demand more powers for themselves, this can be regarded as entirely healthy. Indeed, creating such a political dynamic is probably the only way to attack the over-centralization of the British state; the Westminster parties, left to themselves, will never do it. The high degree of legal and institutional differentiation for Scotland is likely to mean that the Scottish Parliament will have powers and a status greater than that of English regional assemblies, and rather different from the arrangements for Wales. Scotland's status as a nation alone will give greater legitimacy and political weight to its institutions, which is precisely why unionists are so fearful of making any concession; but it is difficult to see where the substantive harm to other parts of the UK arises from this feature alone.

Equality of rights is certainly not a principle well maintained by the UK Parliament, which has allowed exceptional measures in Ireland for well over a hundred years. If there is a problem here, it is best resolved by incorporating the European Convention on Human Rights into the law of the United Kingdom and the devolution settlements.

The issue of spending disparities is not one created by devolution, and the impact of devolution can be argued both ways. English opponents of Scottish devolution in the 1970s insisted that it would give Scotland a financial advantage. Scottish anti-home rulers argued that it would jeopardize Scotland's existing advantage in public expenditure. Even were the Secretary of State for Scotland to remain in the British Cabinet, devolution would remove the Scottish presence from the whole array of Cabinet, interministerial and civil service committees on which Scottish Office representatives currently sit as of right, as a functional department of the central government. The public financial settlement between a devolved

Scottish administration and the centre would be open to more parliamentary and public scrutiny than the present rather furtive arrangements – although the devolution debates of the last quarter century have already put the spotlight on this. Given the way in which public finance works, we are not going to have a brand-new system of fiscal equalization introduced overnight. Experience from elsewhere shows that change tends to be incremental and, even where new formulas are brought in, they are accompanied by dampeners to mitigate their short-term effect. Proposals from the Scottish Constitutional Convention start from the Barnett formula and then argue, rather vaguely, for a system of equalization. This question is still unresolved. The issue of fiscal competition or the use of incentives to attract investment can also perhaps be left to European regulation. Competition does serve to equalize business taxation across jurisdictions and, in any case, none of the devolution proposals includes ceding control of corporate taxation.

Representation at the centre is another difficult matter. Reducing the numbers of Scottish or Welsh MPs in the event of legislative devolution might be justified, but it does not solve the West Lothian question which will be there as long as any non-English MPs remain. This is something with which we will have to live as part of any new union settlement. If Scottish representation is called into question, the matter cannot be resolved without reference to wider questions of representation, notably the electoral system and the composition of the upper house. If proportional representation were introduced for Westminster elections, this could mean the end of the two-party alternation in government. In the new dispensation, minor parties, territorial parties, and territorial factions of UK parties could become more important. This could increase the influence of the minority nations still further, since these are the only places were territorial politics and territorial factions really exist. As Spain has shown, the territorial parties could even become the brokers of national politics. An upper house elected on a territorial basis would similarly strengthen the role of territorial interests in central government.

Not so long ago, political scientists were predicting the end of territorial politics as states completed their social, economic and political integration. In the new Europe, the opposite is happening. Territorial politics is becoming more important and more complex. It can no longer be squeezed into the procrustean bed of the nation state, and constitution-makers will have to get used to the idea.

NOTES

1. The same process is currently occurring in the Basque Country. The *cupo*, or Basque contribution to the central exchequer, has been declining as more services were transferred to the Basque government, and the Basque economy was declining. By 1997, the amount was about to become negative. Since by this time the central government was dependent on a pact with the Basque Nationalist Party, a solution was found which involved some creative accounting. Excise duties, previously collected by the central government, were transferred to the administration of the Basque Country, so giving them some revenue to hand back to the centre and maintaining a positive *cupo* (*El País*, 3 Nov. 1996).
2. Senators are appointed by the federal government but are deemed to represent provinces.
3. Labour governments have always drawn disproportionate support from Wales and, in the 1960s and 1970s, from Scotland. Yet except for the brief Parliaments of 1950–51 and February– October 1974, Labour governments have always had a plurality of seats in England, and Labour governments with working majorities (of which there have only ever been three) have had a majority of English seats. The minority Liberal governments of 1892–5 and 1910–12 owed their pluralities to non-English seats.
4. Scottish Members of the House of Lords are also pressed into service.
5. Lowell, an American, called his book *The Government of England*, and compounded the insult by writing, 'Every Scotchman is an Englishman, but an Englishman is not a Scotchman. The Scotch regard themselves as an elect race who are entitled to all the rights of Englishmen and to their own privileges besides. All English offices ought to be open to them, but Scotch posts are the natural heritage of the Scots. They take part freely in the debates on legislation affecting England alone, but in their opinion acts confined to Scotland ought to be, and in fact they are in the main, governed by the opinion of the Scotch members' (Lowell, 1908, p.138).
6. Crossman, as Secretary of State for Social Services, was about to go into the debate on the Social Work (Scotland) Bill of 1968 but 'Just as we were going in we realized that the Scots would suspect some poisonous English conspiracy... I quote this to show how deep is the separation which already exists between England and Scotland. Willie Ross (Secretary of State for Scotland) and his friends accuse the Scot. Nats. of separatism but what Willie Ross himself actually likes is to keep Scottish business absolutely privy from English business. I am not sure that this system isn't one that gets the worst of both worlds which is why I'm in favour of a Scottish Parliament' (Crossman, 1977, p.48).
7. For example Dicey (1886, p.116) who wrote, 'It were the strangest anomaly for the law to sanction a mode of procedure which convicts a dynamiter in Dublin and not to give the Government the same means for the conviction of the same criminal for the same offence if he has crossed to Liverpool .... An Act which is a law in 1881, but which ceases to be a law in 1882, has neither the impressiveness nor the certainty which gives dignity to the ordinary law of the land.'
8. In order to make this look more like a general policy and less like a special concession, New Brunswick was also allowed to send a delegation, but this has nothing of the significance of Quebec's presence.
9. In 1996, the Partido Popular government agreed to the amendment of the statutes of autonomy of Aragon and Valencia, to recognize them as nationalities. This was taken as an affront by Basque and Catalan nationalists, since it banalized the idea of nationality and so eroded their symbolic special status.
10. On the other hand, it can be argued that all federations are in some way asymmetrical, since they rest on the twin principles of equal representation of citizens in the central government, and on the representation of the federated units, usually in a second legislative chamber.
11. Canada is, of course, a federal state but its system of government also embodies the union principle.
12. This sort of reasoning reaches its apogee in the case of the Ulster Unionists who like to make majoritarian arguments to justify Protestant supremacy. Even liberal Unionists tend to insist that Catholics can be given full rights to participate, if only they first accept the boundaries of the polity and abandon their particularist identity.

13. In a similar way, anti-home rulers have earlier criticized proposals for a Scottish Parliament because they did not include taxing powers and then criticized more recent proposals for having them.

14. From the 1950s, the convention became established that only Scottish MPs sat on Scottish legislative committees. The shortage of Scottish Conservatives since the 1987 election has meant that this convention has been partly abandoned.

REFERENCES

Balfour, A.J. (1912), *Aspects of Home Rule* (London: Routledge).

Constitution Unit (1996), *Scotland's Parliament. Fundamentals for a New Scotland Act* (London: Constitution Unit).

CSA (1988), 'A Claim of Right for Scotland', in O. Dudley Edwards (ed.), *A Claim of Right for Scotland* (Edinburgh: Polygon).

Crossman, Richard (1977), *The Diaries of a Cabinet Minister, Volume Three. Secretary of State for Social Services, 1968–70* (London: Hamish Hamilton).

Crowther Hunt, N. and N. Peacock (1973), *Memorandum of Dissent: Royal Commission on the Constitution, 1969–73, Volume 11*, Cmnd.5460-I (London: HMSO).

Dalyell, T. (1977), *Devolution: The End of Britain?* (London: Jonathan Cape).

De La Granja Sainz, J.L. (1995), *El nacionalismo vasco: un siglo de historia* (Madrid: Tecnos).

Dicey, A.V. (1886), *England's Case Against Irish Home Rule*, reprinted 1973 (Richmond: Richmond Publishing Company).

Dicey, A.V. (1912), *A Leap in the Dark. A Criticism of the Principles of Home Rule as Illustrated by the Bill of 1893*, 3rd edn. (London: John Murray).

Dicey, A.V. and R.S. Rait (1920), *Thoughts on the Union between England and Scotland* (London: Macmillan).

Heald, D. and N. Geaughan (1996), 'Financing a Scottish Parliament', in S. Tindale (ed.), *The State and the Nations: The Politics of Devolution* (London: Institute for Public Policy Research).

M. Keating and B. Jones (1995), 'Nations, Regions and Europe. The UK Experience', in B. Jones and M. Keating (eds),*The European Union and the Regions* (Oxford: Clarendon).

Keating, M and P. Lindley (1981), 'Devolution. The Scotland and Wales Bills', *Public Administration Bulletin*, Vol.37, pp.37–54.

Keating, M. (1975), The Role of the Scottish MP, PhD thesis, Glasgow College of Technology and CNAA.

Keating, M. (1988), *State and Regional Nationalism. Territorial Politics and the European State* (Hemel Hempstead: Harvester Wheatsheaf).

Keating, M. (1996), *Nations against the State: The New Politics of Nationalism in Quebec, Catalonia and Scotland* (London: Macmillan and New York: St. Martin's Press).

Kellas, J. (1988), *The Scottish Political System*, 4th edn. (Cambridge: Cambridge University Press).

Laforest, G. (1992), 'La Charte canadienne des droits et libertés au Québec: nationaliste, injuste et illégitime', in F. Rocher (ed.), Bilan québécois du fédéralisme candien. (Montréal: vlb).

Lowell, A.L. (1908), *The Government of England, Vol.1.* (London and New York: Macmillan).

Lusztig, M. (1995), 'Constitutional Paralysis: Why Canadian Constitutional Initiatives Are Doomed to Fail', *Canadian Journal of Political Science*, Vol.27, No..4, pp.747–72.

Major, J. (1992), 'Forward by the Prime Minister' in *Secretary of State for Scotland, Scotland and the Union* (Edinburgh: HMSO).

McCormick, J. and W. Alexander (1996), 'Firm Foundations – Securing the Scottish Parliament', in S. Tindale (ed.), *The State and the Nations* (London: Institute for Public Policy Research).

McLean, L. (1995), 'Are Scotland and Wales Over-Represented?', *The Political Quarterly*, Vol.66, No.4, pp.250–68.

Midwinter, A., M. Keating, and J. Mitchell (1991), *Politics and Public Policy in Scotland* (London: Macmillan).

Mitchell, J. (1996), *Strategies for Self Government: The Campaigns for a Scottish Parliament*

(Edinburgh: Polygon).

Paterson, L. (1994), *The Autonomy of Modern Scotland* (Edinburgh: Edinburgh University Press).

Requejo, F. (1996), 'Diferencias nacionaes y federalismo asimétrico', Claves de la Razón Práctica, Jan.–Feb., pp.24–37.

Rokkan, S. and D. Urwin (1982), *Economy, Territory, Identity: Politics of West European Peripheries* (London: Sage).

Rossiter, D., R. J. Johnston and C. Pattie (1997), 'New Boundaries, Old Inqualities: The Evolution and Partisan Impact of the Celtic Preference in British Redistricting', *Regional and Federal Studies* (forthcoming).

Tarleton, C.D. (1965), 'Symmetry and Asymmetry As Elements of Federalism: A theoretical Speculation', *Journal of Politics*, Vol.27, No.4, pp.861–74.

Taylor, A.J.P. (1948), *The Habsburg Monarchy, 1809–1918: A History of the Austrian Empire and Austria-Hungary* (London: Hamish Hamilton).

Abstracts

Devolution and Europe: Britain's Double Constutional Problem
Graham Leicester

This article describes Britain's double constitutional problem. Constitutional reform of the British state raised the challenge that sovereignty could be simultaneously drained from the centre in two opposite directions: outwards towards Europe and inwards towards the regions. At a technical level there are lessons to be learned from existing mechanisms in Whitehall for melding a range of interests into a coherent 'national position' for EU negotiations. There are also examples of managing multi-tiered governance within the EU: in Germany, Spain and Belgium for example. But ultimately Britain's double constitutional problem is a consequence of uncertainty about British identity. Britain might well gain insights from the constitutional reform process at home which could be reflected in a more confident performance in Europe. Britain might begin to recognize that it is possible to develop a model of integration which is not federalism, which builds on existing identities and which provides a coherent framework in which practitioners and electors know who is responsible for what, and how and why the democratic elements in the system apply.

Financing Arrangments for UK Devolution
David Heald, Neal Geaughan and **Colin Robb**

This contribution concentrates upon the financial arrangements for the system of devolved government which will be established in Scotland and Wales in 2000, and which may subsequently be parallelled in Northern Ireland. Making devolved government fiscally responsible is shown to be the central issue. It is strongly argued that tax-varying powers are essential, whereas the argument that such devolved governments should raise all the money they spend is shown to be inconsistent with fiscal equalization and impractical in the modern European context. The financing framework devised by the Scottish Constitutional Convention is explained and broadly defended. The debate on the 'tartan tax' (a 3p variation power on income tax in either direction) is reported, and the proposal defended against claims that it would be 'crippling' or 'irrelevant' or both. The major criticism which the article makes of the devolution scheme which will be enacted in

1998 legislation is that a stable fiscal settlement requires an explicit commitment to a future needs assessment and the specification in statute of how the financial arrangements between Westminister and devolved governments will work.

Scottish Home Rule: Radical Break or Pragmatic Adjustment?
Lindsay Paterson

The author argues three main propositions: (1) Scotland's position in the Union – including its position this century – has always involved negotiation and compromise, and so has never been a matter of straightforward assimilation of Scotland to England; (2) the pressure for a Scottish Parliament since the 1960s has been merely the latest phase in the process of negotiation within the union; (3) the autonomy which the new parliament will represent will continue to be constrained by the wider context of both the UK and the EU. The author concludes, therefore, that the autonomy of the parliament might be not much greater than was available informally to Scotland up till the middle of the twentieth century. The biggest impact could, however, be in the reform it could undertake in Scottish policy making, towards more democratic openness.

What Could a Scottish Parliament Do?
James Mitchell

The scope for independent action available to the Scottish Parliament to be elected in 1999 is examined with respect to four types of public policy: redistributive (taxation and welfare benefits), distributive (spending policies of the parliament), regulatory policies (policies designed for the public control of private activities in the public good) and the policy process (how policies are made).

The parliament will have a negligible role in terms of redistributive policies, limited scope in terms of distributive policies (increased spending in any area will only be possible at the expense of cutting another area), potentially considerable in regulatory types of policies and potentially extensive in how policies are actually made. The multi-level nature of policy-making is stressed. Policies will be made by different levels of government including local government, Westminster/Whitehall, European Union as well as the Scottish Parliament.

Reactive Capital: The Scottish Business Community and Devolution
Peter Lynch

Though business has emerged as an important political actor in a variety of policy areas such as the economic development, the environment and trade policy, its role in territorial politics has been less remarked upon, even during periods of constitutional change involving the establishment of regional government. This contribution examines the various market-building and state-building strategies of business organizations towards the issue of Scottish devolution from the 1970s to the late 1990s, culminating in the devolution referendum on 11 September 1997. The study examines a variety of business responses and attitudes to the devolution issue, as well as the likely behaviour of business organizations towards a Scottish Parliament when it is established in 1999–2000. The contribution concludes by examining the reactive and pragmatic nature of business to the devolution issue and its reluctance to become involved in the constitiutional debate as a political actor, with important consequences for business's future relations with the Scottish Parliament.

Deepening Democracy: Women and the Scottish Parliament
Alice Brown

This contribution discusses the involvement of women political activists in Scotland in the campaign for constitutional change and for equal representation in a Scottish Parliament. The way in which women have seized the opportunities opened up by the debate surrounding the establishment of a new legislature is explored. Their desire for a different type of parliament and politics in Scotland is also discussed. Finally the likelihood of success in achieving gender balance in the Scottish Parliament is assessed.

The Devolution Debate in Wales: The Politics of a Developing Union State?
Jonathan Bradbury

The contribution considers the recent historical development of Welsh government, the approach to Welsh government taken by Conservative governments 1979–97, and the reform proposals made by the Labour Party while in opposition, 1992–97. The consideration is made against the criteria of a developing union state model of Wales' place within the British political system. It concludes that contrary to the hopes of advocates of constitutional change the balance of evidence before the 1997 General

Election remained at best supportive only of an equivocal shift in political opinion away from seeing Wales' government as essentially part of a unitary British state towards one which accorded clearer rights of Welsh political autonomy within a union state conception of Britain.

Strategies of Autonomist Agencies in Wales
Jonathan Snicker

This study examines the political consequences of Welsh identity transformation. The role played by key individuals and groups in this process is analyzed in the context of administrative devolution and the development of a specifically Welsh education system.

English Regionalism and New Labour
John Mawson

The contribution considers recent developments in the politics and administration of the English regions and the wider implications for devolution across the United Kingdom. It considers why the regional issue has taken on increasing significance in the past decade and how the challenges of a new form of regional governance have been addressed by Conservative and Labour administrations. It concludes with an assessment of New Labour's emerging approach, arguing that the failure to address the English regional dimension proved to be the 'achilles heel' of Labour's previous devolution initiative and that it could again prove problematic in the reshaping of UK territorial politics.

Territorial Debates about local Government: Or Don't Reorganize! Don't! Don't! Don't!
Howard Elcock

British local government has been repeatedly reorganized since the end of the Second World War, usually with a view to increasing its efficiency or its ability to cope with particular issues, such as economic regeneration. Such reorganizations have on several occasions done violence to long-standing community identities in the interest of more efficient or effective government. The tensions to which such reorganizations give rise when they violate established community identities is explored through the brief and troubled history of the estuarine counties which were created in 1973, in particular the example of Humberside County Council. As the regional institutions of British government develop as a result of the growing importance of regionalism within the European Union, the demands of national (and increasingly international) efficiency must not be allowed to overrule community sentiment to the extent that popular hostility provokes further change in order to dismantle unpopular government structures.

What's Wrong with Asymmetrical Government?

Michael Keating

Proposals for devolution in Scotland and Wales will create an asymmetrical constitution. This raises a number of issues in principle and practice and has been a focus of opposition. Yet asymmetrical features are common in devolved systems, as the experience of Canada and Spain shows, and the existing UK constitution also contains marked asymmetries. No symmetrical solution could satisfy the varied demands from the nations and regions of the UK. In any case asymmetry may be less of a problem in practice than it is in theory.

Notes on Contributors

Howard Elcock is Professor of Government and Honorary Research Fellow at the University of Northumbria at Newcastle. He was educated at The Queen's College, Oxford and previously taught at the University of Hull. He has held visiting teaching positions at the State University of New York at Fredonia, Comenius University, Bratislava, Maktab sains Mara, Kuala Lumpur and the Universities of Warsaw and Würzburg. He is author of several books, including *Local Government: Policy and Management in Local Authorities* and *Change and Decay? Public Administration in the 1990s*. He served as a member of Humberside County Council between 1973 and 1981 and was Chairman of the Planning Committee between 1975 and 1977.

Michael Keating is Professor of Political Science at the University of Western Ontario and Visiting Professor at the University of Strathclyde, has taught in universities in Britain, the United States, France and Spain and held visiting posts in Italy and Norway. He is co-convenor of the European Consortium for Political Research Standing Group on Regionalism, and editor or author of 16 books on urban and regional politics and nationalism.

Graham Leicester is a political consultant and Director of the Scottish Council Foundation, an Edinburgh-based body promoting independent thinking in public policy. With a background in HM diplomatic Service, he was a senior research fellow with the Constitution Unit at University College London in 1995. Recent publications include *Scotland's Parliament: Fundamentals for a New Scotland Act* and *Holistic Government: Options for a Devolved Scotland*.

David Heald is Professor of Accountancy at the University of Aberdeen. His research interests span public expenditure management, government accounting and the financing of devolved government. He is specialist adviser to the Treasury Committee of the House of Commons.

Neal Geaughan is Lecturer in Accountancy at the University of Aberdeen. He has published on accounting change in government and on the financing of devolution.

Colin Robb is currently involved in part-time consultancy and is a member of South Lanarkshire Council. He has wide experience of economic development initiatives, derived from his former roles as board member of East Kilbride Development Corporation and of the Lanarkshire Development Agency.

Lindsay Paterson is Professor of Educational Policy at Moray House Institute of Education, Edinburgh. He has published on many aspects of Scottish politics and the sociology of education. His most recent books are *A Diverse Assembly: the Debate on a Scottish Parliament* (Edinburgh University Press, 1998), and *The Scottish Electorate* (with Alice Brown, David McCrone and Paula Surridge, Macmillan, 1998). He is vice-convener of the Unit for the Study of Government in Scotland, and edits its quarterly journal, *Scottish Affairs*.

James Mitchell is Professor in the Department of Politics at the University of Sheffield. He is the author of *Conservatives and the Union*, 1990; *Strategies for Self-Government*, 1996 and co-author of *Politics and Public Policy*, 1991 and *How Scotland Votes*, 1997.

Peter Lynch is Lecturer in Politics at the University of Stirling. He is author of *Minority Nationalism and European Integration* (University of Wales, 1996) and co-editor of *Out of the Ghetto: The Catholic Community in Modern Scotland* (John Donald, 1998). He has written widely on Scottish devolution and Scottish and Welsh nationalism and is currently working on a book on European Regionalism.

Alice Brown is Professor of Politics at the University of Edinburgh. Her research interests include Scottish politics, women and politics and economic policy, and she has published widely on these topics. She is currently engaged in two ESRC-supported research projects: one as a member of the Scottish team involved in the British Election study; the other as a joint grant-holder in a study of women and local government. Her publications (with others) include *Politics and Society in Scotland* (Macmillan, 2nd edition, 1998) and *The Scottish Electorate* (Macmillan, 1998).

Jonathan Bradbury is Lecturer in Politics at the University of Wales, Swansea and Convenor of the UK Political Studies Association specialist group on British Territorial Politics. His recent publications include *British Regionalism and Devolution* (co-edited with John Mawson, Jessica Kingsley, 1997) and the guest editing of *New Labour and Devolution* for *Regional Studies*, Vol.30, No. 6/7, 1996.

Jonathan Snicker is currently Lecturer in Politics at St. Hilda's College, Oxford. Apart from the politics of Welsh identity, his research interests include sub-state autonomism in Europe and the development of identity in former island colonies.

John Mawson is Professor and Head of the School of Town and Regional Planning at Dundee University, having previously worked as Director of the Public Service MBA programme at Birmingham University. He has professional and senior management experience at the urban and regional scales including serving as Director of Economic Development at West Midlands County Council and Joint Chief Executive of the West Midlands Enterprise Board. He has been editor of the Policy Review Section of the journal *Regional Studies* since 1982 and served as an adviser to the Association of Metropolitan Authorities, the Local Government Association and the House of Commons Environment Committee.

Index

Abercrombie, Sir Patrick 159
Act of Union 1535 24
Act of Union 1707 24
Act of Union 1800 24
Agreement for Cooperation in Community
    Matters 16
Aitken, Jonathon 26, 35
Alberta 199
Amsterdam Treaty 10, 13, 16, 18
Andalucia 16
Andorra 203
Anglo-Scottish Union 2
Asymmetrical Constitution 195, 202, 210
Asymmetry 23, 24, 130, 147, 195, 196, 201,
    203, 204, 205, 206, 213, 214
Audit Commission 77, 78
Austro-Hungarian 205
Australia 31, 44, 45, 113, 209
Azores 203

Baden-Wurttenberg 132
Bagehot 1
Balfour, Peter 88, 205
Bank of Scotland 39, 97, 98
Barnett formula 34, 41, 93, 125, 215
Basque Country 196, 198, 200, 201, 210,
    212
Basque Nationalist Party 204
BBC 166
Belgium 15, 16, 202, 207, 211
Beveridge 138
Blair, Tony 28, 133, 169
Bloc Québécois 200
Bohemia 54
Britain 1, 10, 11, 12, 17, 20, 21, 27, 57, 61,
    62, 64, 74, 78, 81, 112, 121, 122, 123,
    125, 129, 133, 134, 136, 137, 138, 169,
    176, 189, 196, 202, 205
British General Election 120
British Tourist Authority 144
Brown, Gordon 136
Brussels 10, 12, 15, 16, 17, 73, 77, 80, 81,
    190, 201
Business Interest Associations 86, 87, 88,
    93, 97, 99
Business Says Yes 93

Caborne, Dick 169
Campaign for a Scottish Assembly 106, 204
Campaign for a Scottish Assembly's Claim
    of Right (CSA) 204
Campaign for a Scottish Parliament 6, 106,

113
Canada 25, 31, 44, 195, 196, 198, 199, 200,
    202, 204, 206, 208, 209, 212
Canada-hors-Quebec 202
Canary Islands 196
Cardiff 126, 127, 153
Castle, Barbara 183
Catalonia 4, 16, 55, 132, 196, 200, 201, 210
CBI Scotland 87, 88, 89, 90, 91, 92, 93,
    198, 100
Channel Islands 203
Charlottetown Accord 214
Charter 88 6, 113
Charter of Rights 200, 207
Children's Hearings 58
Choice for England, A 167
Church of England 3
Church of Scotland 2
Churchill, Winston 72
Civil society 2, 53, 147
Committee of the Regions 18, 189, 190
Common Agricultural Policy 75
Commonwealth Grants Commission 24, 45
Confederation of British Industry 87, 183
Conservative Party 6, 7, 43, 57, 58, 62,
    103–6, 109, 118, 125, 128, 142, 143, 164,
    165, 174, 177, 185, 190
Conservatives 5, 7, 8, 58, 61, 64, 88, 93,
    104, 125, 126, 128, 131, 143, 153, 165,
    166, 178, 185, 204, 206, 208, 213
Constitutional Court 210
Cooper, Lord Justice 205
Cornwall 4
Corsica 203
Corsican people 203
Cortes 210
Council of Ireland 69
Council of Ministers 18, 80, 210
Countryside Commission in Wales 144
Countryside Council for Wales 144
Crossman 177, 178, 182, 195, 200
Crowther-Hunt, Lord 12, 161
Cunningham, George 161
Curriculum Council for Wales 144, 149
Curry, David 164
Cymreig 141, 150
Cymricization 140, 145, 147, 149
Cymru-Cymraeg 141
Cynraeg- 140, 141, 144, 152

Davies, Denzil 134
Davies, Howard 170

Decentralization 94
Democracy for Scotland 110
Department of Employment 163
Department of Environment 174
Devolution 1, 8, 10, 17, 20, 21, 23, 26, 44,
    46, 72, 81, 86, 88, 94, 96, 120, 131, 153,
    161, 165, 174, 192, 202
Dewar, Donald 96
Dicey 205, 206, 207, 208, 209
Docklands 5, 192
Doomsday scenerio 106
Dorrell, Stephen 25
Dundee and Tayside Chamber of Commerce
    89
Dydd Gwyl Dewi 150

Eastern Europe 96, 176
Edinburgh 7, 9, 13, 14, 29, 30, 35, 54, 70,
    76, 78–82, 86, 93, 101
Edinburgh Summit 13
Education Reform Act 148, 149, 151, 152
Edwards, Sir Nicholas 142
Election Manifesto (1979) 164
Elizabeth I 146
England 1, 2, 5–7, 20, 23–6, 33, 35, 36, 40,
    43–6, 53, 54, 56, 57, 59, 61, 62, 64, 65,
    86, 91, 123–6, 133, 144–6, 149, 151,
    158–62, 164, 166–71, 174, 176–8, 180–4,
    189, 190, 195, 196, 198, 201, 205, 208,
    209, 211, 213
English Partnerships and the Highways
    Agency 170
English Regional Association 171, 174
English regionalism 8, 158, 164, 169
Europe 1, 3, 4–7, 10–12, 21, 55, 59, 60, 64,
    77, 79, 113, 130, 163, 164, 169, 178, 180,
    189, 190, 192, 201–3, 207, 211, 213, 215
Europe and Regional Planning Guidance
    163
Europe of the Regions 163, 190, 191, 193
European Central Bank 18
European Commission 31, 81
European Convention on Human Rights 10,
    207, 214
European elections 20
European integration 4, 19, 80, 132, 202,
    205, 213
European Parliament 18, 76, 105
European Regional Development Fund 80
European Union 4, 10, 11, 18, 20, 21, 23,
    26, 31, 53, 59, 75, 77, 100, 103, 106, 191,
    193, 202, 209, 211, 214
Euskadi 16
Excessive Deficits Protocol 32

Faroes 203
Fawcett, C.B. 159
Federal System 13, 27, 160
Federalism 23, 43
Finland 55, 203
Flemish 202
Foreign Office 201
Forsyth, Michael 33, 39, 41, 44, 59
Forum for Private Business 89
France 19, 179, 202
Francophonie 201
French 160, 176, 201, 202–4
French Revlolution 204

Geddes, Sir Patrick 159
General Government Borrowing
    Requirement 45
German 4, 13, 14, 16, 31, 60, 61, 79, 176,
    198, 202, 210, 211
German Federal Constitution 13
German Lander 4, 31, 60
Germany 15–17, 25, 79, 179, 185, 208, 210,
    211
Gilmour Report 81
Gladstone 131, 209
Glasgow Chamber of Commerce 88
Gonzalez (Prime Minister) 16
Goschen formula 34
Gould, Brian 165
Government of Greater London 177
Government of Ireland Act (1920) 14, 24,
    69, 71
Government Offices for the Regions 165,
    172, 189, 190
Great Britain 7, 24, 45, 205
Greater London Council 178
Green Paper for England: 'The English
    Dimension' 161
Greenland 203
Gummer, John Selwyn 178

Habsburg monarchy 205
Hague, William 126, 127, 142, 143
Hardie, Donald 94
Heath, Edward 2, 151, 160, 164
Herbert Commission 178
Heseltine, Michael 183
House of Commons Trade and Industry
    Committee 169
House of Lords 10, 73, 126, 159, 209
Howells, Kim 134
Humber Estuary 182
Humberside 178, 182–5, 188
Humberside County Fire and Police
    Authority 184
Hunt, David 126, 142, 144

Institute for Fiscal Studies 29, 30, 36
Institute of Directors 87, 89, 94
Integrated Government Offices 189, 190
Integrated Regional Offices 5
Inter-Ministerial Conference for External
    Affairs 15
Irish Free State 159
Irish Home Rule 131
Irish Party 200
Isle of Man 203
Italy 179, 202

Keynes 138
Keynesianism 6
Kilbrandon Commission on the Constitution
    69
Kilbrandon Report 160, 161
Kinross 105

Labour Government 70, 73, 205
Lancashire 177
Lander 15, 79, 80, 210, 211
Lang, Ian 35
Law Society of Scotland/Faculty of
    Advocates 89
LG 134
Lib–Lab Pact 161
Liberal Democrats 5, 12, 64, 97, 103, 105,
    106, 108, 109, 111, 112, 117, 131, 209
Liddell, Helen 105
Liechtenstein 203
Local Government Act (1972) 178, 182, 185
Local Government Boundry Commission
    185
London 5, 7, 9, 17, 25, 29, 30, 35, 54, 55,
    69, 70, 72, 76, 77–82, 132, 138, 151, 154,
    159, 160, 171, 174, 177, 178, 187, 188,
    192, 209
London Borough Councils 177
London Docklands Development Corporation
    187
London Socialists 209
Lowi, Ted 73
Lucky Goldstar 146

Maastricht 10–12, 13, 14, 32, 210
Mackay of Cashfern, Lord 26, 36, 37
MacMillan, Ian 94
Madrid 198
Major, John 7, 166, 204
Manifesto (1983) 164
Mathews, Professor Russell 25
McCormick v Lord Advocate (1953) 205
McLeish, Henry 90, 112
Memorandum of Dissent 12
Millan, Bruce 168

Minister of Housing and Local Government
    177, 192
Ministry of Agriculture 200
Ministry of Energy 200
Monklands East 105
MORI 184
Mudiad Ysgolion Meithrin 148

Napoleanic States 6
Nation-state 4, 76
National Curriculum Welsh Order of
    September 1993 150
National Federation of Small Businesses 96
National Health Service 34
National Labour Party 131
Nationalism 140
Nature of Conservancy Council in Wales 144
Navarre 198
New Labour 6, 25, 100, 122, 129, 130, 131,
    133, 137, 138, 158, 169
New Unitary Authority (1995) 141
Newfoundland 196
Newport 134, 150, 152
Nickson, David 88
Northern Ireland 1, 23, 24, 26, 35, 45, 46,
    69–72, 121, 162, 177, 196, 198, 199, 202,
    204, 205, 207
Northern Ireland Assembly 69, 71
Northern Ireland Parliament 24, 45
Norway 55
Notwithstanding Clause 201
November 1975 White Paper on Devolution
    31

Old Labour 133, 136
On the Record 166
Ontario 196, 198

Paton Office 88
Patullo, Bruce 97
Peacock, Professor Alan 12
Perth 105
Plaid Cymru 129, 130, 141, 143, 144, 147
Poland 176
Poplarism 2
Powell, Sir Ray 134
Prescott, John 136, 164, 168
Procedural subsidiarity 13
Public Order (Amendment) Bill 72
Pwyllgor Datblygu Addyohe Gymaraeg 151

Quango 5, 28, 126–8, 133, 135, 136, 146,
    153, 162, 167, 187 ,189
Quangoization 131, 147
Quebec 60, 196, 198, 201, 202, 204, 206,
    207, 209, 211, 212, 214
Quebec National Assembly 204

Raybould Bill 151
Redcliffe-Maud Commission 177
Redwood, John 126, 127, 142, 144
Referendums 7, 23
Reform Party 209
Regional Affairs Spokesperson 164
Regional and District Councils 177
Regional Arts Associations 189
Regional Development Agencies 5, 8, 165, 168, 169, 171
Regional Director of Employment 163
Regional Economic Planning Councils 160
Regional Governments 1, 15, 30, 192
Regional Sports Councils 167
Regionalism 138, 160, 174
Report of the Regional Policy Commission 168
Rest-of-Canada 202
Rhône-Alpes 132
Ridley, Nicholas 183
Roberts, Sir Wyn 128, 143, 144, 146, 148
Robertson, George 206
Rogers, Allan 134
Rowlands, Ted 134
Royal Commission on Local Government in England 177
Royal Commission on the Constitution 12, 69, 88, 160
Royal Commission on the Distribution of the Industrial Population and Industry 159
Rutland 177, 178

Salisbury, Lord 81
Salveson, Christian 88
Sardinia 203
Scotland 1–3, 5–10, 14, 20–28, 33–46, 53–62, 64, 65, 69, 70, 72, 73, 77–9, 81, 86–94, 96–8, 100, 101, 103–10, 112–17, 121–5, 127, 132–8, 145, 158–62, 165, 177–9, 181, 185, 189, 195, 196, 198–206, 208, 210, 211, 213, 214
Scotland Act 1978 89
Scotland Bill 70
Scotland FORward 112
Scotland Programme 38
Scotland Says No 86, 88
Scotland United 110
Scotland White Paper 27, 45
Scottish Affairs Select Committee 75
Scottish and Newcastle 88
Scottish Arts Council 59
Scottish Chamber of Commerce 89, 94, 98
Scottish Conservatives 57
Scottish Constitutional Commission 110, 111, 117, 206
Scottish Constitutional Convention 14, 25, 27, 32–4, 37, 40, 41, 45, 89, 103, 104,

106, 107–11, 116, 206, 213, 215
Scottish Convention of Women 106
Scottish Council Foundation 37
Scottish Council of Development and Industry 89
Scottish Division of the Institute of Directors 93
Scottish Education and Action for Development 113
Scottish Education Department 56
Scottish Examination Board 57
Scottish National Party 4, 44, 79, 97, 103, 106
Scottish Office 2, 23, 24, 33, 38, 40, 41, 55, 56, 59, 60, 62, 64, 65, 70, 77, 78, 80–82, 97, 112, 116, 124, 196, 200, 211, 214
Scottish Referendum 27
Scottish Secretary 73, 75, 97
Scottish Trades Union Congress 100, 106
Scottish Women's Co-ordination Group 107
Secretary of State for Wales 123, 200
Self-Government 159
Shore, Peter 178
Sicily 202
Sillars, Jim 165
Single Currency 10, 97
Single European Market 132
Single Local Government Association 171
Single Regeneration Budget 163, 173
Single Regeneration Budget Challenge Fund 163
Slovakia 176, 177
Smith, Llew 134
Smith, Nigel 92
Social Work (Scotland) Act of 1968 56
Socrates 146
South Wales 130, 134
South Wales Labour Party 130
Spain 16, 59, 179, 195, 196, 198–202, 204, 208, 210–12, 215
Speakers Conference on Northern Ireland Parliamentary Representation 24
Special Status 202, 203, 212
Stormont 71, 72, 76, 77, 121, 198, 199
Strathclyde Regional Council 178, 186
Sweden 32

Tartan Tax 19, 29, 33, 38, 39,
Think Twice 98
Thomas, Dafydd Ellis 144
Three-Wales Model 144
Training Enterprise Employment Division 163

UK Unionist Party 24
Ulster 159

Uniform Business Rate 91
Union state 213
Unionism 11, 43
Unitary State 1, 44, 120, 121, 123, 125,
    135, 137, 208
United Kingdom Continental Shelf 44
United Kingdom of Great Britain and Ireland
    24
United Kingdom Treasury 89
United States 44, 65, 68, 113, 186, 208, 209
Unwin, Raymond 159
Urdd Gobaith Cymru 141

Valencia 196
Vatican City 203

Wales Tourist Board 144
Walker, Peter 126, 142
Walker–Hunt Era 125, 127, 137
Wallonia 202
Welsh Affairs Select Committee 123, 132
Welsh Grand Committee 120, 123, 124, 127,
    144
Welsh Labour Action 134
Welsh Labour Party 131, 134, 141

Welsh Labour Party's Policy Commission
    133
Welsh Language Act 144
Welsh Liberal Democrats 134
Welsh Local Government Act 126
Welsh Office Personnel Management
    Division 146
West Belfast Question 24
West Lothian Question 24, 208
Wheatley Commission 178
White Paper (1983) 179
White Paper on Devolution (November
    1975) 31
Winning for Britain 168
Withernsea 181
Women's Caucus Group 112

Y Fro Cymruraeg 147
Yarrow, Eric 88
Yarrow's Shipbuilders 88
Yorkshire and Humberside Regional
    Economic Planning Council 183
Young, Lord 59
Younger, George 74
Ysgol Gwynllyw 150

Books of Related Interest

The Regional Dimension of the European Union

Towards a Third Level in Europe?

Charlie Jeffery, *University of Birmingham (Ed)*

The 1990s have seen intense debates about the role of regions in European integration. Changes in EU structural funding rules, the innovations of the Maastricht treaty, and the growing importance of federal and regional government within EU member states have all boosted the significance of regional tiers of government in EU politics. Taken together their effect has been to shift the balance of decision-making responsibility within the EU to a third (regional) level of government emerging in the EU policy process alongside the first (union) and second (nation-state) levels. As a result, a system of multi-level governance can increasingly be identified, in which different levels of government adopt different roles in different fields or phases of the European policy process.

224 pages   1997
0 7146 4748 9   cloth
0 7146 4306 8   paper
Cass Series in Regional and Federal Studies Volume 2
A special issue of the journal Regional & Federal Studies

FRANK CASS PUBLISHERS
Newbury House, 900 Eastern Avenue, Newbury Park, Ilford, Essex IG2 7HH
Tel: +44 (0)181 599 8866 Fax: +44 (0)181 599 0984 E-mail: info@frankcass.com
NORTH AMERICA
c/o ISBS, 5804 NE Hassalo Street, Portland, OR 97213 3644, USA
Tel: 800 944 6190 Fax: 503 280 8832 E-mail cass@isbs.com
Website: http://www.frankcass.com

The Political Economy of Regionalism

Michael Keating, *University of Western Ontario and*
John Loughlin, *University of Wales, Cardiff (Eds)*

This book combines theoretical essays with probing case studies to examine the effects of economic and political restructuring in Europe and North America on regions on these two continents. The main theses are: international economic restructuring and its impact on regions; political realignments at the regional level; questions of territorial identity and their connection with class, gender and neighbourhood identity; policy choices and policy conflicts in regional development.

504 pages   1997
0 7146 4658 X   cloth
0 7146 4187 1　paper
Cass Series in Regional and Federal Studies Volume 1

Britain in the Nineties
The Politics of Paradox

Hugh Berrington, *Emeritus Professor of Politics,*
University of Newcastle upon Tyne (Ed)

This volume looks at the striking changes in British politics and government since the accession of Mrs Thatcher and in particular at the last six or seven years. Its aim is to explore some of these recent changes and to emphasise the recurring paradoxes in the political developments of the last 20 years, for example, the changes of sides by the main parties on Europe.

240 pages   1998
0 7146 4880 9   cloth
0 7146 4434 X   paper
A special issue of the journal West European Politics

FRANK CASS PUBLISHERS
Newbury House, 900 Eastern Avenue, Newbury Park, Ilford, Essex IG2 7HH
Tel: +44 (0)181 599 8866 Fax: +44 (0)181 599 0984 E-mail: info@frankcass.com
NORTH AMERICA
c/o ISBS, 5804 NE Hassalo Street, Portland, OR 97213 3644, USA
Tel: 800 944 6190 Fax: 503 280 8832 E-mail cass@isbs.com
Website: http://www.frankcass.com

Regional Dynamics

The Basis of Electoral Support in Britain

William Field, *Georgian Court College, Lakewood*

'... a pioneering book ...'
> **Vernon Bogdanor,** Oxford University

'... a sophisticated and balanced evaluation'
> Parliamentary Affairs

Many have noticed the 'North-South divide' in British politics. In this book, William Field points out that this divide marks the resurgence of a core-periphery cleavage which was also dominant in British politics in the years before 1914. He shows how astonishingly similar the geographical pattern of the vote was in the general election of 1987 to that in the two general elections of 1910, the last before the outbreak of the First World War. Many of the same constitutional issues – devolution and reform of the second chamber – were coming to the fore then as now.

Are we now seeing the resurgence of a pattern which, from the end of the First World War to the 1980s, was submerged by the politics of class? Is the decline of class leading to the resurrection of older cleavages? Was 'Thatcherism', so dominant in British politics in the 1980s, more a consequence of profound social and geographical changes than a cause? William Field examines these questions, and brings to his analysis a deep understanding of statistics and a rigour not always found in historical analysis.

224 pages   1997
0 7146 4782 9   cloth
0 7146 4336 X   paper

FRANK CASS PUBLISHERS
Newbury House, 900 Eastern Avenue, Newbury Park, Ilford, Essex IG2 7HH
Tel: +44 (0)181 599 8866 Fax: +44 (0)181 599 0984 E-mail: info@frankcass.com
NORTH AMERICA
c/o ISBS, 5804 NE Hassalo Street, Portland, OR 97213 3644, USA
Tel: 800 944 6190 Fax: 503 280 8832 E-mail cass@isbs.com
Website: http://www.frankcass.com

33050724